THE POWER TO MANAGE

THE POWER TO MANAGE

Restructuring the New Zealand Electricity Department as a State-Owned Enterprise
THE ELECTRICORP EXPERIENCE

Barry Spicer, Robert Bowman,
David Emanuel, Alister Hunt

With
Michael Bradbury, Darien Kerkin, Paul Rouse

Auckland
OXFORD UNIVERSITY PRESS
Melbourne Oxford New York

Oxford University Press

Oxford University Press, Walton Street, Oxford OX2 6DP

OXFORD   NEW YORK   TORONTO
DELHI   BOMBAY   CALCUTTA   MADRAS   KARACHI
PETALING JAYA   SINGAPORE   HONG KONG   TOKYO
NAIROBI   DAR ES SALAAM   CAPE TOWN
MELBOURNE   AUCKLAND
and associated companies in
BERLIN   IBADAN

OXFORD is a trade mark of Oxford University Press

First published 1991
© Barry Spicer, Robert Bowman, David Emanuel, Alister Hunt 1991

ISBN 0 19 558233 0

Cover designed by Chris O'Brien
Photoset in Times by Sovereign Print Ltd, Christchurch
and printed in Hong Kong
Published by Oxford University Press
1A Matai Road, Greenlane, Auckland 5, New Zealand

Contents

Figures

Figures 7.1 to 7.20 appear in Appendix C and are listed in the Appendices Contents on page 152.

Notes on the Authors

Barry Spicer   Professor of Management Accounting at the University of Auckland since 1989. He holds a Ph.D. from the University of Washington. He has held appointments at the University of Arizona and the University of Oregon and visiting appointments at the University of Queensland and Manchester University. His teaching and research interests include corporate strategy, the economics of internal organization, and cost and management accounting systems.

Robert (Jerry) Bowman   Professor of Finance at the University of Auckland since 1987. He holds a Ph.D. from Stanford University. He was previously on the faculty at the University of Oregon, and has experience as the chief executive of a start-up company in the USA. His teaching and research interests include investments, capital market behaviour, and the application of financial management techniques.

David Emanuel   Professor of Accounting at the University of Auckland since 1981. He holds a Ph.D. from the University of Auckland. He has acted as a consultant to a number of chartered accounting firms, law firms, and commercial and government organizations. His teaching and research interests cover the relationship between security prices in capital markets and accounting information, and the governance of organizations.

Alister Hunt   Lecturer in Accounting at the University of Auckland since 1990. He holds an M.Com. degree from the University of Auckland. He has worked in chartered accountancy and marketing planning. In 1991 he joined the doctoral programme at the University of Washington.

Other contributors

Michael Bradbury   Associate Professor of Accounting at the University of Auckland. He holds a Ph.D. from the University of Auckland. He has experience in chartered accountancy in Auckland and London. His areas of specialization include financial analysis and financial reporting.

Darien Kerkin   Head, Department of Accountancy and Law at Auckland Technical Institute. She holds an MBS degree from Massey University. Her areas of specialization include management accounting and accounting for public sector organizations.

Paul Rouse   Senior Lecturer in Accounting at the University of Auckland. He holds an M.Com. degree from the University of Auckland. His area of specialization is cost and management accounting.

Preface

In 1986 the New Zealand Parliament enacted the State-Owned Enterprises Act 1986, to reform the trading activities of government departments. The motivation for this reform is well captured in the following statement:

> Over the twenty years to 1985/86 the government invested $5,000 million (in 1986 dollars) of taxpayers' money in the departmental trading activities of the Airways System, the Lands and Survey Department and Forest Service, the Post Office, the State Coal Mines, and the Electricity Division of the Ministry of Energy. In 1985/86 these organisations managed assets valued at over $20 billion but returned no net after tax returns to taxpayers.[1]

A similar statement was made by the then Minister for Justice, the Rt. Hon. Geoffrey Palmer, on the introduction of the State-Owned Enterprises Bill to Parliament on 30 September 1986, together with the comment that '[s]uch a state of affairs cannot continue'.

Under the Act, the New Zealand Government initially established State-Owned Enterprises (SOEs) in electricity generation and transmission; the postal service; telecommunications; coal-mining, forest-ownership, property-owning and management services; and air-traffic control. Other government trading organizations such as computer services, government stores, and radio and television were to follow later. Corporatization involved assets of trading entities being transferred to new organizations which had a corporate form, but with the shares in the corporation owned entirely by the Crown. A clear mandate to be profit-seeking was given to the new SOEs. This mandate, in conjunction with the deregulation of the industries in which they operated, the curtailment of the special protections previously enjoyed by state trading organizations, and the removal of central government controls, provided managers of the new SOEs with the **power to manage**.

In early 1990 the authors were approached by the Industries Branch of the New Zealand Treasury to undertake a study of the comparative performance of SOEs. In consultation with Treasury officials we chose the Electricity Corporation of

---

1. Cited from Stephen Jennings and Rob Cameron, 'State-Owned Enterprise Reform in New Zealand', in Alan Bollard and Robert Buckle (eds), *Economic Liberalisation in New Zealand*, Allen & Unwin, Wellington, 1987. This same statement also appears in Roger Douglas and Louise Callen, *Towards Prosperity*, David Bateman, Auckland, 1987, p.234.

New Zealand Limited or Electricorp as the first SOE to be studied. Our study details the major changes that have taken place in this, the largest of New Zealand's SOEs, as a result of its restructuring from a government trading department.

The opportunity to undertake a study of the effect of a radical change in governance structure in an organization of the size and complexity of Electricorp is rare. Our documentation of the transition period will enable a fuller assessment of the long-term outcomes of the SOE process.

Detailed study of the nature and processes of change in a major organization is difficult without the full co-operation of the people in that organization. We were fortunate in receiving strong support from the Board of Directors of Electricorp, and in particular from its Chief Executive, Dr Roderick Deane. We were provided full access to the Corporation's papers and to its managers and employees. Our contact at Electricorp was the Financial Controller, Martin Holden. We drew on his extensive knowledge of both the former government trading organization and the new corporation to assist our research.

The New Zealand Treasury officials organizing the study were Bruce Carrie and David Hunt. They provided considerable assistance to us over the duration of the study and were a valuable source of advice and constructive criticism.

We received assistance also from a number of faculty members of the University of Auckland in different parts of the project. Paul Rouse contributed to the financial analysis reported in Chapter 7, Darien Kerkin (now at Auckland Technical Institute) made contributions to the institutional and regulatory background discussed in Chapter 2, and to the political and social issues discussed in Chapter 6. Michael Bradbury contributed to the financial analysis and helped with editing of earlier drafts of the study. Special thanks are due to Simon Cauchi for his editorial assistance in preparing our manuscript for publication.

The Electricorp story as it is presented here is rich in details which were drawn from our interviews with board members, managers, and staff who, without exception, agreed to allow us to tape-record our lengthy interviews with them. Our transcription secretary Moir Spicer contributed a great deal by providing accurate transcripts to us shortly after each round of interviews was completed.

The window of opportunity for detailed study of the transition periods of government trading organizations that have been restructured into SOEs is a very small one. The individuals (both in government and in the SOEs) who were in charge of the change-over have begun to move on, as the new SOEs continue to evolve. The institutional learning that can come from a detailed investigation will soon be lost. The time to study and assess the manner in which organizations such as Electricorp initially responded to the new environment provided by the State-Owned Enterprises Act 1986 is now.

Barry H. Spicer
Robert G. Bowman
David M. Emanuel
Alister L. Hunt

Abbreviations

AEPB	Auckland Electric Power Board
BST	Bulk Supply Tariff
CPI	Consumer Price Index
ECNZ	Electricity Corporation of New Zealand
EM	Electricorp Marketing
EMEC	Electricorp Marketing Electricity Contracting
ESAs	electricity supply authorities
ESA NZ	Electricity Supply Association of New Zealand
FMS	financial management system
GW	gigawatt (1,000,000,000 watts)
HVDC	high voltage direct current
kW	kilowatt (1,000 watts)
LRMC	long run marginal cost
MW	megawatt (1,000,000 watts)
NPV	net present value
NZED	New Zealand Electricity Division
PDB	PowerDesignBuild
PSA	Public Service Association
ROE	return on equity
SEPS	Southland Electric Power Supply
SOE	state-owned enterprise
SRMC	short run marginal cost
SSC	State Services Commission

1

Introduction

In 1984 New Zealand's newly elected Labour Government began the most extensive programme of free-market economic reform ever tackled by an OECD country. Over its two terms in office from 1984 to 1990, the Labour Government freed prices, wages and interest rates, floated the exchange rate, progressively removed tariffs and subsidies, deregulated the financial system, slashed income tax rates, and encouraged overseas investment in New Zealand.

As part of this programme of economic reform, the management of government organizations came under intense scrutiny. The government subsequently introduced major structural reforms in the form of the State-Owned Enterprises Act 1986, the State Sector Act 1988 and the Public Finance Act 1989. The first of these reforms was directed at the trading activities of government departments. The second and third were directed at the operation and management of government departments and agencies. In each case the government's overriding objective was to improve the efficiency and effectiveness of the public sector.

To make these state trading organizations more efficient, the government and its advisors recognized that three important changes had to be made. First, the state's trading organizations required clear commercial objectives. Second, they needed to be subject to competitive forces like any private sector organization. Third, their managers needed the power to manage.

These three principles were at the heart of the Labour Government's state-owned enterprises programme and the State-Owned Enterprises Act 1986. Major state trading organizations corporatized under the Act include: electricity generation and transmission; the postal service; telecommunications; a number of government land owning activities including forest ownership, property owning and management services; and air traffic control.[1] In this book we provide a detailed investigation of the restructuring of a major state trading organization into an SOE under the SOE Act 1986. The Electricity Corporation of New Zealand Limited, commonly known as Electricorp or ECNZ, took over the management of the assets of the New Zealand Electricity Division (NZED) of the Ministry of Energy on 1 April 1987.

---

1. The following organizations have been incorporated as SOEs under the SOE Act 1986: Airways Corporation Ltd, Coalcorp Ltd, Electricity Corporation Ltd, Government Computing Services Ltd, Government Property Services Ltd, Government Supply Brokerage Ltd, Land Corporation Ltd, New Zealand Forestry Corporation Ltd, New Zealand Post Ltd, Post Office Bank Ltd, Radio New Zealand Ltd, Telecom Ltd, Television New Zealand Ltd and Works and Development Services Corporation Ltd.

This change coincided with the deregulation of the generation and wholesaling parts of the electricity industry as the Government acted to remove legislative and regulatory barriers to competition.

We chose Electricorp to study for several reasons. First, Electricorp is without doubt the most important of New Zealand's SOEs both in terms of its size and the nature of its product. As a significant and central part of the economy, the performance of this SOE, in one way or another, affects everybody who lives in New Zealand. We had also been assured of the full co-operation of the Chief Executive and Board of Directors. This involved access to confidential internal documents and board papers and the opportunity to conduct open and candid interviews with managers and staff throughout the organization. Lastly, we believed that detailed study of the experiences of this large organization, as it made the transition from government department to SOE, could yield insights that may prove to be useful to other restructurings both in New Zealand and overseas.

Study objectives

Our study is a case investigation of an organization in the process of change from a government department to a state-owned enterprise. It is *not* a study of the electricity industry, nor does it attempt to assess the economic efficiency of the present electricity industry or some of the further restructuring of the industry which has already been decided (such as establishment of the national grid as a separate SOE) or is under consideration (such as the split-up of electricity generation).

Our study had three basic objectives:

(1) To describe and understand the changes in organization and performance that had taken place in ECNZ as a result of incorporation as an SOE.

(2) To draw some tentative conclusions or lessons from ECNZ's experience that might have wider applicability to future restructurings. This includes a general assessment of the SOE process itself.

(3) To provide, through the structure and content of the study, a framework that could provide a basis for future studies of SOE performance.

Our investigation was centred around six sets of questions. The responses to these questions provide the structure for the following chapters:

1 What was the institutional background or context of changes that have taken place at ECNZ as a result of incorporation as an SOE?

To develop understanding of the changes at ECNZ, we first review the broader institutional background or context of these changes. New Zealand's programme of reforms is part of a world-wide trend towards privatization of state-owned trading organizations and the progressive deregulation of industry. Against this broader background the ECNZ experience is best understood as the story of changes wrought in one of New Zealand's largest and most important SOEs as a result of the New Zealand Government's programme of economic restructuring.

Chapter 2 provides a brief overview of the New Zealand programme of reforms against a background of these world-wide trends.

2 How and why was the organization restructured internally and managed differently as an SOE than as a government department?

This broad question was broken down into a set of more detailed questions that involve looking at the formation of strategy, and changes in agency relationships, governance, and measurement resulting from the change in ownership structure caused by incorporation as an SOE:

(a) What important pressures confronted the managers of the new organization at the time of incorporation?

(b) How did ECNZ's new managers respond strategically to the new pressures on the organization? Why did they respond in these ways?

(c) How did ECNZ's new managers change the internal organization, management structures and practices of the organization? Why did they make these changes?

Chapter 3 describes the strategic pressures faced by the corporation after its establishment as an SOE and the corporation's strategic responses to these pressures. Our objective in Chapter 3 is to provide our understanding of how and why the new board of directors and management responded as they did.

First, ECNZ had to respond to the pressures that were placed on it as a result of the SOE restructuring and as a result of deregulation allowing for competition in the electricity market. We identify five pressures on ECNZ which appear to have driven the development of their strategic responses. These include: (1) the excess generating capacity ECNZ acquired from its predecessor, NZED; (2) the new threat of competition in generation from other entities; (3) competition in the end-user market from substitute fuels such as gas and coal; (4) the rate of return on equity objective which is set through a process of negotiation with the Shareholding Ministers; and (5) the threat of regulation of the industry.

These five pressures combined to drive the development of ECNZ's initial competitive strategy. This strategy involved five interrelated responses including: (1) adoption of a pricing strategy to lower electricity prices to deter entry; (2) building market share and volume against competing fuels through pricing strategy and marketing efforts; (3) negotiating with the Shareholding Ministers for a return on equity objective that would maximize the long-run value of the corporation by allowing strategic objectives (1) and (2) to be achieved; (4) 'ring-fencing' the national grid to reduce the threat of regulation; and (5) building a profit-oriented culture throughout the corporation.

Chapter 4 provides a more detailed description and analysis of the extensive, interrelated changes in organization, management structures and practices made by Electricorp's new managers. Wherever it is appropriate, and we were able to obtain relevant information, we provide comparisons between the operations of the old organization (NZED) and the new organization (ECNZ).

Implementation of a strategy of building market share and volume through a combination of pricing policy and aggressive marketing required a fundamental realignment of the organization taken over from NZED. Radical change has taken place in both the organizational structure and management practices and processes of ECNZ.

The basic management principle which is embedded in the SOE Act 1986 can be described by the phrase 'autonomy **within defined areas of responsibility and accountability**'. SOEs were to have a clear commercial objective. Day-to-day political interference was removed so as to provide managers with the autonomy to manage. They were also to be held accountable and responsible for running a successful business. This basic principle also underlies ECNZ's new management structure.

With the organization freed substantially from external control, ECNZ's new managers had the power to manage. ECNZ set about creating a competitive environment for managers and instilling a profit-oriented culture. This was accomplished primarily through organization structure. The organization was divided into relatively autonomous, decentralized business units with profit responsibility. In the case of Trans Power (which operates the national grid), the business unit was initially set up as an 'economic cost centre'. Wherever possible these cost or profit centres were deliberately placed into an environment where they would have to contract out, or compete internally, for the right to supply goods or services.

Significant changes were made in the process of target setting and business planning, and investment planning. Major changes were also made to management information and accounting systems. Perhaps the most important of all has been the introduction of incentive contracting for performance. The use of this mechanism has played an important role in cementing radical changes in management culture into place. It is also likely to be the key to driving cultural change deeper into the organization.

3 What effect has the incorporation of ECNZ had on competitive processes in markets?

Chapter 5 contains our discussion of ECNZ's influence on competitive processes. As we investigated changes in the structure and functioning of ECNZ, it became clear that the process of establishing ECNZ as an SOE and of deregulating the market for electricity generation had not only affected ECNZ's financial performance, but had also influenced competitive processes in the markets in which it operates.

These effects on the competitive process are an integral part of the ECNZ story and are also important to the assessment of the overall corporatization process. Our discussion is based on interviews with ECNZ managers and personnel, our review of documents, and discussions with outside parties. In addressing this question we make no claim to having done a complete analysis. Our intention is simply to draw attention to some wider changes in the extent of competition in the economy that resulted from the establishment of Electricorp as an SOE. In particular, we are interested in describing how ECNZ's actions and behaviour since becoming an SOE have (1) added competitive elements into existing markets, (2) enhanced or diminished the competitive process, or (3) changed the nature of competition. In some cases, such as the market for debt, the market has been enhanced. In others, barriers have been raised as the corporation has sought competitive advantage.

4 What effect has the incorporation of ECNZ had on social and political pressures?
ECNZ has had to respond to both changed commercial and socio-political pressures
as a result of establishment as an SOE. These pressures overlap and interact, but
we have chosen to treat them separately for clarity of exposition. Chapter 3 focuses
primarily on commercial pressures. Chapter 6 describes the social and political
pressures with which ECNZ's managers must contend and their responses to these
pressures.

Political and social pressures are not new to electricity generation in New
Zealand. But since corporatization the political visibility of the organization has
increased. In some cases new pressures have been created, but in most cases the
nature of the existing ones has been changed. ECNZ has commercial incentives
to address these pressures, as well as responsibility under the SOE Act 1986.

5 How has the performance of the organization changed?
Chapter 7 addresses this question. We place our analysis and discussion of this
question as the second to last chapter because changes in reported performance
are, at least in aggregate terms, a consequence of three joint effects: (1) incorporation
as an SOE, (2) the deregulation of the generation and wholesale electricity portions
of the electricity industry, and (3) the numerous changes made by ECNZ's managers
to the organization and operation of the corporation discussed in the preceding
chapters.

We have focused primarily on financial elements of ECNZ's performance which
could be used to build a time-series of performance from 1980 to 1990. ECNZ
was established as an SOE on 1 April 1987. We had in mind that this work might
also form a basis for future work involving comparisons of SOE performance.
While some non-financial measures are included, these types of measures do not
lend themselves to cross-sectional comparisons across SOEs. In our analysis they
serve mainly as a check to rule out degradation in the quality of the delivered
product as one alternative explanation for the observed improvement in financial
performance.

Considerable work had to be done to develop a relatively clean time series of
accounting data before and after incorporation. We also constructed a new measure
called 'return on crown investment' (ROCI) to enable comparisons of a government
trading organization to an incorporated SOE.

Our analysis shows that the financial performance of ECNZ has undergone
considerable improvement since incorporation. Over the period 1980 to 1990, the
1989 and 1990 years (which follow the intervention) show: (1) the highest level
of 'real' profit, (2) the highest rate of profitability measured as return on assets
and return on the crown's investment, and (3) the highest measures of output per
employee. Our analysis also reveals increasing volumes of sales, decreasing real
sales prices per kWh, and decreasing real operating costs per kWh over the
1980-1990 period. These results seem to have been achieved without any obvious
degradation in the 'quality' of the generation and transmission systems.

*6 What conclusions or 'lessons' may be drawn from the study which may have
wider application to future restructurings or investigations of SOE performance?*
Chapter 8 contains our discussion of this question. However, we sound a note

of caution. It is difficult and hazardous to draw firm conclusions from a single case study which describes and explores the experiences of one SOE (even one so rich in detail as ECNZ). Wider study of the experiences of other SOEs in New Zealand is needed to better isolate important factors which may account for the success or lack of success of these restructurings. Having sounded this warning, we provide some reflections on ECNZ's experiences, on the reasons for ECNZ's successful transition to SOE form, and on the SOE process in general.

The first question we address in Chapter 8 is: What events, actions and decisions appear to have been important in the process of transforming ECNZ from a government department to a commercial, profit-oriented corporation within the framework of the SOE Act?

The critical influence of key leaders on the direction and process of change in ECNZ is, in our opinion, the major 'lesson' that emerges from our study. Two individuals played pivotal leadership roles in the establishment and development of Electricorp. These individuals are John Fernyhough, Chairman of the Board, and Roderick Deane, Chief Executive. We believe that the direction and performance of ECNZ is due, in large part, to the vision and complementary leadership and management skills of these two managers. They have been supported by an interested and committed Board of Directors.

The changes made at ECNZ were dramatic, revolutionary, acted upon decisively, and implemented as swiftly as possible by the Board under the leadership of John Fernyhough. The main mechanism used to effect this change was the use of a small task force which worked behind the scenes to develop a new business structure for the new organization. While the process of change that followed certainly had a human cost, the process was generally successful in meeting its objective of placing the best candidates available from inside and outside the organization into the new structure. This resulted in the management culture of the organization changing very quickly.

Our study of ECNZ also highlights the importance of getting the right incentives, motivation and culture in a new organization. Considerable time and attention was given to making the right appointments to senior management positions. A lot of attention was also given to setting up contracts and incentives so as to motivate performance, allow delegation of authority and responsibility, and provide the basis for holding individuals accountable for their performance. This process in ECNZ is best described as performance contracting tied to the achievement of objectives. We believe this incentive contracting was (and is) the key mechanism for institutionalizing the major shift in culture achieved by the initial radical change in organization.

The importance of union relations is also accented. It is clear from ECNZ's handling of union relations that these should be dealt with carefully and comprehensively at the beginning of the life of an SOE. ECNZ's senior managers say they regret that they agreed to a roll over of the majority of existing conditions with respect to union coverage of ECNZ employees. This is one area senior managers say would be handled differently if they had the opportunity to do it all over again.

The second question we discuss in Chapter 8 is: What, if any, comments can be offered about the SOE process itself based on what we have learnt by studying the establishment of ECNZ?

The structural framework put into place by the SOE Act provided the means for changing the governance structure of the organization. In our view it was the institutional change made possible by the SOE Act that played the primary role in the sweeping changes in organization and management described in detail in this book. First, it was the possibility of making these massive changes that was largely responsible for attracting top-calibre managers to the corporation. Second, the longer-run performance of ECNZ is critically dependent on the form of the new institutional arrangements and an ownership structure which separates ownership and control in much the same way as is done by companies in the private sector. Third, it frees the organization from the central control agencies of government and gives managers the power to manage.

While the SOE Act provided a framework for change which has had a profound impact on the operation and performance of ECNZ, there is still a serious debate about the robustness of the SOE model in the longer run. There are weaknesses in the SOE form which arise from a lack of tradeable equity, continued political vulnerability and political constraints on business operations. These factors stimulate the drive for full privatization of SOEs as a way of preserving efficiency gains from future dissipation by politicians and government bureaucrats.

A central feature of the SOE model is the Statement of Corporate Intent. This statement, which is required under section 14 of the SOE Act, provides (among other things) the financial dimensions of the contracting process between the SOEs and the Crown. In the case of ECNZ, three dimensions of profitability are involved – return on equity, return on assets, and growth in 'value'. While we believe the process is generally well specified, some issues which in essence relate to the connection between 'profitability' and 'value-creation' are raised. In particular, it is not clear how different risk characteristics across SOEs get factored systematically into the return target-setting process. Nor is the objective of 'increasing the value of the shareholders' investment at a rate similar to the increase in the market value of comparable large private sector companies' operational for evaluation, particularly on a year-by-year basis.

Methods

In undertaking our study of ECNZ we followed case research methods.[2] Multiple sources of evidence were used. We were fortunate in having access to New Zealand Treasury files on ECNZ which contained correspondence with ECNZ, internal Treasury reports and memoranda to Ministers on issues relating to ECNZ, and reports and correspondence from external parties relating to ECNZ. At ECNZ we were given access to board papers, documents and reports, incentive contracts, long-range plans, business plans, and a wealth of other material. ECNZ managers

---

2. Robert K. Yin, *Case Study Research: Design and Methods*, Sage Publications, 1989.

were remarkably open in providing access to all documents requested in the course of the study. The Treasury and ECNZ materials became the basic data base for our study. These materials were supplemented with reports, newspaper articles, and other documents in the public domain.

Interviews were the other major source of information used in the Electricorp case study. Although we worked to a set of prepared questions, we also followed up particularly interesting leads, asking not only for facts but also for opinions about events and insights into how and why the interviewee thought change had taken place. Quite often our intention in interviews was to corroborate statements made by others or found in our review of documents. We probed further when inconsistencies or different perspectives on the same event surfaced. In other instances we used documents to corroborate what we had been told in interviews.

Interviewing was conducted in three phases. The first phase involved meeting with the chief executive and his senior managers to discuss the scope of the project and to agree on administrative details. The second stage involved writing to all senior operating and corporate managers indicating areas we would like to explore with them. We interviewed staff in each of ECNZ's four main business units and made trips into the field to interview some plant managers and operating personnel. We also interviewed people in organizations outside ECNZ such as the Electricity Supply Association. The third and final phase consisted of two sets of interviews. The first set was aimed at filling in gaps in our understanding that arose out of the second round of interviews and our review of documents. The second set of interviews involved wide-ranging interviews with the chairman of the board, other board members and the chief executive. This set of interviews was deliberately left until last so that we would have sufficient knowledge of the organization to sharpen the focus of our questions and gain further insights into *why* changes had taken place.

During the course of the study we were given access to commercially sensitive and confidential information by the New Zealand Treasury and Electricorp. Interviews with ECNZ's managers and board members were wide-ranging and sometimes they too resulted in the revelation of commercially sensitive information or the expression of personally sensitive opinions. We were sometimes asked to keep details and sources confidential. In writing this book we have tried to be sensitive to the nature of the material that was provided to us and the trust and candour of the many individuals we interviewed. We do not feel that the value of our study is diminished because of our respect for this confidentiality.

2

The Reform Process

Introduction

In this chapter we sketch the background of the reform process in New Zealand. Our objective is to provide an overview of the legislative changes that resulted in the corporatization of SOEs and created the regulatory environment in which they were expected to operate. An understanding of these reforms assists in placing the changes which have taken place at Electricorp and the strengths and weaknesses of the SOE structure into perspective.

The conceptual basis for reform

The current wave of public sector reform, both in New Zealand and in developed (and developing) countries around the world, is principally driven by the objective of economic efficiency as a means to increase the well-being of citizens. There are several lines of argument on how best to achieve economic efficiency in public sector activities. Four concepts have provided the intellectual foundation for most recent efficiency-seeking efforts. These four concepts are:
- Property rights
- Agency
- Governance structures
- Measurement issues

These concepts are not mutually exclusive. The first two focus on incentives. The second two focus on transaction costs. Collectively they provide the conceptual underpinnings of economic restructuring programmes. In particular, each of these concepts has played an important role in the development of the SOE programme of reform and restructuring carried out by the New Zealand Government. Therefore, each is useful in understanding the application of the SOE programme and each has been valuable in informing our analysis of Electricorp's experiences as an SOE. They are introduced here as general concepts which underlay the development of the SOE programme.[1]

At the centre of the debate is the role of the state in the ownership of trading assets. Property rights theory argues that private ownership of enterprise will result

---

1. More extensive reviews of the theoretical underpinnings of public sector reform and the SOE programme in New Zealand are to be found in Boston (1991), Deane (1991), and Jennings and Cameron (1987).

in superior profitability and efficiency. Private ownership confers the right to use and retain the proceeds from the use of an asset, the right to exclude others from its use, and the right to transfer the bundle of rights which makes up the asset to others. Private ownership tends to increase economic efficiency as the owner of the asset also bears the consequences of the employment of the asset. Thus private ownership builds in incentives for the efficient use of assets. Reviews of the property rights literature which expound on these themes are to be found in Furubotn and Pejovich (1972), and De Alessi (1983). While by no means conclusive, what empirical evidence there is on the relative efficiency of private versus public enterprise suggests that, in competitive environments, private companies tend to outperform similar public sector enterprises (Boardman and Vining 1989).

What have come to be known as agency issues arise from a separation of economic roles. Discussions of agency problems, and ultimately agency costs, are typically developed around the separation of ownership from control in private firms (Jensen and Meckling 1976, Fama 1980, Fama and Jensen 1983). However, the concept is useful in understanding a wide range of relationships including those between owner and manager, employer and employee, and − more loosely − citizen and politician. In each case one view of the relationship of the parties is that of principal and agent with divergent interests. Agency costs encompass the costs of monitoring and controlling the divergences as well as the consequence of the divergence (referred to as the 'residual loss').

The economics of governance is based upon a view that there are different ways of organizing economic activities (e.g. within entities such as firms or government departments or in markets). These are viewed as governance structures and it recognizes that the form of organization structure (of which ownership structure is a critical component) chosen to arrange transactions can have important economic consequences. The focus is upon the contracting processes and transaction costs which result from the alternative structures. Thus a change from government department to SOE is a change in governance structure. This paradigm is a branch of transaction cost economics which has emerged from the work of Coase (1937), Cheung (1982), Alchian and Demsetz (1972) and in particular Williamson (1975, 1979, 1985).

Measurement is the other branch of transaction cost economics. Here the concern is with ambiguities in the measurement of performance and quality associated with the provision of goods or services. This is clearly an important issue in government reform at all levels, as measurement costs and governance structures are interdependent. In particular, the form of the organization or governance structure can affect the ease with which performance can be measured. Measurement issues are addressed in Alchian and Demsetz (1972), Ouchi (1980) and Barzel (1982).

These are not the only conceptual underpinnings of public sector reform in New Zealand. As Boston (1991) points out, there are many intellectual currents and counter-currents that have had an influence. In addition to agency and transaction cost economics, Boston provides a useful review of the influence of public choice theory and what he refers to as managerialism and the 'new public management'. However, there is little doubt that the design and implementation of the New

Zealand SOE programme has been most heavily influenced by the concepts of property rights, agency and transaction cost economics.[2]

Levels of reform

Around the world, economic reform which has sought a reduction of state involvement in commercial activities has generally been of three levels, each with different implications for the role of government. The three levels are commercialization, corporatization, and privatization. Taken together they involve significant changes in property rights, agency costs, governance structures and measurement.

Commercialization can be considered as the lowest level of reform. It involves the restructuring of government departments and functions so as to introduce accountability and economic efficiency into government activities. The reform is generally characterized by various attempts to bring market forces to bear on the agents of government. The State Sector Act 1988 and the Public Finance Act 1989 provide the principal legislative components in New Zealand for the commercialization and financial management reform of government departments.

Corporatization is an intermediate level of reform. It is a process whereby the trading activities of government departments are transferred to state-owned corporations. Corporatization in New Zealand has been given structure by the State-Owned Enterprises Act 1986. Under this legislation SOEs are assigned the principal objective of operating as successful businesses. Although ultimate ownership of trading activities does not change under corporatization, the *form* of the ownership structure does. The design puts in place the corporate form of ownership structure and necessary market mechanisms so that the SOE will function similarly to comparable commercial businesses. The study reported in the following chapters focuses on the 1987 corporatization of the Electricity Division of the Ministry of Energy into the Electricity Corporation of New Zealand Limited.

Privatization is the highest level of reform. It involves the withdrawal of the state from the production of goods and services. It typically involves the government selling off the assets (such as plant, land or forests) or its equity in corporatized trading entities. This level of reform has been the most publicized with major events such as the United Kingdom sale of British Telecom and the recent sale of Telecom in New Zealand. Vuylsteke (1988), in a study for the World Bank, identified 1300 cases of enterprise and asset privatization in 86 countries. A more recent survey would show a large increase in the number of privatizations taking place in Western Europe, Asia, Eastern Europe, and Latin America.[3] In Eastern Europe, for

---

2. Treasury officials indicate that it was Cameron and Duigan's (1984) review of property rights, agency and transaction cost economics and their suggested application of these concepts to government owned enterprises that provided the intellectual basis for the resulting SOE reform process.

3. 'Around the world, governments are dumping an unprecedented array of state-owned assets onto the open market', *Time*, 8 April 1991, pp. 34-9.

example, the unwinding of state ownership of productive assets is proceeding at a pace that was unthinkable a short time ago. Poland alone is reported to have 2500 state-owned enterprises that should be candidates for privatization.[4] Privatizations are also underway in Western Europe, most notably the United Kingdom where, since the first sale in 1981, almost 50 state-owned trading entities and corporations have been sold. A further dozen are slated for privatization. A wave of privatization of state-owned enterprises is also reported to be sweeping Latin American countries such as Mexico, Argentina, Brazil, Venezuela, and Honduras.[5]

Reform in New Zealand

As McKinlay (1987) points out, the development of New Zealand's public sector, especially the intervention of the government in trading enterprises, has a long history and is rather different from the experience in the United Kingdom and other countries. New Zealand being a small country with a limited population and skill-base, the common rationale for government intervention was that only government had the resources and stability required to provide the needed service.

Although the original need for such intervention has diminished, the institutions providing the goods and services remained in the public sector. Bureaucratic departments with their vertical organization structures, rules and regulations were difficult to change. Over time serious concerns developed about the efficiency and effectiveness of government departments. These included concern over inappropriate and unnecessary bureaucratic controls, lack of managerial autonomy, unclear and conflicting objectives, lack of proper accountability, and inappropriate organizational structures. A major concern was the lack of clear objectives and the confusion that arose from the mixture of commercial, social, regulatory, and policy roles of government departments.

Attempts were made to introduce better management practices and the Audit Office and the State Services Commission started to develop means of assessing performance of managers and departments (value-for-money or comprehensive performance audits). But progress was slow. By the beginning of the 1980s, those wanting to reform the public sector came to believe that radical change was needed.

New Zealand's fourth Labour Government came into power in July 1984 and embarked on an ambitious programme of economic and public sector reforms. Although they recognized that New Zealand's slow economic growth at the time was influenced by world trends, they also believed the nation's economy was severely hampered by existing policies and controls. To free the economy from what it viewed as the over-regulation imposed by prior governments, the Labour Government implemented a series of initiatives directed at improving trade

---

4. 'Eastern Europe's Economies: What is to be Done?', *The Economist*, 13 January 1990, p. 22.
5. 'Privatisation in Latin America', *The Economist*, 23 March 1991, pp. 82-4.

conditions and the balance of payments. The exchange rate was floated, a programme of the progressive removal of subsidies and tariffs was put into place, income tax rates were slashed, and international investment was encouraged.

A major concern of the Labour Government was the high level of government spending and indebtedness. Fiscal restraint and improved management of public sector entities was thought to be needed to check spending and reduce indebtedness. To improve the efficiency and effectiveness of government entities, they decided to adopt, insofar as possible, a private sector model of management and control. Implementation of new governance structures was considered to be imperative if sustainable improvements to economic efficiency were to be achieved.

Some evolutionary initiatives had been introduced within departments in the early 1980s but the Labour Government dramatically escalated the pace of change. They initiated programmes which were revolutionary rather than evolutionary. The intent was to achieve radical improvements which would encourage cost savings in either of two ways:

Elimination of unnecessary activities. As in other countries, politicians (as well as interest groups and individuals) were questioning the role of government and its involvement in a wide range of activities. Tasks performed and services provided by departments and trading entities were targeted for scrutiny. This was not a new concern. There were many critics of unnecessary government involvement, which required a high tax take to fund its level of spending. These critics generally were of the view that many government services were either unnecessary, or were redundantly supplied by more than one department, or simply would be better supplied by the private sector.

Improved efficiencies. There was also much criticism of the excessive cost of the services due to inefficiency, the unwieldiness of bureaucratic organizations, and the lack of autonomy of the providers from Government. Government organizations were seen as being slow and inflexible in their dealings with the public, and the tales of inefficiency were apparently being supported by fact.

Commercialization of trading entities

The philosophy behind the early changes to the public sector was outlined by Government in two documents: the Economic Statement issued in December 1985[6] and the Expenditure Reform document issued in May 1986.[7] The Economic Statement explicitly described a new way of viewing trading entities, with a much more commercial orientation than had previously been the case. Four key principles were identified to encourage the new commercial approach to management of SOEs:

*1 Responsibility for **non-commercial** functions was to be transferred from major trading state-owned enterprises.*

Removal of conflict between social and commercial objectives improves

---

6. Hon. R.O. Douglas, *Economic Statement*, Statement to the House of Representatives, 12 December 1985.

7. Hon. R. O. Douglas, *Statement on Government Expenditure Reform 1986*, 19 May 1986.

performance measurement. Where these objectives are not separated, managers could not be held accountable for performance. Under the new scheme, politicians make social policy and the Government may then contract with and pay the appropriate entities for its implementation. The departments or corporations involved would then receive a fair price for providing the service. Managers become free to make commercial decisions and can thus be properly assessed on their performance. Commercial and non-commercial activities are to be funded and accounted for separately. The separation should provide transparency by disclosing the true costs of providing subsidized services. The achievement of social goals could be funded through direct subsidy. If a social service is considered desirable, Government would purchase the service, thus entering the arena as a customer.

A fear quickly surfaced in the community, and is still prevalent, that non-profitable functions and services of departments would be ended. This concern was subsequently validated by a number of events. Perhaps the most emotive was the closing down of many small Post Offices throughout the country because they were considered non-viable commercial units. This separation of socio-political goals from commercial objectives has had an important impact on NZED.

2 The principal objective of managers of state-owned enterprises is to operate them as successful businesses.

The SOEs became limited liability corporations and, as such, were subject to relevant company, securities and other laws. They were also required to pay taxes. The chain of responsibility and authority is modelled on private corporations where managers report to Boards of Directors who are accountable to shareholders. In the case of SOEs, the Government is the shareholder. It was believed that trading organizations, by acting in the best private-sector tradition, would provide an appropriate return for Government investment. Cash flow (i.e. 'income' from a government accounting viewpoint) would be derived from taxes and dividends from earnings. The State's investment in the SOE would also be increased by the reinvestment of retained profits. Experienced business people were sought for many of the management positions as they were expected to be more aligned to this objective. Boards of Directors were selected predominantly from the private sector, although people from public sector backgrounds were not precluded from selection.

3 Managers are given the responsibility for decisions on the use of inputs and on pricing and marketing of their outputs.

Managers are given the freedom to make commercial decisions without political interference. SOEs prepare a Statement of Corporate Intent which specifies the scope and nature of activities, performance targets and sets out dividend policy. They are then responsible to Parliament through the appropriate Minister, who is to monitor their adherence to plans. In this way the Government is able to administer its investment but is restricted from intervention in the operations of the SOE. Another important facet of this arrangement was the greater freedom of decision making and accountability given to managers. By separating trading activities from government departments, Treasury and the State Services Commission no longer dominated financial and personnel policies.

The intended effects are better defined responsibility and quicker decision making. For example, the hiring of personnel is now under the control of the entity. This recognizes that managers within the organization should be better able to assess human resource needs than an officer of the State Services Commission.

Similarly, there are fewer opportunities for intervention by Treasury, which now has a new relationship with SOEs. Treasury's new role is that of economic adviser and financial analyst to the Shareholding Ministers. It no longer has the specific economic and accounting controls it exerted prior to corporatization. Management of financial affairs means greater control of funds held within corporation bank accounts, and greater ability to deal in financial markets to get the best possible borrowing rates and to control risk with hedging instruments. However, as a part of the new found freedom, SOEs are no longer the beneficiaries of Government's guarantee of its debts. This has been made explicit by Government, although implicit guarantees are still presumed to exist by some lenders. Arranging borrowings in the commercial markets without the benefit of explicit Government guarantees placed SOEs squarely in a commercial environment.

This extensive accountability process, including full disclosure of both Statement of Corporate Intent and operating results, is designed to address inherent agency problems. It should encourage the efficient and effective use of resources.

4 Unnecessary barriers to competition are being removed so that commercial criteria will provide a fair assessment of managerial performance.

Many SOEs operated in an environment where they had enjoyed monopoly status or derived other benefits from state ownership. The resulting potential for misuse of this power was a major concern. In addition, it would be difficult to assess managerial performance if market forces were not pressing upon the corporations. Studies of various industries were commissioned and, where appropriate, a process of deregulation was started. Creation of commercial and competitive environments for SOEs, wherever possible, was essential to the whole programme. Potential competitors had to be allowed freedom of entry, and surrogates for competitive pressures had to be designed. Government was endeavouring to adjust the regulatory environment so that there would be competitive neutrality between Government and commercial entities. The catch phrase used to describe the goal of these efforts was the 'level playing field'. Competitive forces would drive SOEs to efficiency and effectiveness.

However, merely imposing change on existing organizations was unlikely to result in the required improvements. The governance structure had to be right. If SOEs were to be run as businesses in a normal commercial fashion, they would need to be restructured internally as well as externally. Political and bureaucratic control that had restricted the actions of the predecessor departments had to be removed or limited. It would be up to the new managements of the SOEs to reorganize themselves to compete in their new environments. How an SOE should organize itself was not dictated to managers. SOEs were responsible for achieving their performance objectives, with the means being determined within the organization.

These four key principles of the Economic Statement of December 1985 became the cornerstones of the State-Owned Enterprises Act 1986. However, before we move to a discussion of that Act, it is worth noting the related efforts being directed at non-trading areas of Government.

Commercialization of non-trading entities

The May 1986 Expenditure Reform document outlined more initiatives for reform. This extended a commercial approach to some non-trading departments and indirectly encouraged privatization of SOEs. A major objective was to subject non-trading activities of Government to commercial pressures.

To encourage the process, the budget speech in 1986 gave due notice of longer-term cuts in funding which were proposed for some departments. By implication, these departments would have to reduce the level of their activities unless they were able to find funding from alternative sources. An obvious source of funds for many departments was through recovery of costs from recipients of the services, either individuals in the community or other government departments. Many activities provided free of charge previously would now become 'user pays'. Charging for traditionally 'free' services would presumably determine whether the activity was worthwhile. It would also encourage private enterprise to expand into these areas once the level playing field was established.

The resulting experience in New Zealand was similar to what had been experienced in other countries. Many tasks being undertaken by the public sector could be provided more effectively and efficiently in other ways. In addition, costs could be cut while maintaining appropriate levels of service and recipients of Government services were often willing and able to pay for the benefits they received.

State-Owned Enterprises Act 1986

The State-Owned Enterprises Act 1986 became law in December 1986. The SOE Act embodied the principles outlined in the Economic Statement of December 1985. The purpose of the Act was to officially legislate the framework needed to put into effect the Government's policies on the management of SOEs. Principles for management and control of Government trading entities and their commercial orientation were now law. The primary objective of each SOE is to be a successful business. They are to be as profitable and efficient as comparable private sector businesses. In addition, the SOE is required to be a good employer and to act in a socially responsible manner.

Ownership of SOEs on behalf of the Government is by the Minister of Finance and the responsible Minister. All shares are held by them with the exception (if issued) of redeemable (non-convertible) preference shares which do not confer any voting rights. Similarly, any equity bonds issued by resolution of the House of Representatives do not confer voting rights. Annual audited financial statements are required. These annual reports are released to the public.

As owners, the Government is interested in earning a risk-adjusted return on its investments. SOEs were being asked to succeed in commercial markets; to change their perspective from that of civil-service organizations to that of profit-oriented businesses. To be successful, there would have to be enormous alterations in the objectives of the entities and pervasive adjustments throughout the organizations. Having established an overall framework for change, the Government then wanted to avoid dictating issues of implementation to the SOEs. However, it was considered essential that SOEs have clear statements of purpose, and that their achievements be measurable and transparent. Performance was primarily to be evaluated on profitability, thus imposing commercial incentives upon management.

A draft Statement of Corporate Intent with plans for the current and subsequent two years must be delivered to the Shareholding Ministers within a month of the start of a financial year. Responsibility for this is with the Board of Directors of the SOE. The Statement of Corporate Intent includes objectives of the corporation, nature and scope of activities to be undertaken, accounting policies, performance targets, and other measures by which performance may be judged in relation to its objectives.

The Statement of Corporate Intent ensures that objectives are clearly stated and appropriate resources acquired and utilized for the long term good of the organization. It also provides a means for evaluating the efficiency and effectiveness of SOEs by comparison of actual results to plan. To ensure that the corporations were free to pursue commercial goals without reference to the many social and political goals which had been part of their roles as government departments, non-commercial objectives were explicitly removed as a responsibility. Where the Crown wants to have an SOE provide goods or services to any persons or other Government entities, they will specifically purchase the goods or services. The Crown and the SOE can enter into an agreement for the provision in return for payment.

The SOE Act consists of four components which are critical to its success. These components relate directly to the four concepts described above, which underlie all of the reform. Ownership is separated from control in the conventional corporate fashion: equity holders, board of directors, and managers. Business planning is required, particularly through the Statement of Corporate Intent. Monitoring is implemented through annual audits, reports to the Shareholding Ministers, and public reporting. Accountability is direct from managers to the Board to shareholders and is based upon conformance to plan.

Electricity Corporation of New Zealand Limited

Electricity Corporation of New Zealand Limited was formally registered as a limited liability company in February 1987 and commenced operations on 1 April 1987. ECNZ is a state-owned enterprise whose shares are held by the Minister of Finance and the responsible Minister on behalf of Government. ECNZ was the successor to the Electricity Division of the Ministry of Energy. The overriding objective of NZED was to ensure that a reliable supply of electricity was made available to the country and its consumers. This orientation, over many years, had led to an oversupply of electrical generating capacity, non-commercial pricing, a high degree of cross-subsidizing in favour of residential consumers, and a lack of focus upon cost containment and efficiency. NZED provides an excellent illustration of the commingling of economic, social and political objectives which was discussed above. Consistent with the SOE Act, the objective of ECNZ is to operate as a successful commercial enterprise.

The electricity industry in New Zealand

The electricity industry in New Zealand is overwhelmingly dominated by two organizations: ECNZ (formerly NZED) and the electricity supply authorities (ESAs). ECNZ is responsible for virtually all generation, transmission and wholesaling of electricity in New Zealand. Retail distribution is handled by local-monopoly electricity supply authorities. ECNZ generates over 95 percent of New Zealand's electricity and virtually all electricity is transmitted through the national grid.

In 1986, under NZED, the country's generating capacity of 7435 MW was sourced 63 percent from hydroelectric, 28 percent from steam (including geothermal) and 9 percent from combustion turbines. Approximately 72 percent of total energy produced by this system that year was hydroelectric. The system is characterized by geographic imbalances. Well over half of the hydro capacity is located in the South Island where only a quarter of the population resides. Fossil fuel generation is entirely on the North Island. The two islands are linked through a high voltage direct current line. In 1988, ECNZ estimated that excess capacity was 15-20 percent.

To encourage competition, the generating and wholesaling portions of the industry have been deregulated since 1986. Government attempted to create a competitively neutral setting where threat of entry is real. It is clear that ECNZ is overwhelmingly dominant in the industry. However, it is not clear that they are a natural monopoly in all areas of operation. It is generally agreed that transmission, through the national grid, constitutes a natural monopoly. It is less clear and arguable whether the monopoly power exists in generation. This issue is discussed in more detail at a number of points in this report.

Establishment of Electricity Corporation of New Zealand Limited

An Establishment Board was founded to lay the ground work for corporatization of NZED. This group became the Board of Directors upon incorporation. Mr C.J. Fernyhough was appointed Chairman of the Board in August 1986. None of the Board members were from NZED. The company functioned through the leadership of Mr Fernyhough and committees of the Board until May 1987, when Dr Roderick Deane assumed the position of Chief Executive. The majority of the new Senior Management team were not previously employed by NZED. In addition to the obvious need to maintain the operations of the company, two tasks initially absorbed the Board and management.

The organization required extensive restructuring, as is discussed in the following chapters. It was also necessary to negotiate the terms under which ECNZ would assume assets, liabilities and operating responsibilities of NZED. The contentious and critically important issue was the value of the assets to be transferred. The value set would have important implications for the ability of the new firm to earn a target rate of return. The book value of the NZED assets was \$3,766 million at 1 April 1987. However, Treasury, acting as consultants to the shareholder, argued for a substantially larger amount. The two sides were unable to reach agreement. Therefore, ECNZ operated under a licence arrangement for its first year to 31 March 1988. As of that date, agreement was reached between the Government and the Board of Directors of ECNZ as to the value of the assets to be transferred and the related liability structure. A fixed asset valuation of \$6.3 billion was agreed to, backdated to 1 April 1987. In addition, long-term debt was adjusted to \$3.0 billion. Implications of this valuation are considered in Chapter 7.

References

Alchian, Armen, and Harold Demsetz (1972) 'Production, Information Costs, and Economic Organisation', *American Economic Review* 62 (December), pp. 777-95.

Barzel, Yoram (1982) 'Measurement Cost and Organization of Markets', *Journal of Law and Economics* 25 (April), pp. 27-48.

Boardman, Anthony and Aidan Vining (1989) 'Ownership and Performance in Competitive Environments: A Comparison of the Performance of Private, Mixed and State-Owned Enterprises', *Journal of Law and Economics* 32 (April), pp. 1-32.

Boston, Jonathan (1991) 'The Theoretical Underpinnings of Public Sector Restructuring in New Zealand', in Jonathan Boston, John Martin, June Pallot, and Pat Walsh (eds) *Reshaping the State: New Zealand's Bureaucratic Revolution*, Auckland, Oxford University Press.

Cameron, R.L and P.J. Duigan (1984) 'Government Owned Enterprises: Theory Performance and Efficiency', Paper presented to New Zealand Association of Economists' Conference, February.

Cheung, Stephen (1982) 'The Contractual Nature of the Firm', *Journal of Law and Economics* 26 (April), pp. 1-22.

Coase, Ronald (1937) 'The Nature of the Firm', *Economica N.S.* 4, pp. 386-405.

Deane, Roderick (1991) *Reflections on Privatisation*, Occasional Paper 32, Auckland, The Centre for Independent Studies.

De Alessi, Louis (1983) 'Property Rights, Transactions Costs and X-Efficiency: An Essay in Economic Theory', *American Economic Review* 73 (March), pp. 64-81.

Fama, Eugene (1980) 'Agency Problems and the Theory of the Firm', *Journal of Political Economy* 88 (April), pp. 288-307.

Fama, Eugene and Michael Jensen (1983) 'Separation of Ownership and Control', *Journal of Law and Economics* 26 (June), pp. 301-26.

Furubotn, E., and S. Pejovich (1972) 'Property Rights and Economic Theory: A Survey of Recent Literature', *Journal of Economic Literature* 10 (December) pp. 1137-62.

Jensen, Michael and William Meckling (1976) 'Theory of the Firm: Managerial Behavior, Agency Costs and Capital Structure', *Journal of Financial Economics* 3 (October), pp. 305-60.

Jennings, Stephen and Rob Cameron (1987) 'State-Owned Enterprise Reform in New Zealand' in Alan Bollard and Robert Buckle (eds) *Economic Liberalisation in New Zealand* Wellington, Allen and Unwin.

McKinlay, Peter (1987) *Corporatisation: The Solution for State Owned Enterprise?* Wellington, Institute of Policy Studies.

Ouchi, William (1980) 'Markets, Bureaucracies and Clans', *Administrative Science Quarterly* 25 (March) pp. 120-42.

Vuylsteke, C. (1988) 'Techniques of Privatisation of State-Owned Enterprises', World Bank Technical Paper Number 88, World Bank, Washington.

Williamson, Oliver (1975) *Markets and Hierarchies: Analysis and Antitrust Implications* New York, Free Press.

Williamson, Oliver (1979) 'Transaction-cost Economics: The Governance of Contractual Relations', *The Journal of Law and Economics* 22 (October) pp. 3-61.

Williamson, Oliver (1985) *The Economic Institutions of Capitalism* New York, Free Press.

3

Strategic Response of the New Corporation

As noted in Chapter 2, ECNZ is required by the SOE Act to operate as a commercial business, subject only to the normal constraints imposed on private enterprise in New Zealand. This includes the payment of taxes. The main difference between ECNZ and a private sector corporation is the ownership structure. As a corporation, ECNZ is wholly owned by the State with the Ministers of Finance and the responsible Minister (in this case the Minister for State-Owned Enterprises) acting as the Shareholding Ministers.

At the same time as ECNZ was established, the generation side of the electricity industry was deregulated. Removal of economic licensing of new generating facilities and the lack of explicit controls over the price of electricity meant that ECNZ did not enjoy government protection from competition as did its predecessor. These two events have had significant effects on the strategy and structure of this organization.

Our purpose in this chapter is to identify and describe the key pressures faced by ECNZ just after its establishment as an SOE and its strategic responses to these pressures. We consider how and why the new Board and management responded as they did. We focus on the time of the establishment of ECNZ and a period of roughly two years thereafter. Since that time, some of the key pressures discussed in this chapter have changed in intensity, partly as a result of ECNZ's own strategic responses and partly because of the continuing restructuring of the electricity industry. Some of these key pressures are discussed again in Chapter 5 in relation to how they have influenced competition in ECNZ's generation and wholesale electricity markets.

Key pressures driving the development of ECNZ competitive strategy

As Figure 3.1 shows, we treat the the problem of surplus generating capacity as a pressure internal to ECNZ, and the remaining four pressures as external. Threat of entry in generation and competition from substitutes are market-based pressures, and the rate of return objective and the threat of regulation are government-based pressures.

Surplus generating capacity
For a number of reasons — including the oil shock in the early 1970s, inflation, the need of the government of the day to deal with unemployment, and the

Figure 3.1

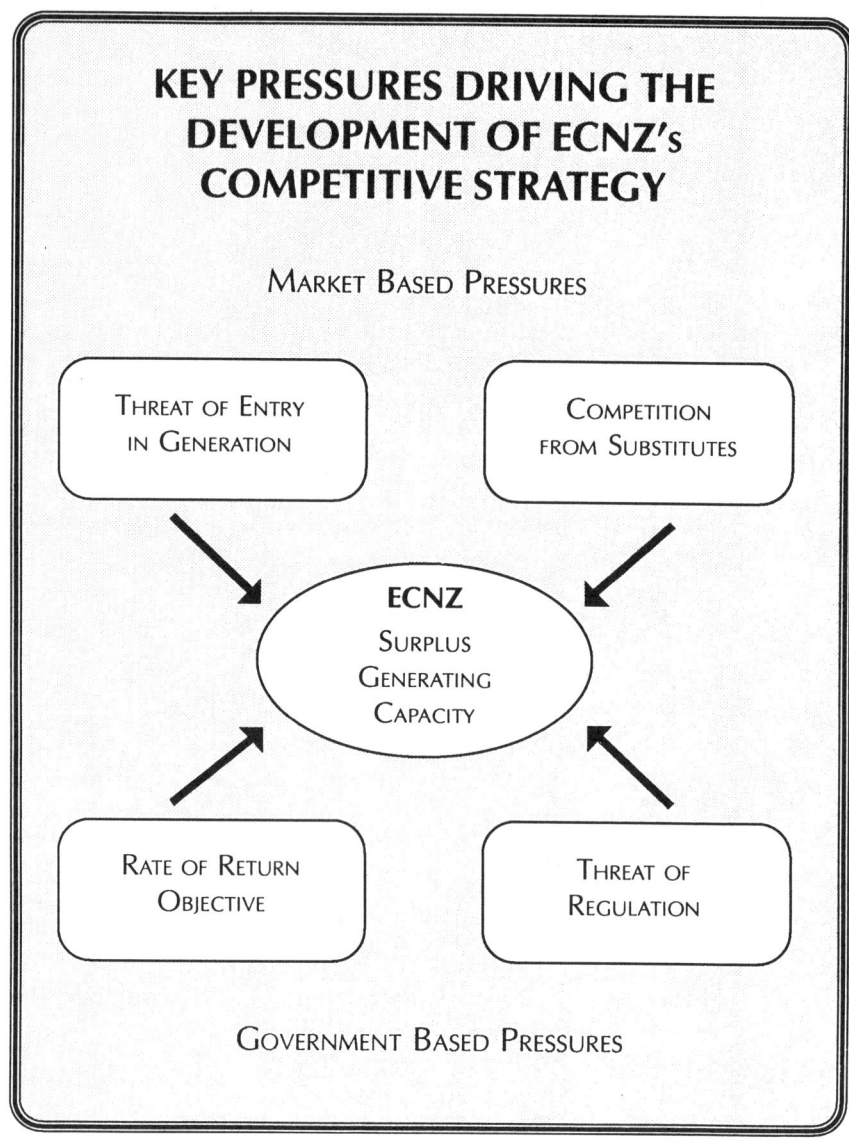

KEY PRESSURES DRIVING THE
DEVELOPMENT OF ECNZ's
COMPETITIVE STRATEGY

MARKET BASED PRESSURES

THREAT OF ENTRY
IN GENERATION

COMPETITION
FROM SUBSTITUTES

ECNZ
SURPLUS
GENERATING
CAPACITY

RATE OF RETURN
OBJECTIVE

THREAT OF
REGULATION

GOVERNMENT BASED PRESSURES

engineering orientation of the old organization – substantial overbuilding of generating capacity occurred prior to the establishment of ECNZ. As a result, the generating capacity taken over by ECNZ from NZED was far greater than that needed to meet current demands for electricity. The extent of this surplus capacity was addressed by *The Task Force Report on Electricity Corporation Organisation Structure,*[1] which reported that:

Contrasting the load forecasts with existing capacity suggests that no extra generating capacity will be required for some time. This is particularly pertinent for thermal; it is unlikely a major thermal station will be required in this century. (p. 23)

Management's desire to maximize the use of this surplus generating capacity became a key consideration in the development of ECNZ's strategic response to its environment.

The threat of entry in generation

Before deregulation of the electricity industry, NZED enjoyed a monopoly in electricity generation. The need to obtain government consent for the production of electricity made it extremely difficult for anyone, including licensed supply authorities, to produce electricity from any source. As a result NZED generated 96% of all electricity produced in New Zealand.

Although ECNZ was in no danger of losing its dominant-firm status immediately after incorporation, the removal of economic licensing made the market for generation contestable. The only remaining barriers to entry were economic ones. ECNZ faced the threat of entry in generation from various potential competitors: supply authorities building their own generating facilities, firms with cogeneration opportunities, and private corporations seeking to enter the generation market. This threat put at risk ECNZ's ability to maximize the use of its surplus generating capacity, and created a powerful pressure on ECNZ's managers to develop a competitive strategy that would act to deter entry.

That the threat was taken seriously by ECNZ's managers and was a key motive in the development of ECNZ's strategy is clear from a number of sources. These include: (1) the 1987 *Task Force Report*; (2) key strategy papers prepared in 1988 for the Board of ECNZ; and (3) interviews with a number of senior managers and Board members.

Some relevant excerpts from the 1987 *Task Force Report* read as follows:

If the assets of the new corporation are close to book value and a reasonable financial gearing level is set there is likely to be some comparative cost advantage to the Corporation [in generation] . . . However, asset values and the gearing level have yet to be determined and organisations will have the freedom to invest in generation — whether they are supply authorities, cogeneration opportunities or private organisations. There will be an increased potential level of competition for generation. (p. 15)

---

1. *The Task Force Report on Electricity Corporation Organisation Structure* which reported their recommendations in February 1987 provides the blueprint for the initial establishment and structure of the new Electricity Corporation. It is an important document which contains a fairly complete discussion of the management philosophy involved in developing the structure of the Corporation. It will be referred to in the text simply as the *Task Force Report*. An overview of some of the management principles and criteria underlying the Task Force recommendations is contained in Appendix A (pages 153–5).

It would be prudent planning to allow for increased competition. (p. 23)

> . . . the threat, and possible later reality of competing generators will be a significant
> spur. And many other effective competitive elements can exist . . . (p. 58)

The strategic planning papers prepared for the Board of ECNZ in mid-1988 reviewed in detail a number of major and minor proposals for the construction of competing generating plants in New Zealand. The proposals included: (1) a 500 megawatt coal-fired CRA plant at Marsden; (2) a 160 megawatt gas-fired combined-cycle plant by Auckland Electric Power Board; (3) a 25 megawatt geothermal plant by Fletcher Challenge at Tauhara; (4) a maximum 40 megawatt geothermal plant by McLachlan adjacent to Wairakei; (5) a gas-fired combined-cycle plant proposed by Hutt Valley Energy Board; (6) a 6.5 megawatt geothermal plant at Rotokawa proposed by the Gas and Geothermal Trading Group; and (7) a 25-50 megawatt geothermal plant proposed by Fletchers at Mokai.

These proposals triggered a number of strategic analyses by the Corporation, including:

(1) The investigation of price profiles designed to deter entry and of their impacts on ECNZ's own return and profitability.

(2) The simulation of the financial effects on ECNZ of entry by other major generators and of potential pricing responses to new entry.

(3) Studies of the economics of major proposals from the perspective of the potential competitor.

The strategic planning papers and the analyses they contain make it clear that the Corporation, with its surplus generating capacity, was very concerned about the prospects for new entry into generation in both the short and medium terms. Managers therefore took steps to collect market intelligence on potential entrants and to analyse the potential effect of different strategic responses to new entry on the future profitability of the Corporation. One conclusion drawn from these analyses was that the Corporation's delivered price of electricity was above the cost of generation for a new entrant. Another was that the Corporation's net worth would be increased by deterring potential entrants, even if this involved a real reduction in the average delivered wholesale price of electricity.

Our interviews with senior managers and Board members corroborated what we found in the documents. None of the people we interviewed believed that the threat of new entry faced by ECNZ shortly after its incorporation had been overstated. They were also adamant in their belief that, given the Corporation's surplus generating capacity, new entry of the sort being proposed by Auckland Electric Power Board (a 160 megawatt plant) or CRA (a 500 megawatt plant) would, if it occurred, materially affect the Corporation's future return on assets. Keith Turner, Corporate Development Manager, put this view to us in the following way:

> The sort of surplus capacity we have means that we have under-utilised plant lying
> around that we are having to pay the standing costs on from our existing revenue

Figure 3.2 Market growth and market shares in the non-transport energy market 1980-1986 and estimated 1987-1989

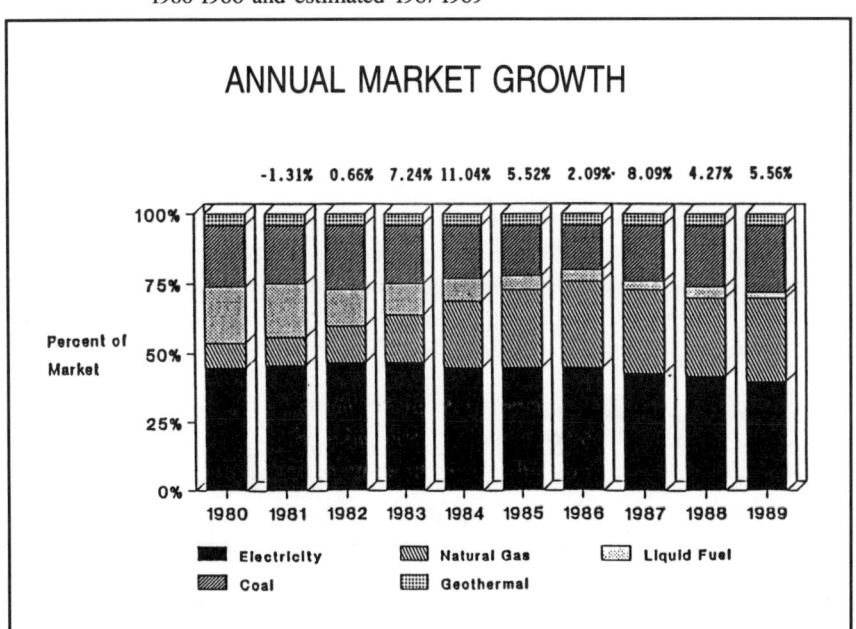

base. If someone comes along and reduces our revenue by building a new generating plant, that's a reduction in the funds needed to pay for those surplus plants. If for example, a new plant from Auckland came in it would have a life of 25-30 years and so we are at risk of losing that revenue for at least that time period.

Competition from substitutes

While the threat of competition from new entry in generation was a direct consequence of the deregulation of the electricity industry by the removal of economic licensing, electricity as a product has always been subject to competition from other fuels such as gas and coal.

The most recent hard data on the non-transport energy market was prepared by the Ministry of Energy in 1986. Electricorp Marketing used this as the basis for the graph shown in Figure 3.2. It shows that, even though the overall market for non-transport energy was growing, the share of this market held by the electricity industry has been declining. In a memorandum to the Chairman and Board of Directors of ECNZ dated 18 January 1988, the General Manager of Electricorp Marketing commented as follows:

The details of the [Ministry of Energy] 1986 forecast are presented in [Figure 3.2], where it can be seen that even then, although a steady growth in electricity volume was predicted, our market share decline was forecast to continue at the rate of 1%

per annum. This loss in market share can be attributed to NZ Steel contracts secured by Coalcorp and continued market penetration by natural gas. The greater degree of commercial confidentiality now practised by the energy industry has meant that no definitive energy forecasts are currently available and thus market share figures are estimated.

As a result of our specific marketing strategies we anticipate that the predicted decline in market share will be arrested and that a small improvement in market share will be achieved during the latter half of the 1988/89 financial year.

In the quasi-commercial environment they operated in, the loss of market share to competing fuels was of little consequence to NZED managers. ECNZ's managers, on the other hand, concerned about the surplus generating capacity taken over by the new Corporation, considered the need to win back market share to be a key factor in the profits equation.

The rate of return objective
Under the SOE Act, ECNZ is expected to earn a commercial return on shareholder's funds. Pressure for meeting rate of return objectives has come from both inside as well as outside the Corporation. Initial pressure came from the new Chairman of the Board, the Board itself, and the Chief Executive. As Roderick Deane, Chief Executive, explained:

> I think that the biggest pressure on the organisation came from the Chairman of the Board wanting better commercial performance. He wasn't under so much pressure from Ministers as from his own self motivation and the wish to prove that this task he'd taken on could be done. I felt a lot of that personally as well.

However, pressure was also to come from a disagreement between the Shareholding Ministers and ECNZ over the Corporation's rate of return objective. Correspondence between the Shareholding Ministers and ECNZ's Board Chairman and Chief Executive shows that pressure was placed on ECNZ to raise the rate of return on shareholder's funds to at least the average level for major non-government-owned corporations. The problem faced by ECNZ managers was how to achieve higher rates of return on an asset base valued at $6.3 billion (which was considerably higher than the Corporation had negotiated for), while at the same time competing for increased market share and volume against other fuels and deterring new entry in generation.

The threat of regulation
There were two regulatory threats that placed pressure on ECNZ. The first related to the operation of the national grid. The second related to ECNZ's behaviour as the dominant firm in the electricity industry.

The national grid is the main arterial network covering New Zealand and includes the HVDC (high voltage direct current) link across Cook Strait. The function of the grid is to transmit electricity to different regions of the North and South Islands. Because of its highly specific nature and the size of the investment, the national grid is considered to be the 'natural monopoly' part of the restructured electricity industry. It faces no real threat of competition, although any development of on-site generation and cogeneration would reduce the demand for the transmission services of the grid. For competition in generation to be a viable threat, however, other generators must be allowed open access to the national grid on non-discriminatory terms. ECNZ's managers understood that failure to provide this access could result in regulatory action against them under the Commerce Act. Consequently, the threat of regulatory action to curb monopolistic behaviour with respect to the operation of the national grid constituted a key constraint on the behaviour and performance of ECNZ.

Similarly, ECNZ's managers understood that any attempt by the Corporation to exploit its dominant-firm position (and the high switching costs of existing end-users of electricity) by raising prices unreasonably and out of line with movements in costs could result in legal action taken under the provisions of the Commerce Act or in the creation of electricity price regulations.

ECNZ's strategic responses to key pressures

Figure 3.1 and the associated discussion outlined the five key pressures which combined to drive the development of ECNZ's competitive strategy. Figure 3.3 depicts ECNZ's strategic responses to these pressures.

Contain the trend of electricity prices

Although there were a number of actions ECNZ took to deal with the threat of new entry into generation, the heart of their strategy has been to send out a clear *signal* of their determination to hold prices in real terms at least in the short to medium term. The development of this pricing strategy was based on the analysis discussed above. The conclusion drawn was that the net worth of the Corporation would be greater under a decision to reduce prices in order to deter entry by a major competitor (such as Auckland Electric Power Board) than it would be if new entry occurred and the Corporation suffered a corresponding loss of revenue. Keith Turner, Corporate Development Manager, commented as follows:

> Pricing policy is a pretty fundamental issue to the company. Without any regulation on us there is theoretically no cap on prices. We could set our price almost at whatever we wish as a dominant company. However, when the Government set us up they also deregulated generation so this means that anyone can now build power stations. If those proposing power stations look on them as commercial investments then they will build a power station when they can produce power at a price which is equal to or lower than our supply price. For example, if Auckland Electric Power Board can produce power at a price lower than our supply price there is an incentive for them to do so. It is not really as simple as that because it is also tied up with load factors, reliabilities and system support as well, but it does illustrate the basic economics we face.

Board documents and business plans corroborate the central importance of pricing strategy to the current and future performance of ECNZ.

Figure 3.3

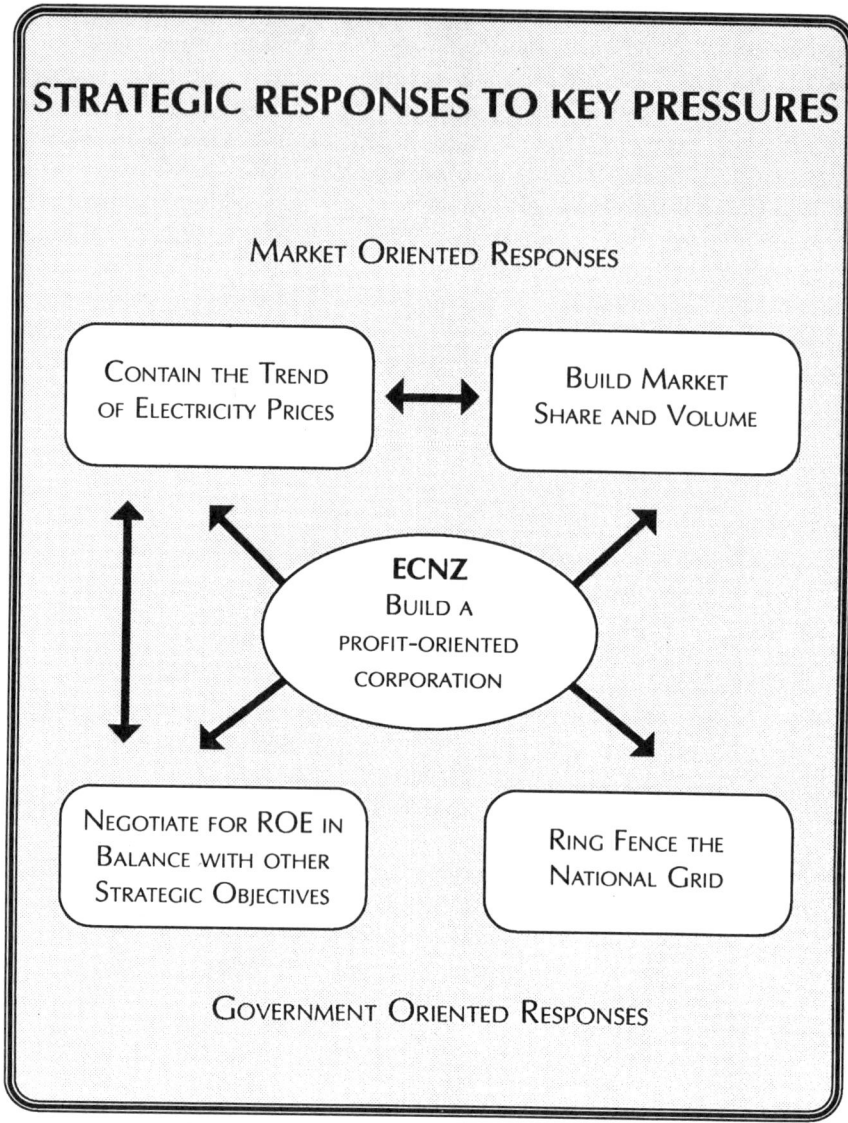

A major policy decision taken by the Board in 1989 shows the continuing emphasis placed on pricing policy as a means of deterring entry. The Board's decision was to adopt a declining real price trend for average wholesale electricity prices. The stated objective of this policy was to ensure that the delivered price of base-load energy moves below the entry cost of new generation plant. The target date for achieving this result was 1992.

As a step towards implementation of this policy, ECNZ's marketing plan called for it to hold average wholesale prices in *nominal* terms throughout 1990/91. The objective of this pricing policy was to constrain nominal prices in order that the base-load price of delivered energy in the North Island is competitive with the average price expected from a new base-load station. ECNZ managers report that the company has substantially achieved these objectives. They believe that containment of the price trend has been instrumental in lowering the probability of a competitor entering and building a major new generating plant.[2] Marketing managers believe that price containment has allowed them to influence the outcome of a number of cogeneration studies (involving in excess of 200 GWh per annum) by providing information about the outlook for electricity prices in the medium to long term, and/or by offering to participate as joint-venture partners at an appropriate time.

A crucial difference between pricing policy under ECNZ and NZED is that business strategy is now the driving force in deciding on pricing trends and structures. While the Shareholding Ministers placed upwards pressure on prices through the initial asset valuation and their expectations with respect to rate of return, the Government has relinquished direct control over pricing to ECNZ's Board of Directors. Competitive strategy became paramount in deliberations about pricing policy, with the Corporation's rate of return objective acting as a constraint. This is considerably different from the prior situation in which pricing was heavily influenced by political and fiscal considerations. As a result, price movements often had little association with movements in generation costs or the need to be competitive.

Build market share and volume

As illustrated in Figure 3.3, ECNZ's two market-oriented responses of containing electricity prices and building market share and volume are interrelated. The view of ECNZ's top managers was that pricing policy was as crucial to winning back market share from competing energy products such as gas and coal as it was to deterring competitors from entering the market for electricity generation. Containing prices was seen as a necessary but not a sufficient condition for reclaiming market share and building the volume needed to maximize the use of its surplus generating capacity. ECNZ also developed an aggressive marketing programme aimed at developing market intelligence and flexible pricing structures, and at improving customer relations, advertising and promotion skills. These were considered critical to the successful marketing of electricity in an increasingly competitive energy marketplace.

---

2. Reference can be made to the financial analysis of ECNZ's performance in Chapter 7. By looking at Figure 7.8 showing Sales Volume 1980-1990 and Figure 7.10 showing Sales Revenue 1980-1990 it can be readily seen that ECNZ has been successful in holding average wholesale prices constant in *real* terms. Also, internal company data made available to us shows that during 1990/91 ECNZ actually managed to *reduce* average wholesale prices in *nominal* terms.

A surprisingly strong and successful marketing presence was developed by ECNZ in a relatively short period of time. As a result Electricorp Marketing, the new marketing division, has consistently exceeded market share and volume performance targets set in the business-planning process. Major competitors have started to 'feel the heat', as is evidenced by the following excerpt from Derek A. Johnson's Presidential address to the annual conference of the Gas Association of New Zealand on 19 February 1990. Using an aquatic metaphor, Mr Johnson commented:

> Coming across the horizon and sharply into focus is that smoothly hulled catamaran, captained by Electricorp Marketing and crewed by members of the ESA. An odd craft this, sponsored by the Government but it displays a compelling competitive urge to get its regulatory rigging untangled and to rundown the increasingly popular aquatic gas duo of Miss Cogeneration and Miss Airconditioning.

The emphasis ECNZ put on building market share and volume through marketing efforts involved a significant change in the orientation of the organization, moving it in the direction of a market-driven company. This has involved employing marketing professionals and developing a marketing orientation in the Corporation, while retaining the considerable skills possessed by its professional engineers. This shift in the direction and 'culture' of the Corporation will be discussed more fully below.

To summarize, the reasons given by ECNZ's managers for their pricing strategy of holding average wholesale electricity prices in real terms are that this was being done (1) to reduce the threat of entry in generation and (2) to build volume against competing fuels so as to maximize the use of its excess generating capacity. However, it should be noted here that we encountered scepticism outside the Corporation about the reasoning behind ECNZ's pricing strategy – particularly insofar as it is based on the need to deter entry. Outside observers express the opinion that the threat of entry has been consistently overstated by ECNZ. Accordingly we carried out further investigations and discussions, and return to this topic in Chapter 5.

Negotiate for a rate of return expectation in balance with other strategic objectives

The vertical arrows in Figure 3.3 between the boxes on the left hand side of the diagram represent the balance that needed to be struck in ECNZ's pricing strategy between deterring entry and building market share and volume on the one hand, and meeting rate of return objectives on the other.

One strategic response of ECNZ to this tension was to negotiate with the Shareholding Ministers for a rate of return requirement in line with the competitive situation of the Corporation. Other responses have involved attempts to increase revenues by driving up volume and to focus internal management attention on cost containment strategies and programmes. Only the first strategic response will be discussed here. The last two responses will be discussed in later sections of the report.

The argument presented by the Corporation for a short-run reduction in the rate of return expectations of the Shareholding Ministers was that forcing higher rates of return would result in putting upwards pressure on prices which, given the competitive situation faced by the company, could result in a long-run diminution in the overall net worth of the Corporation. As noted above, there has been disagreement between the Board of ECNZ and the Shareholding Ministers on this matter. Ministers assert the need for ECNZ to lift its rate of return to bring it into line with average levels earned by major non-government-owned corporations in New Zealand. ECNZ argues that this expectation would be hard to achieve given the high valuation placed on assets at incorporation and its competitive need to reduce average real electricity prices.

This process of negotiation can be seen in the following exchange of letters between the Shareholding Ministers and ECNZ over the 1989/90 performance target in the Statement of Corporate Intent. On 8 June 1989 John Fernyhough, Board Chairman, wrote to the Shareholding Ministers:

> . . . there was some reluctance on the part of the Board to move from the [Return on Equity] figure of 10% to 11% as contained within our plan given that this range has only been decided upon after exhaustive analysis by the Board of the plan submitted by management, and bearing in mind that the Plan provides for what we would regard as a demanding increase in sales volume and a further substantial drop in real unit costs. However, the Board would be prepared to live with the compromise I suggested in my letter of 10.5% to 11.5% for the year and I suggest that we now move to agree on this range.

In a letter dated 23 June 1989 the Minister of Finance replied:

> It is a matter of considerable concern to us that ECNZ, having achieved an excellent performance in going from a 4% return on shareholder's funds in 1987/88 to an 11% return in 1988/89, is now proposing a potentially lower return for 1989/90, which, we understand, is unlikely to increase in subsequent years on the basis of your current plans. These proposed profitability levels are some way below the average level for major non-Government owned corporations in New Zealand. While we are pleased that you have made small increase in your proposed level of performance, we would ask you to consider a performance target that is no lower than an 11.5% rate of return on shareholder's funds.

ECNZ's Corporate Finance Manager sent a fax to the Treasury on 29 June 1989 indicating that ECNZ was proposing to include a target range of 11.0% to 11.5%. On the following day, ECNZ's Chief Executive, Roderick Deane, wrote to the Minister of Finance:

> As you will realise from previous correspondence, the 11.5% return on shareholder's funds which you are seeking for the current financial year 1989/90 is higher than had been proposed at the time of the presentation of the plan in our meeting with you, and is likely to be a difficult target to achieve, given the competitive need for us to reduce prices in real terms. However, as a matter of urgency we are approaching Directors individually to see whether they are prepared to live with the target you suggest.

Ring-fence the national grid

The need to ring-fence the national grid by organizational and/or accounting separation was recognized by the Task Force in its recommendations for the initial organizational structure of ECNZ. Some relevant excerpts from their *Report* are as follows:

> In some aspects of its [ECNZ's] business, it is likely that its actions and costs should be transparent to avoid claims of using its monopoly position unfairly. This could be critical in the area of transmission where other organisations may wish to use the facilities. Cost identification and transparency of decisions and actions are likely to be essential elements to avoid becoming regulated by the Government. In summary the Corporation will be an organisation that is overtly competitive but sufficiently transparent to avoid claims of using its monopoly position. (p. 22)

> There is no potential for competition with the National Grid organisation. It is a natural monopoly with high entry costs. Therefore there is a need to create an organisation structure that ensures the operation of the National Grid is seen to be 'transparent' and hence less open to criticism of profiteering or discrimination. (p. 71)

Initially, ECNZ organized the national grid as a cost centre within Production, controlled through a fixed budget. In addition to normal operation and maintenance, its costs were to include servicing of all borrowings, taxes, and a required return on equity. It was proposed that these costs would be included in the internal contractual agreements that the Production division negotiated with the Marketing division for electricity transfers.

It was a short step from this organizational arrangement to the establishment of the national grid as a separate subsidiary company wholly owned by ECNZ. The reason for this new structure was stated in a letter from the Corporation to the Minister of Finance on 14 January 1988:

> The principal reason for establishment of a subsidiary company is to ensure the independence of the National Grid division by creating a main electricity transmission system in New Zealand which is open to any party's use for the transmission of electrical energy and has a transparent cost structure. This is seen to be an important factor in establishing competition in the electricity industry in New Zealand.

Since incorporation of ECNZ, there have been progressive refinements in transmission pricing. Transmission and energy components have now been separated out as distinct charges. This is something which had never been attempted under the NZED. The new subsidiary, Trans Power New Zealand Limited, has been working on transmission pricing with the objective of developing and implementing a more competitive and equitable transmission pricing structure.

Total legal separation of Trans Power from ECNZ has now been announced by the Government, with ownership to be held by a 'club' of ECNZ, the electricity supply authorities, and direct supply customers. When this takes place, the problem of the threat of regulation of the national grid will shift to Trans Power as an autonomous organization. ECNZ will still have an interest as a joint owner and as the dominant generator relying on the grid. However, when Trans Power is separated, a more immediate issue will be the need to write contracts to deal with the day-to-day integration of power generation and distribution. Because contracts involving complex interrelationships cannot be written to cover every eventuality, conflicts will inevitably occur. Whereas conflict could always be controlled by administrative fiat while Trans Power was part of ECNZ, this will no longer be the case when Trans Power is split off. Internal administrative processes will be replaced with (potentially) more costly arms-length bargaining and other external arbitration mechanisms.

Build a profit-oriented organization

Implementation of a strategy of building market share and volume through a combination of pricing policy and aggressive marketing required a fundamental realignment of the organization taken over by ECNZ. The objective of this realignment was to build a profit-oriented mindset in the managers with a strong focus on detailed understanding of the Corporation's markets and on cost control.

Accomplishing a radical shift in the objectives, orientation, and culture of an engineering organization with a strong public-service ethic was not to be an easy task, nor was it one that could be completed overnight. Just setting up the infrastructure within which attitudinal and cultural change could take place involved making radical changes in the structure of the organization, in management personnel, and in the basic ways in which the organization was managed.

Changing the structure of the organization

Figure 3.4 shows the basic form of ECNZ's current organizational structure and the nature of some of the major internal contracting and control relationships. This structure was based on the recommendations of the *Task Force Report* referred to above. Direct comparison with NZED's organization structure is complicated by the major organizational restructuring that was in process at the time of incorporation. Details of the transitions in organizational structures and the major management concepts and principles underlying the current structure are reported in Appendix A (pages 153–5). Appendix B (pages 156–7) contains a formal organization chart of ECNZ. Here we provide a general overview of ECNZ's new organizational structure and discuss the major organizational points of difference with NZED.

The general form of the new organizational structure is fairly conventional, with four operating divisions – Production, Trans Power (transmission), Marketing, and PowerDesignBuild (design and construction) – accountable to a Chief Executive who is, in turn, responsible to a Board of Directors.

(1) Marketing

The establishment of a professional marketing organization to market electricity to retailers and other major customers throughout the country was perhaps the most fundamental change to the old NZED structure, which had no real marketing

Figure 3.4

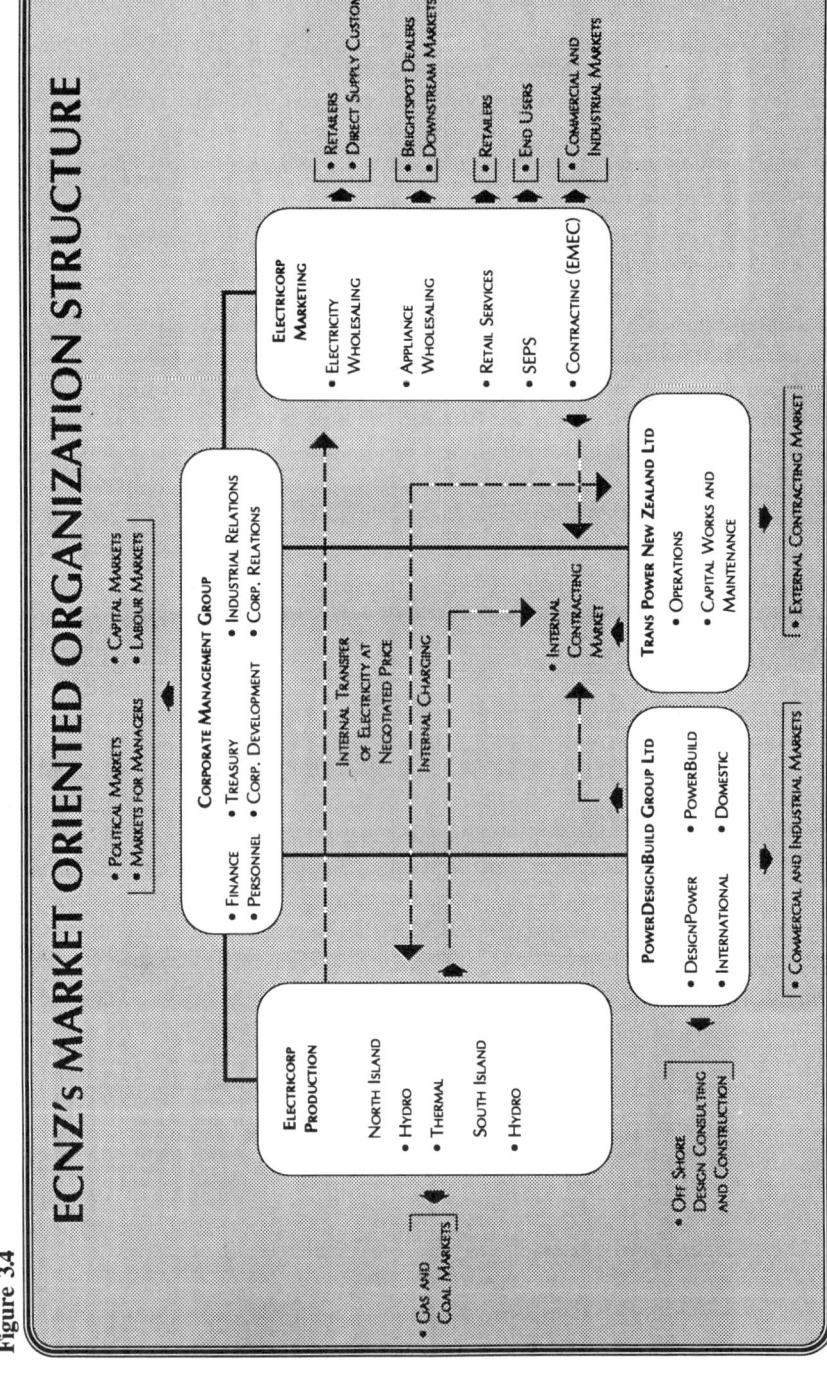

ECNZ's MARKET ORIENTED ORGANIZATION STRUCTURE

capability. NZED produced and delivered electricity as a public service at prices set by the government of the day. With the formation of this division, ECNZ sent out a strong signal that electricity was now a product to be aggressively marketed against competing energy sources such as gas, coal, and liquid fuels.

Originally organized in 1987 along regional lines, Marketing was reorganized in November 1989 into functional business units — Electricity Wholesaling, Appliance Wholesaling, Retail Services, Contracting, and SEPS[3] — each of which was to operate as an internal profit centre. As is shown in Figure 3.4, each of these business units was oriented towards selling particular products or services into specific markets. Each business unit is now better able to develop marketing plans for penetrating and serving those markets. Organizing around markets also allows for the development of indicators which measure the success of activities in particular markets.

(2) Production

Production is responsible for the operation of the Corporation's generating plants. It was given a regional organization by type of power plant. There are separate hydro groups for the North and South Islands and two thermal groups in the North Island. The separation of transmission into another business unit was a major change in the organization of production. Another major difference was its relationship with the new Marketing division. Although Production and Marketing were, for all intents and purposes, completely vertically integrated, a decision was made to establish both divisions as profit centres with explicit rate of return requirements rather than establishing Production as a cost centre and Marketing as a profit centre. Managers of these divisions were left to negotiate supply and transfer price contracts with each other.

Setting up Production as a profit centre was predicated on the belief that it would help instil a market-driven, profit-oriented mindset in Production managers by subjecting the division to a profit discipline. Although this arrangement has had some success in developing a profit-oriented culture in Production, the negotiations between Production and Marketing over transfer prices are primarily discussions of how to distribute profits from external sales. As a result, significant managerial attention has been given to dealing with the conflicts associated with the setting of transfer prices and the sharing of cost information. This has, at the margin, drawn attention away from the real business of the Corporation, which is (1) to make profits by driving up external (not internal) sales and (2) to improve efficiencies by driving down the cost of external (not internal) inputs. (Chapter 4 contains further discussion of internal transfer pricing and how initial problems were dealt with.)

---

3. SEPS is Southland Electric Power Supply, the one retail supplier that is operated by the Corporation. While the Crown retains ownership of its assets, ECNZ staff manage the organization under an arms-length contract negotiated between Electricorp Marketing and the responsible Minister.

(3) Trans Power New Zealand Limited
This subsidiary business unit is responsible for the high voltage transmission system throughout the North and South Islands and the Cook Strait cables. The unique feature of Trans Power's structure is that it was purposely set up without its own works and maintenance capability. This has required it to contract out all its substantial capital and maintenance work to its sister units (Marketing's Contracting unit, Production, and PowerDesignBuild) and to external contractors. This has resulted in both internal and external competition for this work.

The contracting out process is considered to be very successful by Trans Power's managers, who report that it has forced them to review and specify their maintenance requirements, develop business skills in contracting, and gain knowledge of the capabilities of internal and external contractors – resulting in estimated cost savings of 35-40% over operations under NZED. While senior managers we interviewed believe this internal competition has helped to instil a market-driven, profit-oriented culture in the Corporation's works and maintenance groups, some managers outside Trans Power believe that the extent of internal competition has now become harmful and that they are spending too much time dealing with internal disputes rather than concentrating on the business of being strongly competitive. In order to avoid having internal units bidding against each other for external work, this situation has recently been reviewed prior to Trans Power becoming an autonomous company. (Chapter 4 contains further discussion of the contracting-out process.)

(4) PowerDesignBuild Group Limited
In the light of current predicted load growth, ECNZ is not planning to embark on the construction of any new power stations in the next 6-10 years. With attention focused on the management of assets-in-place and the utilization of surplus capacity, design and construction was no longer a central activity of the Corporation. For this reason, design and construction was organized as a separate business unit called PowerDesignBuild (PDB) which was to survive on its own merits.

Initially, PDB was partially protected from competition for the capital works of the Corporation under the terms of a transition agreement. However, since April 1989 PDB has had to compete for this work against all competitors, internal and external. This has provided a powerful impetus for PDB to learn how to market its design consulting skills and its projects and construction capabilities to its sister units and to industrial, commercial and governmental organizations outside the company. The small size of the domestic market has led PDB managers to devote considerable attention to developing opportunities in the offshore market for heavy power engineering. Without the protection afforded by dominant-firm status, the ability of PDB to survive and prosper as a stand-alone business unit has been crucially dependent on a rapid change in orientation. As the National Manager of PowerBuild put it:

> Our business is life and death to our staff and they've got to learn this after 30 or 40 years working in a government department where their futures were secure and

they hardly ever sacked or removed anybody. Our whole future hangs on being able to get business. Everybody has got to keep an ear open for business — not just three or four managers and the business development manager. Everybody has got to be thinking about it and talking about it. It is a real change for them to actually understand that their bread and butter is going to depend on not only the work they do but also the work they can get in.

(5) Corporate Management Group

The responsibility of the corporate management group is to oversee central functions such as finance, treasury, and corporate relations, and to act as advisors to the Chief Executive. As shown in Figure 3.4, the corporate group can be looked on as having responsibility for marketing the Corporation to political markets (the Shareholding Ministers and the public), capital markets (currently limited to debt markets), the market for managers, and labour markets.

Business units were deliberately set up with their own support staffs in order to keep the Corporate staffing levels lean and to enhance the decentralized nature of the Corporation. Strong financial control was exercised by the Chief Executive with the advice of his corporate managers. The corporate managers do not have line authority over operating departments. This structure has had a profound influence on the manner in which the organization is managed and is strikingly different from the centralized management structures of the NZED.

Changing management personnel and the process of management

Changes in top management personnel brought radical change to the organization as they sought to adapt the Corporation to the new environment. While there were many features of the old organization which they sought to retain (e.g. the high levels of engineering professionalism), the message communicated to lower levels of management and employees was that the organization would no longer be managed in the same way.

Key appointments from *outside* the old organization included John Fernyhough as Chairman of the Board, Roderick Deane as Chief Executive, Drew Stein as General Manager of Marketing, Steven Blanch as Managing Director of PowerDesignBuild, Jim Ryniker as Corporate Finance Manager, Guy Manuell as Treasurer, David Bedford as Corporate Industrial Relations Manager, Jeff Lycett as Corporate Personnel Manager, Geraldine Baumann as Company Secretary, Juliet Hensley as Corporate Relations Manager, and Ralph Pyatt as Internal Auditor. Senior managers appointed from *within* the organization included Bob Thompson as Managing Director of Trans Power, David Frow as General Manager of Production, Keith Turner as Corporate Development Manager, and Martin Holden as Financial Controller.

These new leaders and, in particular, the new Chairman of the Board and the new Chief Executive, set the direction of change. Senior operating managers and corporate managers were then able to develop strategies (e.g. pricing strategy) and policies (e.g. industrial relations policy) which provided a framework within which more detailed investment and business planning could take place. In this way it became possible to make decisions about major issues (e.g. the HVDC link) which had frustrated the decision-making processes of the old organization and the institutions of government.

With a change in direction underway, the new senior management team set about altering the processes to empower managers throughout the new organization structure to manage. This involved a number of interrelated changes:

(1) The removal of the central control agencies of government (in particular the State Services Commission and the Treasury) from the management of the Corporation.

This had already come about as a consequence of being incorporated as an SOE and was one of the reasons for the SOE programme. The removal of the ability of the Public Service Association (PSA) to act as a second tier of management in the Corporation took longer but was no less crucial.

(2) The establishment of an organizational structure within which managers would be expected to manage and were provided with appropriate incentives to do so.

The new managers believed this required a decentralized management structure with a lean corporate services section that would have insufficient resources to become actively involved in the operational management of the operating divisions. They also believed that it required placing responsibility and accountability on individual managers rather than on committees, as had been so often the case under the NZED. The number of management layers in the organization was reduced so that decisions could be made quickly and as close to the source of information as possible.

(3) The development of a business culture that stressed both a greater awareness of markets and customer needs as well as the the need for continuing cost containment and productivity improvement programmes.

New processes of investment, business planning, target setting and incentive contracting were implemented and have helped focus attention on key external and internal factors which are critical to the success of the Corporation.

(4) The building of an environment which supported and rewarded innovation, experimentation and entrepreneurial behaviour on the part of managers.

The following are just a few examples of the new entrepreneurial or innovative activities of the new Corporation's managers: the development of week-ahead 'spot' market prices; the establishment of the Brightspot franchise; innovative advertising and promotions; the establishment of retail services; the pursuit by PDB of offshore consulting and construction work; the establishment of PDB's copy shop as a commercial for-profit operation; and the use by Trans Power of contracting out. Other more ambitious plans for diversification into large-scale energy-related ventures have been rejected or dropped because of advice from the Treasury to the Shareholding Ministers. All these plans, however, are evidence of the success of ECNZ in releasing the entrepreneurial energies of its managers – old and new.

We return to the first three of these topics in Chapter 4, and to the fourth in Chapter 5.

A middle-level manager's perspective

The sweeping away of old bureaucratic philosophies, centralized structures, and arcane management processes, and their replacement with new profit-oriented philosophies, decentralized structures, and more commercial management processes, rapidly created an environment where middle- and lower-level managers could have a significant impact on how their part of the organization was operated. This was very satisfying to those managers and professional staff who were re-employed by the new Corporation and accepted the new management philosophies.

What follows is an extended quotation from an interview with one middle-level manager in Trans Power which provides a perspective on these changes. While the statement is simplistic, it is generally representative of the feelings about the change which were expressed to us by a number of the managers who had also worked for the old NZED.

The NZED:

> It was a funny world in the old organisation because you led two lives. On the one hand a manager could be responsible for making technical decisions that may involve tremendous economic consequences such as taking lines out of service or power stations off-line. Look at New Plymouth, it cost $4 million a month to run and if you had to take something out of service to maintain it, you could make those decisions. But to buy a bottle of white correcting fluid or something, you couldn't do that! No way could you have a clutch pencil, only draughtsmen could have clutch pencils. That is the sort of world we lived in. In the old organisation there were two external controls — one through the stores manager and the other through personnel. Personnel was really a mouthpiece for the State Services Commission and they actually controlled everything — the number of staff you had, the grades that were paid, everything. You really were in a strait-jacket. What tended to happen was that technical people got their enjoyment out of the technical world. That is possibly part of the reason that in the old organisation we tended to gold-plate things. We overdesigned because we'd strive for technical excellence. It was something those buggers over there had no control over! It was a funny world.

The new corporation:

> In the new organisation there is a lot of enthusiasm and the ability to actually achieve. People can see the need for something, get it done and see the results. If problems arise they can be resolved pretty quickly. There were problems that have been around the organisation for years and years and here you can actually solve them. I'm not saying we've solved all the problems but at least now you can solve them! It has been quite rewarding. In the old organisation we had something like thirteen or fourteen levels and nobody could make a decision. In order to do things that were obviously needed to be done decisions got referred up and up and ultimately got to the point where the people who made the decisions didn't have a clue about the issues involved. They would often be conservative and say no.

4

Managing the New Corporation

Some of the most striking comparisons between NZED and ECNZ are internal and involve the way in which the two organizations were managed. Therefore, in this chapter we concentrate on planning, control and incentive mechanisms which are applicable to the whole organization. It is through the use of these mechanisms that manager attention is focused on the efficient and effective implementation of corporate strategy.

The basic management principle

The SOE Act provided the framework for change in the governance structure of ECNZ. The Act did this by defining the objectives and autonomy of SOEs, their responsibilities and their accountabilities.

First, the SOE Act gave ECNZ the clear objective of operating as a successful business. It was to pursue profitability and efficiency just like any comparable private sector organization. Second, the SOE Act provided ECNZ's Board and top managers with the autonomy needed to manage by removing them from day-to-day political interference and from centralized government control. Lastly, the Act made ECNZ's Board of Directors responsible and accountable to the Shareholding Ministers. Section 5 of the SOE Act requires the Board of Directors to act in accordance with its Statement of Corporate Intent, which lays out the objectives of the Corporation for a three-year period.

The principle of *autonomy within defined areas of responsibility and accountability*, which is embedded in the SOE Act 1986, is also the basic management principle which underlies ECNZ's new management structure. As shown in Figure 4.1, the implementation strategy used by ECNZ's new managers had three parts:

(1) Working to enhance the autonomy of managers throughout the organization by furthering the process of removing the centralized control of external organizations.

(2) Creating a competitive environment for internal management. The organization was structured to set up internal competition between parts of the new organization. Internal competition was facilitated by setting up Trans Power without works and maintenance staff, thereby forcing them to contract out for these services. Transfer pricing and internal charging arrangements were also introduced.

Figure 4.1

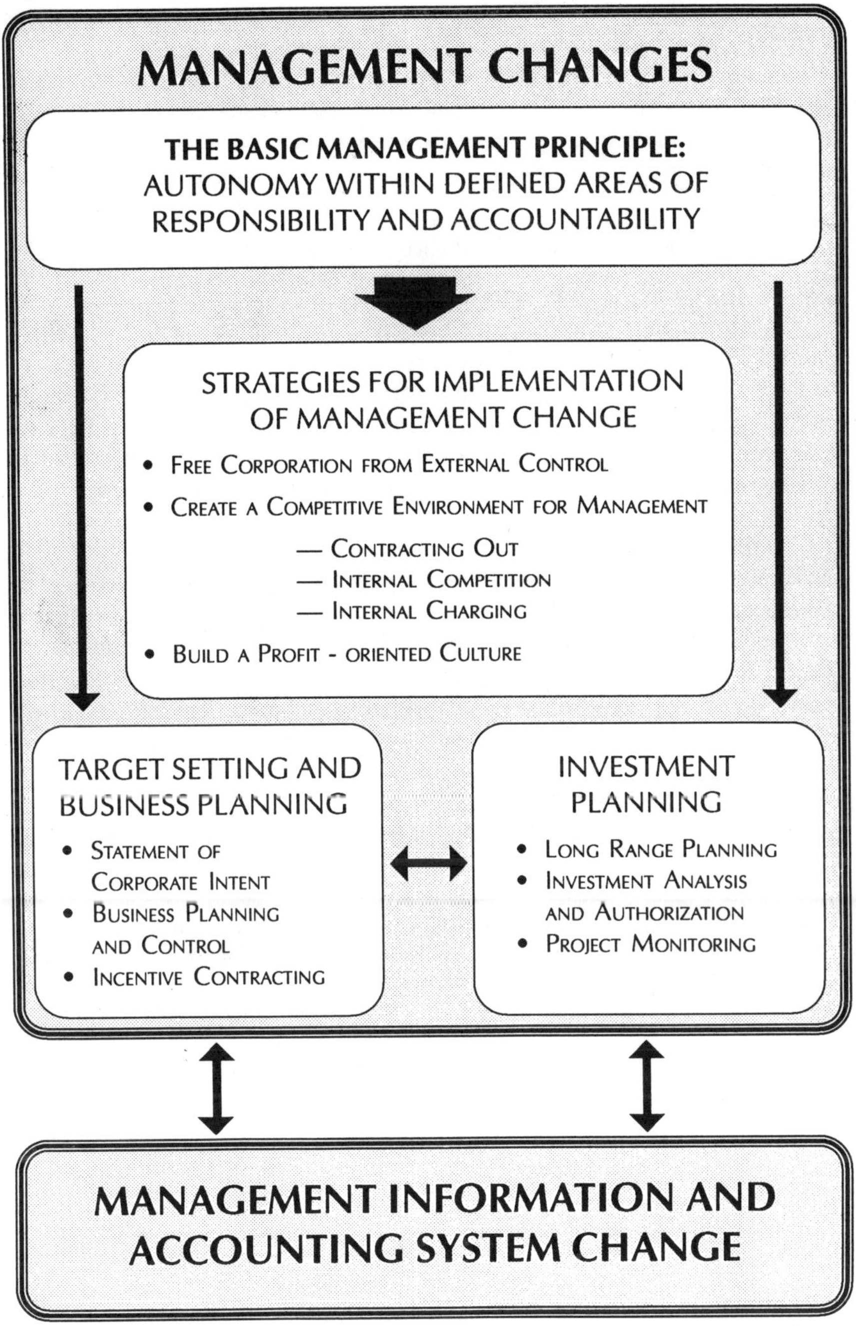

MANAGEMENT CHANGES

THE BASIC MANAGEMENT PRINCIPLE:
AUTONOMY WITHIN DEFINED AREAS OF
RESPONSIBILITY AND ACCOUNTABILITY

STRATEGIES FOR IMPLEMENTATION
OF MANAGEMENT CHANGE

- Free Corporation from External Control
- Create a Competitive Environment for Management
  - Contracting Out
  - Internal Competition
  - Internal Charging
- Build a Profit - oriented Culture

TARGET SETTING AND
BUSINESS PLANNING

- Statement of
  Corporate Intent
- Business Planning
  and Control
- Incentive Contracting

INVESTMENT
PLANNING

- Long Range Planning
- Investment Analysis
  and Authorization
- Project Monitoring

MANAGEMENT INFORMATION AND
ACCOUNTING SYSTEM CHANGE

(3) Building a profit-oriented culture by delegating and defining responsibility and accountability for the achievement of profit and cost containment targets throughout the organization.

Autonomy within defined areas of responsibility and accountability is also embedded in the way ECNZ has organized its major management processes of (1) target setting and business planning and (2) investment planning, and is reflected in the changes made to its internal accounting and information systems.

Strategies for implementation of management change

Free the Corporation from external control

Prior to incorporation as an SOE, the Electricity Division was subject to external control by the central control agencies of Government (especially the Treasury and the State Services Commission) and by the PSA. The latter operated as a quasi-control agency and was actively involved in management decision making. Removal of the centralized control of these external organizations has been crucial to providing an environment in which managers have the power to manage.

(1) Government control agencies

The autonomy of NZED managers was severely constrained by Ministers and by the influence of the central control agencies of Government. Control was exercised over electricity pricing, finance, personnel, industrial relations, and information systems. Revenue projections, capital planning and operating budgets, staff numbers, staff and pay gradings, capital planning and operations budgets, award negotiations, and computer system development: these were all subject to control and/or approval from outside the organization. This significantly compromised the freedom of managers to manage. It also made it difficult to hold them responsible and accountable for their performance. One senior manager who had been an Assistant General Manager of the old Electricity Division told us:

> We were getting into an impossible situation with the State Service Commission and the Treasury and other control agencies. They were all bearing down on us and it was impossible to make any worthwhile internal decisions. All the decisions were effectively made for us by people who could best influence the Cabinet Committees.

Often the actions of these control agencies related to the Public Service as a whole, and were made without due regard for specific businesses such as NZED. Martin Holden, the Chief Accountant at NZED and now Financial Controller of ECNZ, points out with respect to centralized negotiation by the SSC:

> Often the negotiators had little knowledge of the department, business or industry for which they were making the decisions or doing the negotiations.

The decision-making apparatus of government departments could also be agonizingly slow. Another accounting manager at ECNZ described his experience with information system development in NZED:

I served on a committee on information systems in the old organisation. At one time computerised accounting systems ranked third in a priority listing behind inventory systems and plant history systems. What happened was that the project ran out of funds on the inventory system! One of the problems was that we were linking into the Government Computer Services Division and they were not very customer oriented so progress was slow. It was mandatory that we use the Government Computer Services Division for software. Even though that did change in late 1984-85 you still had the dead hand of the State Services Commission and the Government Computer Services Division involvement. It is my personal opinion that they held back computing in the Public Service for ten years. There is no doubt in my mind about it.

The SOE Act provided the framework for freeing the Corporation from the central control of government agencies and from the involvement of Ministers and politicians in the setting of electricity prices. The direction and management of ECNZ are now the province of a commercially oriented Board of Directors operating through a Chief Executive. Corporate strategies and management policies are formulated according to the business needs of Electricorp and changed as circumstances change.

Treasury is still officially involved with ECNZ but the focus is now on the overall results of the Corporation rather than on the control of inputs. Treasury officials monitor entity performance and advise the Shareholding Ministers, whose previous direct control function has been replaced with an ownership interest. The Shareholding Ministers appoint the Directors who are responsible for the management of the Corporation. Negotiation between the Shareholding Ministers and the Directors takes place with respect to the Statement of Corporate Intent.

Treasury is also involved in longer-run issues involving the continued restructuring of the electricity industry. The announced split-off of Trans Power as an autonomous corporation and the question of whether generation will be broken up will have significant impacts on the Corporation and its management. As a consequence, ECNZ is still vulnerable to interventions by Government officials and politicians. The uncertainty this injects into the organization makes planning difficult as it makes the outcomes of management decisions hard to determine.

(2) The Public Service Association

The PSA is the key union in government departments. Over the years it gained a significant amount of centralized influence and control over the management of NZED. The PSA had a powerful Electricity Group Management Committee which met in Wellington once a month with NZED's senior head office managers to discuss management and operating issues relating to any part of the organization. NZED's operating managers throughout the organization would then be informed of what had been resolved. If the PSA Committee was dissatisfied with the outcome of their discussions with NZED, they would appeal to the State Services Commission, which had maintenance of the electricity supply as a political priority. The need to have the agreement of the PSA before any substantive management decision could be made gave the PSA a role somewhat similar to that of a Board of Directors. At the time of ECNZ's incorporation, 42 different occupational determinations and 50 agreements with the PSA had been made over the years.

ECNZ's new managers saw clearly that their ability to manage the Corporation would rest on completing the task of removing the centralized control of external organizations that the SOE Act had started. Therefore, in the first round of wage negotiations with the PSA, the Corporation pressed for an enterprise approach to bargaining, with separate agreements for each business unit. The objective was to pursue a decentralized approach to industrial relations which paralleled the decentralized management structure. Line operating managers throughout the organization would thus be given the power to manage and could be held responsible and accountable for results.

This created considerable tension with the PSA and a difficult time for the new management. However, in the end ECNZ prevailed and separate agreements for each business unit were negotiated. ECNZ was the first SOE to negotiate business units agreements. In a speech to a conference of the Institute of International Research held in August 1989, David Bedford, ECNZ's Corporate Industrial Relations Manager, commented on the changed relationship between the PSA and ECNZ as follows:

> Within the Electricity Corporation there has been a radical change to our management of industrial relations:
>
> — where the NZED was a centralised organization largely dominated industrially by the PSA, the Electricity Corporation has a decentralised management approach and nine enterprise based agreements;
> — the role of the PSA has been largely diminished and it no longer performs the 'management' role that it previously had;
> — the Corporation's management had no intention of sharing its management role with the union;
> — the management of the Corporation now have a strong desire to speak directly to staff rather than to use the PSA as a conduit for such communication.

Another excellent example of the power the PSA had over management decisions is contained in the Contracting Out Agreement. This Agreement was 'imposed' on the old organization in 1981 through a series of strikes over letting contracts to outside contractors. The issue of potential loss of employment to PSA members was of paramount concern to the union. The major provisions of the agreement bound the Electricity Division to consult with the PSA whenever work was to be let outside the Division. The restraining influence of this Agreement on the ability of managers to contain costs is reflected in Clause 5 of the Agreement which reads:

> Recognising the undesirability of contract labour receiving rates of pay and conditions which are significantly at variance with those paid to permanent staff for similar work, the Division undertakes to require the contractor, when tendering, to disclose the proposed rates of pay and conditions of employment for his contract employees. Subsequently, when letting the contract, the Division will undertake to adhere to

the principle that the nominated contractor's rates should be broadly in line with those paid to Public Service staff for similar work.

Incentives for contractors to compete on price in labour-intensive work, and the ability of the organization to manage its costs through contracting out, are both clearly circumscribed by such a requirement.

The Contracting Out Agreement was incompatible with the way ECNZ was to be managed. The PSA argued that the 'spirit of the agreement' should be adhered to and requested consultation. ECNZ therefore 'consulted' with the PSA by providing them with 14 days notice each time they intended to employ outside contractors which, given the organization of Trans Power, was regularly. The PSA never replied, so in time the 'consultation' ceased and the Agreement became defunct.

Create a competitive environment for management

The Task Force on Electricity Corporation Organisation Structure believed that in order to control costs in ECNZ it was necessary to create a competitive environment for internal management. The *Task Force Report* contains the following statements:

> To assist the Board with its objective of producing and transmitting electricity at the cheapest cost, and thus keeping prices at a minimum, the encouragement of competition both internally and externally to the Corporation was seen to be of major importance. Competition between internal units doing similar work was seen to be of benefit in keeping internal costs down. To have the Corporation operating in a competitive electricity market was also seen of benefit in putting pressure on internal costs plus removing the propensity for large electric utilities to be highly regulated. (p. 32)

> The commercial mechanisms illustrated . . . demonstrate the internal adversary approach to internal pricing at all stages through the organisation – from generating power through 'delivering' of the 'product' to customers. Thus all sections of the organisation will need to market their products on a competitive, commercial basis, working within cost structures calculated on commercial bases. (p. 71)

Within NZED, managers had been insulated from markets and competition by the objectives and structure of the organization and the centralized provision of support services. With no 'bottom line', there were no strong incentives for managers to consider the services they consumed on a cost/benefit basis. ECNZ has endeavoured to remove this insulation, and to create competitive tensions inside the Corporation, in three ways: (1) contracting out for services was required and/or encouraged; (2) internal (and external) competition to supply services was stimulated; and (3) wherever possible, internal charging was introduced for the transfer of goods or services between parts of the organization.

(1) Contracting out for services

There was very little contracting out for services in the NZED. Even had there been an incentive for operating managers to employ external contractors for efficiency reasons, this was effectively precluded by the terms of the Contracting Out Agreement 'imposed' on NZED by the PSA.

The most comprehensive contracting out programme in ECNZ has been developed in the Trans Power subsidiary. This was accomplished by purposely setting up Trans Power as a separate and substantially autonomous subsidiary of ECNZ, and giving it responsibility for the operation and maintenance of the national grid. It was not, however, provided with its own maintenance staff, as it was felt that greater efficiency and a greater degree of control over costs could be obtained by having all this work contracted out. As a result a very large market for services of roughly $80 million per year was instantly established. These contracts are being let internally to other qualified sub-units and to qualified external contractors.

One of the benefits of contracting out has been to force Trans Power managers to define what maintenance on the national grid is required and to specify standards for that work. The Operations and Maintenance Manager for Trans Power explains this benefit:

> One of the things that contracting out has actually done is force the organisation to define what it wants. If you don't define it, you won't get it. It's as simple as that. I think there has been a lot of savings because we've had to stand back and say, 'What do we really want?', and write it down exactly because that's what you get and that's what you pay for. Doing this has been really beneficial.

Another benefit has been to shift the emphasis from fault finding and repair to the development of a programme of preventative maintenance. The Operations and Maintenance Manager indicated that some attempts were made in NZED 'to have linesmen change their fundamental philosophy from "fire brigade" to a preventative maintenance philosophy'. These attempts were not generally successful. Also, in the old organization, maintenance performed tended to depend on the number of maintenance staff available rather than on need.

The first contracts let by Trans Power after it came into existence in early 1988 were awarded for a one-year period and went almost exclusively in-house to Electricorp's other business units. This was a necessary period of learning because Trans Power managers had little experience in awarding contracts. For the first round the standards and specifications were not as explicit as they might have been. However, it did provide an opportunity to gather cost information and to review maintenance services received relative to cost. This allowed specifications to be tightened and non-essential services which were not returning value for money to be pared away. Subsequently, maintenance work has been advertised throughout New Zealand and Australia, and Trans Power is now letting three-year contracts to both internal and external contractors. Although only about 10 percent of routine operations and maintenance work has been let to external contractors, this proportion is expected to rise significantly in the future, especially now that Trans Power is to be separated from ECNZ and made an independent corporation.

To keep costs down while maintaining standards, Trans Power managers are of the opinion that they need to have three or four strong external contractors actively competing for contracts against each other and against internal contractors. To this end they have sometimes awarded a contract simply to promote and encourage competition. In some areas, such as buildings and grounds maintenance, there is no shortage of competition. However, in areas which involve high-voltage work, only a limited number of contractors have the necessary capabilities. Some existing contractors are now improving their capabilities to do high-voltage work, and some Power Boards are also starting to build on their expertise in low-voltage work to acquire high-voltage capabilities, so that they can compete in this area.

Comparison of maintenance costs between NZED and ECNZ is complicated for a number of reasons. These include a change in emphasis from 'fire fighting' to preventative maintenance and problems of cost allocation and measurement. Even so, Trans Power managers argue that there have been significant reductions of between 30%-40% in operations and maintenance costs. These are not hard numbers; they are subjective estimates. The Operations and Maintenance Manager explains how he arrives at this estimate of the cost saving percentage:

> In the old organisation the only costs that were traced directly to maintenance were direct costs and there was no attempt to allocate overhead costs to this work. Even the direct costs had measurement error because there was no good job costing system. Also the direct costs were recorded in a pretty broad way. Perhaps the cleanest one to make a comparison on is the maintenance of transmission lines because that is still more or less the same. You could look at that and say OK it cost us about $13-$14 million in direct costs. There was an exercise done by one of the accounting people just before we broke up. He came to the conclusion that the indirect costs, if you actually went through and apportioned them out, would be about equal to direct costs. That was probably not unreasonable. In the old organisation you had no tax and no profit so to get a reasonable figure you would have to multiply direct costs by a factor of 2.2 to 2.3. If you do that and compare it to what our costs are currently, you are looking at a reduction of around 30-40%.

Some further idea of the trend in maintenance and service costs can be gained from a recent Report to the Trans Power Board of Directors by the Operations and Maintenance Manager. This report stated that for the 1988/89 year, overall contract costs for routine work was approximately $31.7 million compared with $20.7 million (est) for the 1989/90 year. The reduction was attributed to:
- A clearer definition of the work required by Trans Power, particularly in relation to station grounds and building maintenance, protection maintenance and communications maintenance.
- Competition and the threat of competition.
- A more realistic allocation of overheads by business units.
- Growing productivity from Electricorp business units and a willingness to work towards reducing costs by improving work methods.
- Commitment by Trans Power to a longer term contract.

To conclude, Trans Power's managers claim that creating a competitive environment through contracting out has enabled them (1) to better define what tasks are necessary, (2) to move from a focus on post-event emergency repairs to preventative maintenance, (3) to measure and reduce costs, and (4) to deal with inefficiencies more easily. To illustrate this latter point, Bob Thompson, the Managing Director of Trans Power, tells the following story:

> There was one maintenance group where Marketing had about 30 men. The staff there were notorious for doing 'homers' — doing jobs for home, making trailers or furniture that sort of thing. It was rampant and NZED seemed unable to control it. We simply decided to close them down by not awarding them any work. In the old days we never could have done that.

(2) Internal competition to supply services
Internal competition to supply services was used to complement the contracting out process. The organization was deliberately designed with duplication and overlap between the capabilities of sub-units in order to promote internal competition.

Currently, three sub-units compete amongst themselves and with external contractors for contracts to supply operations and maintenance services to Trans Power. A breakdown of 101 operations and maintenance contracts awarded for the period April 1989 - March 1992 is as follows:

Internal contractors:		
Marketing (EMEC)	51	
Production	32	
PowerDesignBuild	4	87
External contractors:		
Supply authorities	9	
Other contractors	5	14
		101

Internal competition seems to have been used primarily as a device to create and reinforce a cultural change within the organization and the 'mindset' of managers. It was important to have this change take place quickly and to have it strongly reinforced by holding managers responsible and accountable for profits of their business units. In this sense internal competition seems to have accomplished its objective.

However, there are counter-productive aspects of internal competition that should not be overlooked. Over time these aspects can increase in importance and need to be weighed against the future benefits. To illustrate, internal contractors currently bid against each other and against external contractors for contracts with Trans Power. With the coming separation of Trans Power, it will make little organizational sense to have two or more internal units competing against each other for what will then be external work involving external cash flows. Similarly, PDB and EMEC (Electricorp Marketing Electricity Contracting) have competed against each other in New Zealand for external contracts. This is counter-productive because it can drive down bid prices and potentially lose the contract for the Corporation. If neither internal bidder wins the contract, the Corporation bears the cost of preparing two bids rather than one. Such a situation can be likened to family members bidding against each other at the same auction.

This situation has now been reviewed by ECNZ, with the result being the amalgamation of EMEC into PDB. One General Manager commented on the need for change in this area as follows:

> There was a philosophy running through the organisation at the time of incorporation which said 'You've got to have competition, its great! it makes you go!' It's like any revolution; the pendulum swings a bit too far. I hope we're going to see it coming back to a more pragmatic approach.

(3) Internal charging for the transfer of goods and services

Competitive tensions were also introduced into the Corporation by the introduction of internal charging for the transfer of goods and services. Internal charging takes place in three main areas: transfer pricing between Production and Marketing for the transfer of electricity; internal charging between Trans Power and Production in relation to the dispatching of power stations and the transmission of electricity; and internal charging for central services.

Transfer pricing between Production and Marketing: The need for transfer pricing between Production and Marketing arises because both business units were set up as profit centres with a rate of return objective. The managers of the two business units were left to negotiate the transfer price for electricity.

Setting up Production as a profit centre has helped Production managers to think of the division as an autonomous business, with a focus on the bottom line. However, Production and Marketing are vertically integrated businesses. Without practical access to large outside markets for the sale or purchase of electricity, negotiations about transfer prices are basically negotiations over the internal distribution of profits from external sales. The usual result of such organizational arrangements in vertically integrated firms is conflict between divisions. Predictably, ECNZ has not been spared this conflict. One senior manager in Electricorp Marketing indicated that 'a hell of a lot of conflict' had taken place over transfer pricing, so much so in fact that some staff directly involved with transfer price negotiations had asked to transfer out of that section.

Internal conflict between Marketing and Production also acted to reduce the information flows between them, and resulted in divergence between the individual objectives of the divisions and the overall interests of the Corporation. One of the objectives of Marketing is to promote the off-peak use of electricity so as to increase total demand. (This stems directly from the corporate objective of using surplus capacity). To do this, Marketing needs detailed short-run marginal cost information in order to set 'time-of-use' and 'spot market' prices. They also wanted incremental purchases of electricity above the business plan to be transferred to them from Production at short-run marginal cost. However, Production took the position that all internal transfers should be transferred at average production cost plus profit margin, and were reluctant to provide short-run marginal cost information to Marketing.

As a result, Production captured most of the gains from the efforts of Marketing to build market share and volume over and above the agreed volumes in the business plan. Also, the lack of short-run cost information made it difficult for Marketing to pursue their pricing strategy for building volume through 'time-of-use' charges and 'spot market' prices. Without clear and detailed information on the ever-changing cost structure of electricity generation, development of flexible pricing structures is not possible.

Not surprisingly, a period of damaging internal conflict between Marketing and Production resulted from this attempt at creating internal competitive tensions. Apart from a belief that competitive tension between Production and Marketing was philosophically appealing, there seems to have been no clear vision as to what transfer pricing between these two vertically integrated divisions was supposed to accomplish. The *Task Force Report* placed a great deal of stress on building quasi-competitive mechanisms into the organization wherever possible, but no consideration was given to the possibility that corporate objectives might be defeated by the ensuing conflict between divisions. This is a curious omission. We were told that senior managers are aware of the difficulties between Marketing and Production and have it on their agenda for further consideration.

Interestingly, Marketing and Production have now negotiated an agreement that provides incentives for each division that are more in line with corporate objectives. The parties have agreed to contract initially for those electricity volumes which are contained in the approved business plan. This volume will be priced to provide Production with its required target return on assets. Incremental volume purchased by Marketing above this agreed volume will be priced on a short-run marginal cost basis. This incremental volume is then eligible to be added to the base volume in subsequent years and priced accordingly. In addition, agreement has been reached on a greater sharing of cost data between Production and Marketing to enable the implementation of pricing structures that signal short-run marginal costs to customers.

With this transfer pricing arrangement, Production still has an incentive to reduce costs in order to increase profits above the level in the business plan. Such an incentive is reinforced by the personal incentive contract written with the Production General Manager. Similarly, Marketing has an incentive to achieve incremental sales as the profits on these sales go straight into its income statement in the year of sales. Again, this incentive is reinforced by the personal objectives of the Marketing General Manager.

Internal charging between Trans Power and Production: In addition to Marketing, Production also interacts extensively with Trans Power. Trans Power has responsibility for bringing (dispatching) generating stations in and out of service so as to satisfy demand. It will also 'dispatch' generating stations as needed, to meet the system operating requirements of the national grid. For instance, generating stations are sometimes required to control voltage on the national grid. They are also required to provide 'spinning reserve' to provide insurance against breakdowns and surges in demand.

Trans Power is provided with short-run marginal cost information by each power station connected to the grid. This enables them to schedule and dispatch stations in merit (least cost) order. If Trans Power for some reason dispatches a power station in other than least cost order, then it is charged internally for these 'out-of-merit' costs. Trans Power is also charged by Production for the costs of controlling voltage and providing spinning reserve.

Internal charging provides Trans Power with an incentive to reduce or control these transmission-related costs. Interestingly, the costs of purchasing spinning reserve have reduced significantly, thanks to a critical examination of spinning reserve requirements and the introduction of contracts for major customers that provide price concessions for the interruptibility of power supply. Such interruptible contracts reduce the need for spinning reserve. Similarly, Trans Power charges Production for any transmission losses which are associated with the non-availability of a generating station. In this way Production is provided with an incentive to reduce or control these costs by ensuring availability.

However, Trans Power operates on a full cost recovery basis. Proposed pricing structures for Trans Power are being devised to recover all costs from generators or distributors. Although the more detailed specification of these charges can be expected to place cost pressure on Trans Power, there is still a need for direct control of costs through stringent budgets. Documents and correspondence indicate that Trans Power has been under strong pressure from the Chief Executive to contain costs. In one of a series of letters on this topic to the Managing Director of Trans Power in the last half of 1989, the Chief Executive included the following statement:

> On cost containment, I see this as a high priority objective in the sense that maintaining expenses within budget and achieving profit targets is something which all business unit managers are expected to deliver on regardless of any performance incentive arrangements. Failure to keep costs within budget on either current or capital account would be regarded as a potentially severe penalty with respect to performance entitlement. On the other hand, to the extent that costs are contained well within budget, this would be regarded as a contributor to a positive outcome with respect to the potential performance payment. This implies a skewed weighing with respect to the issue of costs and the performance payment as I have explained to you orally.

Internal charging for central services: The scope and extent of services provided centrally within NZED were considerable, but without cost information there was no mechanism to ensure that these services were provided efficiently. With the reorganization of ECNZ, many services provided centrally became the responsibility of profit-oriented business units.

However, some services are still provided centrally (e.g. management training programmes and legal services). Internal charges are supposed to reflect the full cost of the provision of the service plus a return (although the rates for legal services are substantially less than external rates). Business units are free to decide whether to use internal services on the basis of cost and quality. The rationale is that if the internal services are uneconomic or substandard, then they will not be used. In this way internal charging provides one important signal as to whether central services are competitive and whether they should be continued. Such a mechanism was not used in NZED.

Internal charging for services can also be a springboard for entrepreneurial activity. Within ECNZ there are a number of services that started out by being offered internally and are now also being offered externally. For example, the Corporate Personnel section developed training programmes to offer to the business units. They are now endeavouring to market them outside the Corporation. Other examples can be found in PowerDesignBuild. Computer Aided Design facilities beyond the present requirements of PDB are offered outside the Corporation as a service at commercial rates. Their plan copy service used to be exclusively a service to other business units within the Corporation. Plan copying services are now offered to the general public through a copy shop located on the ground floor of their building. Steven Blanch, Managing Director of PDB, explains the decision to turn the plan copying service into a profit centre:

> Our plan copy shop was costing us a lot of money. It is needed for our work but I said 'I'm not prepared to let this business stay the way it is. It makes a profit or it goes'. So we made it into a profit centre and put a manager in there with the job of turning it around. We put some money into it and we got the latest gear. It is now making a nice profit and the morale is incredible. It's got a fabulous reputation. We get a lot of work from Electricorp. I think the quality of the service is excellent. They produce high quality work for us and we make money.

While some control by senior management and the Board over the proliferation of entrepreneurial activity outside the core business of the organization is needed, the selling of services externally may be useful as a means of using temporary excess capacity or achieving economies of scale. In such cases the costs to the Corporation of providing the service internally are lowered.

Build a profit-oriented culture

Considerable attention has been given in ECNZ to building a profit-oriented culture and changing the 'mind-set' of managers and employees. This has involved bringing in outside managers who already had this profit orientation and, wherever possible, appointing managers from within the Corporation who were enthusiastic for change. It has also involved the creation, wherever possible, of business units that would be treated as profit centres, with managers held responsible and accountable for a bottom-line profit figure.

Setting and monitoring profit and cost containment targets receives considerable managerial attention in the new Corporation. This is achieved through processes involving business planning and incentive contracting to motivate performance by managers. It is also embedded in the long-run investment planning process and the manner in which information systems are selected and managed.

What should be mentioned at this point is that change in the management culture at ECNZ came very quickly. As Doug Dell, the Manager of EMEC, explained:

> All of the sorts of things which were an effort to us as public servants we've now had to embrace. The ideas of advertising, promotion, account management, client service, sales negotiation, and contract negotiation are all things we've had to build in.

However, driving this cultural change deep into the core of the organization is taking longer to accomplish. Certainly, some significant change has taken place. Doug Dell again:

> The lower you go down in the organisation, the less comprehensively the internal competition philosophies are understood. It is fair to say that at the lower levels employees puzzle if we lose a job to PDB that they have traditionally done. They say, 'we're all part of the one organisation. They [Trans Power] are endangering my job when they give that work to another part of the organisation'.
>
> However, overall there has been a dramatic modification of attitudes. Even at the lower levels. If you go back to where we were [in NZED], that perception of job loss would have been followed by immediate outrage and union involvement and all the rest of it. There is none of that now. Even at the lowest levels, people now understand that we are in a competitive business, that PDB is a major competitor, and that what they must do is perform as well as they can in order to get the maximum amount of work so we can expand.

However, senior managers admit that the cultural change has not penetrated all parts of the organization to a satisfactory level. This was confirmed by observations we made on the generating plant 'production floor'. The question of how to change the culture at the lower levels in the Corporation is now being given attention. Board Chairman, John Fernyhough, has stated that it is 'our biggest piece of unfinished business'.

Target setting and business planning

Target setting and business planning are important processes in ECNZ. They encompass the Statement of Corporate Intent, business and investment planning and control, and incentive contracting within the Corporation.

The Statement of Corporate Intent

The Statement of Corporate Intent is the critical element in the target setting and planning process. It supplies a central commercial objective for the organization, which was lacking in NZED. Of primary interest to the Shareholding Ministers is the target rate of return on equity and the scope of activities of the Corporation. In the absence of an equity capital market, an accounting-based rate of return on equity is used as the primary measure of effectiveness of management. Pressure from the Shareholding Ministers for ECNZ to achieve a target return on equity surrogates for the equity capital market forces which private sector corporate managers normally face to maximize the value of the owners' interests.

As noted in Chapter 3, ECNZ has negotiated with the Shareholding Ministers for a return on equity target which is in line with the Corporation's strategy of reducing prices in real terms. ECNZ argues that this action, while reducing the return on equity in the short term, will act to maximize the long-run value of the Corporation by raising future returns on equity. In a letter to us of 17 July 1990, the Chief Executive, Roderick Deane, wrote:

> Extensive analysis which has been carried out by Corporate Development, and which you would be welcome to have a look at, demonstrates clearly that we would maximise the short run gains to the Corporation over the next several years by simply increasing the price [of electricity], and certainly maintaining it in line with the rate of inflation, and thus increasing our profit rate. On the other hand, by taking a medium to longer term view of the way in which we would maximise the value of the shareholders' investment in the business, we are making a significant short run profit rate sacrifice in order to reduce prices in real terms. This will take several years to pay-off in terms of increasing the profit rate over the medium to longer term.

Treasury officials remain sceptical and take the position that, in the absence of true capital market pressures, management will always be able to come up with compelling reasons why the owners will not receive a commercial rate of return. Hence, the result of Treasury advice to the Shareholding Ministers has been to put pressure on ECNZ to lift its current return on equity targets to bring it more into line with what officials consider is a commercial return on equity.

Business planning and control

Considerable planning took place in the Electricity Division. Indeed, the ten-year financial model that is presently used by ECNZ was developed in the old organization and grew out of the ten-year electricity demand forecasts and power planning.

However, the primary weakness of the planning and budgeting that took place in NZED was that it lacked clear objectives and was connected to the political process of preparing estimates for the Budget. Aside from the provision of a public service and the building of generating facilities to meet the forecast demand for electricity, there was no clear business objective to plan towards. As a result, directed business plans of the sort normally made within large commercial corporations were not prepared. One senior divisional accounting manager, who had been with the old Electricity Division, listed the following characteristics of the old approach to planning and budgeting:

1. A business plan did not exist.
2. Financial objectives were unclear.
3. An incremental approach to budgeting was adopted (i.e. 'last year plus a bit').
4. There was little emphasis placed on removing budgetary slack.
5. Planning was not related to markets, competitors or customers.
6. Department budgets were approved by Cabinet.
7. Department budgets were not timely, being issued well after the start of the financial year.

An extensive process of business planning and budgeting now takes place in Electricorp. This has required a lot of learning about how to plan and form budgets in a business environment. Profit-oriented budgeting was not a skill that was heavily emphasized in the old organization.

The process of target setting and identifying measurable performance targets begins when each General Manager and Corporate Manager provides a review of the current year and plans for the coming year. The timetable for the plan commences in September when Corporate Finance issue guidelines within which the business planning process is to proceed. These guidelines include overall targets such as sales volumes, electricity prices, wages increases, inflation rates, and a view of the economy. Using these guidelines, each business unit prepares a business plan that reflects the demands of the market for their product or service, the state of the competition, and rate of return requirements. Similarly, major sub-units within business units formulate business plans within guidelines set for them.

Individual business unit plans are required by Corporate in mid-November for consolidation and peer review before formal challenge meetings attended by General Managers of the other business units, senior Corporate Managers, and the Chief Executive. The challenge round is a crucial part of the business-planning process. It provides an opportunity for General Managers to defend their plans and provides a forum in which problems of integration and co-ordination can surface and be quickly resolved. Another important aim is to discourage and eliminate any opportunistic attempts by ECNZ's business units to inject slack into their budgets. Some senior managers find the process of having their business plans subject to vigorous challenge an uncomfortable experience but readily concede that the process is a valuable part of the overall target-setting and business-planning process.

Business plans are updated in late December for changes agreed to in the challenge meetings and then finalized during late January for presentation to the Board for their approval in the February meeting. Following Board approval, the Statement of Corporate Intent is finalized and agreed with the Shareholding Ministers.

Performance is monitored monthly by the Chief Executive, his corporate advisors, and the Board. Business units report monthly on progress towards meeting financial and technical operational performance targets. In addition, management meetings of the Chief Executive, the four General Managers, all Corporate Managers and the Financial Controller are held immediately after each Board meeting to report on Board decisions and identify issues which require additional work. This management group meets again two weeks later to finalize the next Board meeting agenda and report on progress on outstanding issues. Each manager has a list of action points which is reviewed at each meeting. This focuses the manager's attention and provides a means by which the Chief Executive can monitor performance.

It is interesting to note that while General Managers are privy to the business plans of other business units, there is a corporate policy not to share details of other units' plans below the General Manager level. The objective of this policy is to preserve the integrity of internal competition at the level of those line managers actually involved in the details of the competitive activities. For the same reasons, business plans may be deliberately short on details which could help an internal competitor or contractor gain competitive advantage.

Incentive contracting

Lack of clear business objectives and the intrusion of external control agencies into areas of management made the evaluation of the performance of NZED and its individual managers either infeasible or very difficult. Assessment of managers in the old system was not based on performance with respect to objectives but rather on the qualities of the individual, using criteria such as work knowledge, organization at work, dependability, versatility, punctuality, and staff relations.

Business planning now plays an important role in setting personal performance objectives for management. After the business plan has been approved by the Board and the Statement of Corporate Intent by the Shareholding Ministers, the people process starts with the negotiation and setting of the Chief Executive's performance objectives by the Board Chairman in consultation with the Remuneration Committee of the Board. A substantial part of the Chief Executive's total remuneration package is tied to the achievement of these objectives in the form of a bonus payment.

The same general process is then carried on down to the General Managers of the four business units and the Corporate Managers. These objectives are arrived at by negotiation between the Chief Executive and each manager. This usually involves individual meetings and an exchange of letters formally listing the performance objectives. Points of difference are negotiated and a final set of objectives agreed. These objectives are either derived directly from the business plan or are personal objectives, some of which may involve 'stretching' beyond the business plan (e.g. the plan may call for a 1.5% increase in sales volume, the 'stretch' objective may call for an additional .5% above this). Objectives are divided into Priority A and Priority B groupings. This is done in order to direct management attention towards the objectives considered to be most important. One General Manager described the general process as follows:

> We start off with the Business Plan which has the company objectives in it. I then negotiate my objectives with the Chief Executive. I take a number of objectives directly out of the Business Plan, add some additional ones and send them to him. He will come back to me and say 'I like three of them, some of these others are not tough enough, I've got another fifteen here I'd like you to think about'. We then negotiate and agree to a set of objectives.

Once senior managers have agreed their incentive contracts, they in turn use much the same process for the managers who report directly to them. The form of these contracts is similar and they are written to contain performance objectives that will enable the senior managers to fulfil their objectives. This process can be carried on down into the regional segments of each business unit.

Bonuses are tied directly to the meeting of the agreed performance objectives. Objectives are stated in financial and non-financial terms, but are measurable wherever possible. Bonus levels vary from around 30% of the total remuneration package for the Chief Executive to around 20% at the General Manager level and around 10%-12% for managers reporting directly to a General Manager. Bonus levels decline for successively lower levels in the organization. There is pressure to increase the bonus portion of the remuneration so as to increase its motivating influence.

Once performance objectives are set, they are expected to be met or exceeded in order to receive 100% of the available bonus. As the General Manager of one business unit puts it:

> It is very hard to get 100% of the bonus. I have a clause [in my performance contract] which says that 100% of the bonus is achieved by 'walking on water'. You can't get more than 100% but you don't get 100% for achieving objectives; the only way you get 100% is by exceeding them to blazes!

This statement raises an interesting point about ECNZ's present incentive contracting process. A manager's bonus payment may be reduced if personal performance objectives are not met, but there is no provision for the bonus to be increased when objectives are exceeded. To quote another General Manager:

> There is no incentive to overachieve. That's the problem with the incentive package at the present time. If you overachieve you don't get rewarded for it. You are overachieving by even getting these objectives but if you do overachieve the objectives there is no extra incentive. The incentives flex downward but they don't flex upwards. I think that is a mistake.

This General Manager expressed the concern that such an incentive contracting regime can create situations where managers may be penalized in the year they make a decision that has large short-run costs in that year (e.g. staff layoffs which require large redundancy payouts) but not rewarded for payoffs which are deferred to later years and which may result in overachievement of objectives in those later years. Other General Managers expressed similar concerns with respect to expenditures on research and development and on maintenance.

The question has to be asked whether the present incentive contracting regime, by failing to reward overachievement of objectives, may lead managers to make decisions which are not in the best long-term interests of the Corporation. Although we are not in a position to assess the extent to which this has actually happened, it is clear that such a possibility exists. Indeed, the problem is not confined to the way incentives are structured for managers within ECNZ. The question may also be asked of the Corporation's return on equity target, which is stated in the Statement of Corporate Intent. What incentive does the Board have to attempt to *exceed* this target?

One final issue is the number of personal objectives written into an incentive contract. Some managers have to contend with over 25 objectives. Some General Managers would like to see the number of objectives reduced because they feel unable to focus on so many. One General Manager argued that he would be 'more inclined to work on about half a dozen'. Another General Manager described his coping strategy: 'it's really a matter of concentrating on five or six things that are important and letting all the rest swim along'. The Chief Executive shares the concern about the number of personal objectives being used and told us that the trend is now 'to reduce the number of explicit objectives and to identify the key parameters and their priority order more explicitly'.

Although the incentive contracting process at ECNZ is still evolving, it does seem to have had a major influence on the behaviour and motivation of managers. Unless some mechanism such as incentive contracting is used to cement cultural change into place, it is possible to have a change in culture without resultant performance increases. Incentive contracting is also likely to be a key mechanism for driving the profit orientation deeper into the Corporation. The major inhibiting factor to extending the use of bonuses in business units such as PowerDesignBuild is the union memberships held by professional staff. To pay more under the union's pay structure requires upgrading which, in a consulting organization, raises the problem of moral hazard. The Managing Director of PDB explains:

> The only way to pay more under a union-based pay structure is to put someone up a grade. So someone has worked brilliantly for a year and you upgrade them and they decide they'll have a year off. Theoretically, you could downgrade them but it's camel through the eye of a needle stuff – very hard to do. Tying pay to performance is the way to go, but I am opposed to having collective bargaining in bonus performance based systems. So I only have bonuses tied to performance for non-union people.

Investment planning

Investment planning is of considerable importance in large, vertically integrated, capital-intensive utilities such as ECNZ. Here we describe the process of investment planning in the new Corporation, comparing it where possible to investment planning in the old Electricity Division. We discuss in turn (1) the critical nature of long-range planning and development in ECNZ, (2) the changes and improvements made in investment analysis and authorization systems, and (3) the developing process of project monitoring and post-audit reviews.

Long-range planning

Planning for the integrated electricity system operated by ECNZ is complex and long-term. It is complex because planning involves dealing with multiple uncertainties involving demand growth, availability of resources and fuels, actions of competitors, and community acceptance of possible investments. It is necessarily long-term because of these complexities and the time needed to make any major change to the generating and transmission systems. For example, the lead time for major investments such as a new generating plant is fifteen years from the date of the initial study to commissioning. Long-range planning studies can cover up to a thirty-year planning horizon.

Considerable long-range planning with respect to the system took place within the NZED. Long-term thinking is not new to the organization. But there is a major difference. It is not in the nature of uncertainties faced, although these have changed with the establishment of ECNZ as an SOE and deregulation of generation. Nor is it in the analytical and modelling capabilities of planning personnel — these abilities existed and were applied in the old organization. The major difference lies in the clearer commercial objectives of the long-range planning and development process under ECNZ. As Chief Executive, Roderick Deane, who is a professional economist, points out:

> I used to build econometric models. The modelling resources and analytical power in this place is fantastic and second to none. That is one of the inheritances from the past. When Electricorp took over they were all set to apply this power to more commercial type problems just as they'd applied them to other issues in the past. That is the sort of strength that the old organization had which people underestimated.

The strategic and commercial approach to long-range planning in ECNZ is what stands in sharp contrast to the long-range planning of the NZED, where major pricing and investment decisions were subject to political intervention and where the planning focus tended to be on developing the system to meet long-term forecasts of demand for electricity. Now the technical analytical ability of ECNZ's planners is being developed to give the Corporation a competitive advantage in order to retain the Corporation's dominance in electricity generation.

There are a number of good examples of how long-range planning is being conducted in the new Corporation and its impact on decisions. Long-run strategic planning analyses were used to arrive at ECNZ's current pricing policy. They are notable because, for the first time, the possible effects on the long-run profitability of the organization of new competitors entering the market for generation were explicitly modelled.

Another example of long-range planning is contained in surveys the Corporation has conducted on all its thermal power stations to decide, given the present surplus of generating capacity, whether each station should be kept in operation, mothballed, or permanently closed down. These analyses take a ten- to twenty-year view and consider not only the economics of the stations and system operating and security requirements but also strategic considerations about the reaction of potential competitors to these decisions. On the strength of these analyses, the Corporation has decided to maintain a number of thermal stations even though they were, at the time of survey, in excess of current generating requirements. ECNZ's planners believe that the Corporation has gained a competitive advantage as to the timing of future capital investment because it has decided not to discard surplus generating plant. The low marginal cost of recommissioning plant provides a financial advantage to the Corporation as well as a timing advantage, because it can make capital investments closer in time to when capacity is needed.

The Corporation has also recently completed a long-term development plan which covers a thirty-year planning period. This is a major piece of long-run planning that develops plans for a number of scenarios and options. Scenarios include: (1) a conservation future which is based on the premise that market intervention of some form will be applied with growing concern about global fossil fuel pollution problems; (2) a thermal future based on coal which assumes little in the way of new gas discoveries; and (3) a thermal future based on gas which assumes that more gas is found and Maui gas reserves turn out on the high side.

Each scenario has been simulated for assumptions of high, mid and low demand growths using Corporate Development's PRISM model. This model uses fifty years of hydrological data to optimize the use of limited water inflows and storage to avoid excessive spills or expensive fuel burns. To compare alternative plans, the operation of the whole power system is simulated over the next thirty years to calculate expected fuel usages and costs. This enables an optimal plan to be developed for each scenario by balancing these expected fuel costs with the capital expenditures required for future projects. One outcome of this long-range planning exercise is an increased emphasis on maximizing the use of existing stations through upgrades rather than on planning new developments. This shift in emphasis is a significant outcome of the planning process and reflects the strongly commercial approach to long-range planning now used.

Major investment projects are conducted within the context of the Corporation's long-range plan with the substantial cost of investigations being managed through a staged investigations programme.

Investment analysis and authorizations

A number of changes have been made to investment analysis and authorization procedures in the new Corporation. They include a much wider use of net present value (NPV) techniques to analyse capital projects, a more intense process of internal scrutiny, and clearer and more systematic financial delegation and authorization procedures.

The first and perhaps most important change is the more extensive use of NPV analysis throughout the organization to evaluate capital expenditures. Whereas in the old organization it was really only major projects such as new power stations that were subject to such analysis, it is now required throughout the entire organization for all proposed capital investments. As Warren Taylor, Accounting Manager of Electricorp Production, notes about the old system:

> There was no NPV analysis used to set up the priorities within [the] programme. So what did you aim for? That was one of the first things we had to resolve.

All projects being considered are now supported by full discounted cash flow analysis and prepared in both 'real' and 'nominal' formats. A real rate of return after tax is used and results are presented for NPV, internal rate of return and profitability index. The project evaluation is supported by sensitivity analyses and a narrative which highlights the principal features and sources of risk of the project. A full review of the appropriate discount factor (currently 7% real, after tax) has been undertaken to allow for changes in interest rates and risk premia, but particularly to allow for taxation changes. This has been undertaken from the perspective of ECNZ being a fully 'privatized' corporation, as if it had shareholders who were subject to New Zealand income taxation. Electricorp Production has prepared a manual that contains clear instructions to managers and analysts on how to undertake economic analyses of both capital and maintenance projects.

Second, evaluations of capital works and major maintenance projects are also subject to more intense scrutiny than they were in the old Electricity Division. NZED had a works programme which was a five-year plan of all proposed work, both large and small. Because of its size, the works programme was very difficult to review and prioritize. Martin Holden, who had been Chief Accountant at NZED, comments:

> Some projects had been in the programme for years and years and hadn't ever been done. Some people would say it was an important job and others would say it didn't need to be done. So it never hit the priority list and never got done.

He believes that in the new Corporation there is now a much more intensive review of projects in the business units, thus reducing the number of projects put forward. This contrasts with the NZED works programme, which he describes as a 'bit of a wish list'. Although all the projects on this 'wish list' may have been technically worthwhile, many of them could not withstand commercial scrutiny. Capital expenditure proposals are now put forward by the General Managers of business units to the Corporate Development and Finance Managers, who make a recommendation to the Chief Executive. The Chief Executive may then carry the proposals forward to the Board.

Finally, the financial delegation and authorization process is now considerably changed. Prior to incorporation, financial delegations were heavily centralized. Cabinet, Ministers, and the central control agencies were involved, with only limited delegations to managers. Every submission going forward to be authorized by Ministers or a Cabinet Committee required a Treasury Report. Although there was rigour in the system, it was confined mainly to checking that the proposed financial return was in line with policy. Treasury officers were not in a position to evaluate the technical aspects of the project or to assess its wider organizational and strategic impact on the Division.

Financial delegation is now more extensively decentralized and authorities are clearly defined. Authority flows from the Shareholding Ministers as shareholders to the Board of Directors, with extensive delegations to the Chief Executive, senior managers, and the Boards of the two subsidiary companies. The overall review role of the Cabinet Committee is now assumed by the Board and Chief Executive of ECNZ.

Financial delegation begins with approval of the business plan and capital expenditure budgets by the Board of Directors. This provides 'approval in principle' for activities during the year. The Chief Executive and senior managers have delegated authority to approve expenditures within the approved budget. They also have authority to approve expenditures not within the approved budget, using funds available from savings on other approved works, but the delegated authority here is significantly less than for expenditures within the approved budget. Further sub-delegation of authority takes place in order to push decision making and participation in management as low as possible.

Project monitoring and post-audit

Each business unit is required to monitor projects under its control and report to the Board on a regular basis. There is an intention to move to monthly reporting in the near future. The objective is to control capital expenditure by monitoring expenditure approvals against the business plan throughout the financial year. For example, within Production, capital expenditures on individual projects are reported directly to Electricorp Production's headquarters. Reports are then sent to Corporate each month for projects over $200,000 and those using substituted funds (i.e. projects that were not in the approved budget).

Post-audit procedures were not part of the old system. Although for major projects Treasury would investigate to ensure that a new project would show an acceptable return, at least on a predicted basis, there was no mechanism in place for a review of the actual performance of the project against the earlier predictions. A set of procedures for the post-audit review of projects is being developed for projects approved by the Chief Executive and the Board. The first major project initiated and finished by the Corporation is the upgrade of the HVDC link across Cook Strait. This project will be the subject of the first major post-audit review conducted by the Corporation. It is planned that 25% of all major maintenance and capital projects in Production that were approved by the General Manager, the Chief Executive or the Board will be the subject of post-audit reviews. The 25% to be reviewed will be selected by the General Manager but projects that are 'in trouble' may be subject to immediate review. The purposes of these post-audit reviews are defined in the new Capital Expenditure Manual. They include:

(1) checking that project profitability matches or exceeds the claimed profitability level at the time of approval, (2) the investigation of variations in profitability aimed at improving future capital investment decisions, (3) determining if projects undertaken for non-financial reasons e.g. safety, return the required results, (4) checking if realized results are consistent with the mission, goals and objectives of Electricorp Production, and (5) information systems were adequate to determine and signal the development of adverse trends with respect to projects.

Management information and accounting systems

At the time of incorporation, information system development was a centralized, specialist group in the organization that had been set up to implement accounting and financial management systems, a plant history system, and other administrative and technical systems. The Electricity Division had a long history of unsuccessful development of financial and administrative systems. They generally faltered on the size of the request, and even when an attempt was made to progress in smaller increments, the large database approach took over in the end.

One of the first major decisions faced by the Board Chairman and the Establishment Board was whether to proceed with the expenditure of funds for the development of centralized computer facilities for the information systems group. Even though a new computerized accounting system (known as FMS) was nearly complete and being piloted reasonably successfully, a decision was made to close the facility and disband the centralized information systems group. Although it took the Board a little time to conclude that this was the correct decision, the basis for their decision in the end was simple and clear cut – continued operation of a centralized information system group was contrary to a decentralized management philosophy and the basic management principle of 'autonomy within defined areas of responsibility and accountability'.

Instead, General Managers of business units were given responsibility for meeting their own management information and accounting system needs. Progress was rapid. More accountants were hired from the private sector and, because of the need to get financial systems up and running quickly, standard off-the-shelf software was chosen and quickly installed. Corporate, Production, Marketing and Trans Power chose to install the same business system software on Datacom bureau equipment. PowerDesignBuild chose other software because they wanted job-costing capabilities. This approach was carried even further in the Production Groups where the General Manager made it optional for his four Group Managers to accept the choice of the divisional accountant or to pursue their own strategy. One accounting manager commented on these changes as follows:

> Previously we'd spent about 10 years trying to develop one giant data base system which was basically a general ledger system called FMS. The speed with which we were able to install new accounting systems is one indication of a significant efficiency gain that's come out of the establishment of the Electricity Corporation as an SOE. The reason why the change was done so quickly and successfully was firstly because they made the accountant responsible for the system as opposed to a committee (which was the previous arrangement), and secondly, because a very tight deadline was imposed.

One of the first tasks was to get decentralized accounting control over revenue, expense, and cash flows for the newly established business units. Another was to set up fixed asset registers. This required allocating individual assets to business units and placing a value on each of them. The valuation of individual assets was to be derived from the overall asset valuation. The outcome of this allocation and valuation exercise was to be important to the business units, because their performance as profit centres was to be evaluated using rate of return measures. This proved to be a difficult task as tracking of assets in the old organization was haphazard. Another accounting manager, one who was hired in from the private sector, describes his reaction to the situation he found on joining the Corporation shortly after its establishment:

> The record keeping was a bit of an eye opener for me coming in from private enterprise. There was often very little communication between the engineering and operational side and the accounting side. Literally, whole items of plant, even buildings (houses, etc) would be moved around the countryside, erected or knocked down and

there was no accounting record to match. So a transformer that could be on the books at Christchurch might end up in Auckland but nobody knew except the engineer doing the job. A major exercise since I came was to try to develop a fixed asset register.

He went on to describe the allocation of assets to the new business units:

The actual allocation of assets between the business units was done in an interesting way. It was semi-political with people arguing whether they wanted an asset or whether they didn't. There was no sound accounting basis for the decisions in a lot of cases. Finally, it was settled by a corporate management meeting which was referred to as the 'Quality Inn Agreement' because it was held in a Quality Inn. This meeting decided which assets would go where. The idea was that once the assets had been identified we could list them out and start to value them. The feedback I was getting from my regional accountants was 'Hang on, I'm not too sure about the historic records we've got and it may not be that easy'. So we got in a firm of public accountants to help us, gave them two months to do it and two years later it is nearly finished. In Palmerston, for example, there was something like ten trays of old ledger machine cards with information going back to the 1920's.

It was all somewhat arbitrary — we had no choice. For example we found that when we looked through the records comparing certain transmission lines we found that a line of similar length, same number of poles, similar voltage, built at roughly the same time could have three times the value of another. On inquiry we found that the lines might have been built at the same time but the work camp was closer to one of them so all the costs of labour etc. were put into the line which was closest.

It would be incorrect to leave the impression that there was little accounting, record-keeping, financial reporting or control in the old organization. NZED ran a plant site based accrual ledger system and routinely prepared a district expenditure return, a revenue and operating return, and cost statements for non-recurring maintenance and capital projects. All of these reports were designed to have districts continually review their actual expenditures against estimates. The Electricity Division was also required to report revenue and expenditure to the Minister and had a statutory requirement to prepare a balance sheet and profit and loss account for each year.

The old accounting and reporting system reflected the nature of NZED as a division of the Ministry of Energy. The main purpose of the reports was to maintain fiscal control over inputs. They were certainly not timely. For example, the district expenditure report usually took two months to finish from the end of the month to which it related. One accountant that had been with NZED summed up the district expenditure report as 'acres of figures, no commentary and boring as hell to read'.

A middle-level manager who has been with the organization for seventeen years and had been a power station manager made the following comment:

We were, I believe, quite a good trading department in terms of meeting capital and revenue requirements. However, I don't think many of us knew whether we actually did make a profit or a loss or on what basis it was worked out.

The emphasis now is on producing reports that are useful for management decision making. Therefore, they must be produced speedily so that decision making can be timely. The nature of the reports is determined primarily by internal management needs rather than by the requirements of external control agencies. However, not all accounting and information system problems have been solved within the new organization. Difficulties are still being experienced with accounting, budgeting, and performance reporting systems. Many of these systems were rushed into place under time pressure, and although they have performed adequately, the Financial Controller indicated to us that a review of these systems is about to take place to 'improve the capability of the Corporation to analyse and report more effectively and efficiently'.

There has been considerable improvement in accounting and information systems, reporting structures and control systems since the establishment of Electricorp. The systems are now better designed to focus attention on the 'bottom-line' effects of actions and decisions, unlike the systems in NZED which were focused on fiscal control of inputs. Provided that the Corporation can manage to avoid resistance to change in its decentralized accounting and information systems' groups, the systems should continue to evolve to meet management needs.

5

ECNZ and the Competitive Process

Our purpose in this chapter is to draw attention to the wider impacts on the form and extent of competition in the economy resulting from ECNZ's incorporation. In particular, we describe how some of ECNZ's managers' decisions, actions and behaviour since ECNZ became an SOE have (1) added competitive elements into existing markets, (2) enhanced the competitive process, or (3) changed the nature of competition.

Figure 5.1 provides a visual overview of the Chapter. Attention will be given first to input markets, then to competition in generation, and finally to output markets. The discussion is not intended to be exhaustive.

Markets for inputs

ECNZ's major input markets include the markets for capital (debt), fuel supply, labour, managers, maintenance services, and capital works.

Capital (debt) markets

Changes initiated by ECNZ have enhanced New Zealand debt markets and increased New Zealand's involvement in international capital markets. ECNZ has created markets in debt instruments that simply did not exist before. When ECNZ acquired the assets of NZED, the initial valuation placed on these assets was approximately $6.3 billion and a debt equity ratio of 1:1 was established. The initial $3 billion owed to the Government was to be refinanced and converted to 'private' debt within about three years.

While NZED had some financial management expertise, it had no need for a treasury function, because this was handled centrally for all government departments by the Treasury. In ECNZ, however, where between 20 and 30 cents of every dollar of revenue was being expended on interest, it was vital to have an efficient and sophisticated treasury function in order to contain costs and meet rate of return objectives. The following considerations determined ECNZ's approach to the treasury function and to debt markets:

(1) ECNZ's asset structure is dominated by power stations and transmission lines with extremely long lives. Therefore there was a need for long-term debt to finance that asset structure.

(2) ECNZ's cost structure is dominated by New Zealand dollar costs. Therefore the interest expense should also be denominated in New Zealand dollars.

(3) The long-term fixed asset structure, and the nature of the contracting between

Figure 5.1

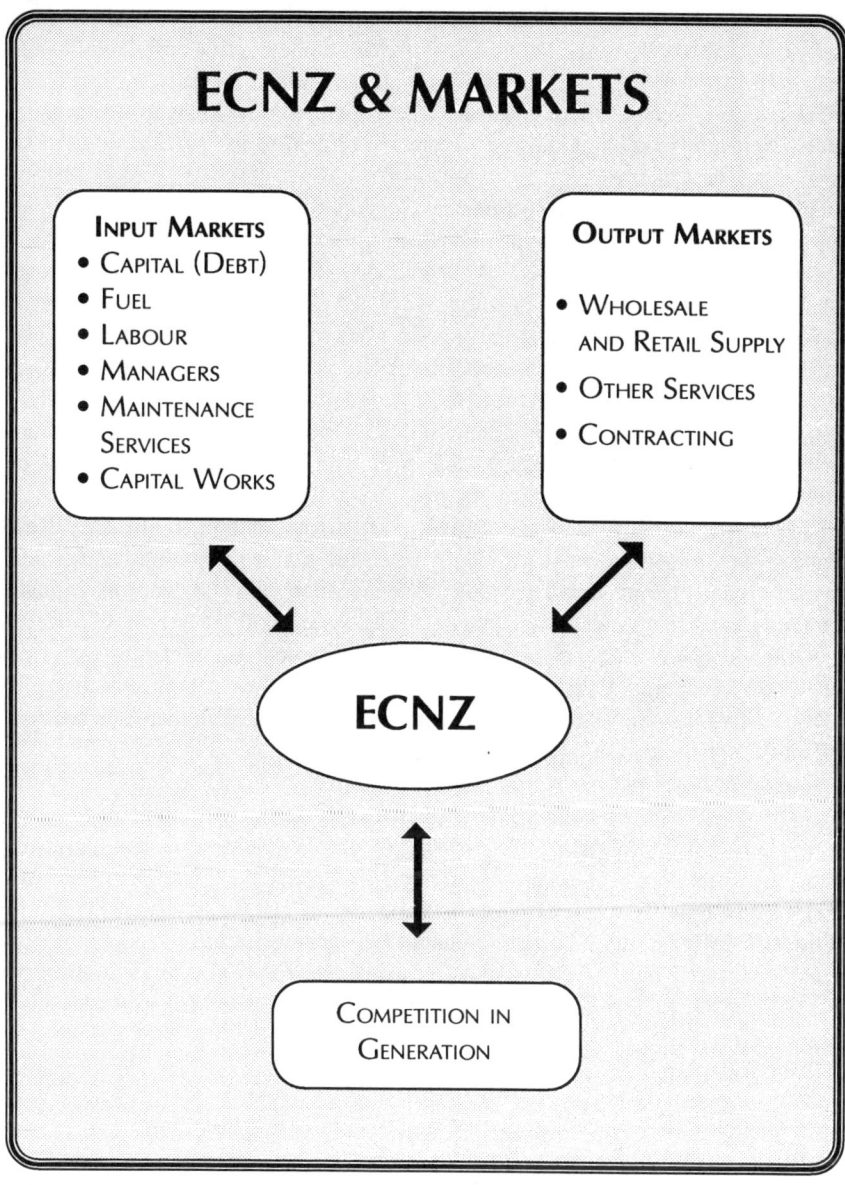

ECNZ and its major customers, required a fixed rather than a floating interest rate.

First, it was necessary to have the debt of ECNZ rated, as this would establish the interest rates at which debt could be issued and resold. International rating was necessary to give ECNZ access to the international bond markets. The ratings were carried out jointly by the US-based international rating agencies of Standard & Poor's and Moody's. ECNZ's short-term debt was rated A+1 by the former and P1 (i.e. Prime 1) by the latter. These are the highest ratings available. Long-term ratings for foreign currency issues were AA- and Aa3 respectively. These are also high ratings, about on a par with those given to New Zealand Government debt. High ratings such as these were clearly critical to the success of ECNZ's bond issue programme.

Following the Development Finance Corporation débâcle, the bonds were reassessed in November 1989 at the same levels. Moody's also rated the New Zealand denominated debt at Aa2. An indication of the high 'status' of these ratings can be gained by comparing them with those of 381 US industrials rated by Standard & Poor's at B or better (i.e. in the top six grades). Of these only 22% earned ratings of AAA or AA, the top two grades.[1] Figure 5.2 shows the relationship between the yield to maturity on ECNZ's bonds over time relative to the yield on Government Bonds of similar duration. During most of this period, the premium for risk is about 70 basis points, a clear indication of the relatively low risk of these bonds.

Second, there was a need to establish a secondary market for ECNZ's New Zealand denominated debt instruments, since the major institutions that would be interested in holding such debt would, as part of their purchase decision, evaluate the ability to resell such debt back into the market-place. Although there was clearly a market for New Zealand Government debt instruments, a market for large amounts of corporate debt did not exist.

Third, it was necessary to establish appropriate networks with merchant bankers and sharebrokers, particularly those offshore, as it was clear that some of ECNZ's debt requirements would be financed from outside New Zealand. There was therefore going to be a demand for funds, and a need to manage the foreign currency exposure that would result from borrowing offshore. This would mean that there would be a need to swap some of the foreign currency debt with New Zealand denominated debt. Foreign currency and fixed interest rate swaps change the nature of the risk ECNZ faces. The risk of changes in variable exchange and/or interest rates is replaced by the risk arising from dealing with the swap counterparty. ECNZ's exposure to counterparty risk (which emerges in many contexts other than swaps) is regularly assessed by the Finance Committee of ECNZ's Board.

The dealer panel established by ECNZ consists of 'market makers' prepared to stand in the market to buy and sell ECNZ's bonds. ECNZ has also been active in buying back the shorter duration bonds. The simple nature of the bonds ('plain vanilla bonds') and the volume of issue have created a liquidity in the market that was absent before. Because of this liquidity, the bonds are typically quoted with an extremely low bid-ask spread of about four basis points. Guy Manuell, ECNZ's Treasurer, comments:

---

1. See Ahmed Belkouai, *Industrial Bonds and the Rating Process* (Quorum Books, Greenwood Press, Westport CT, 1983), pp. 104-5.

Figure 5.2 Comparative yields on ECNZ bonds and government bonds

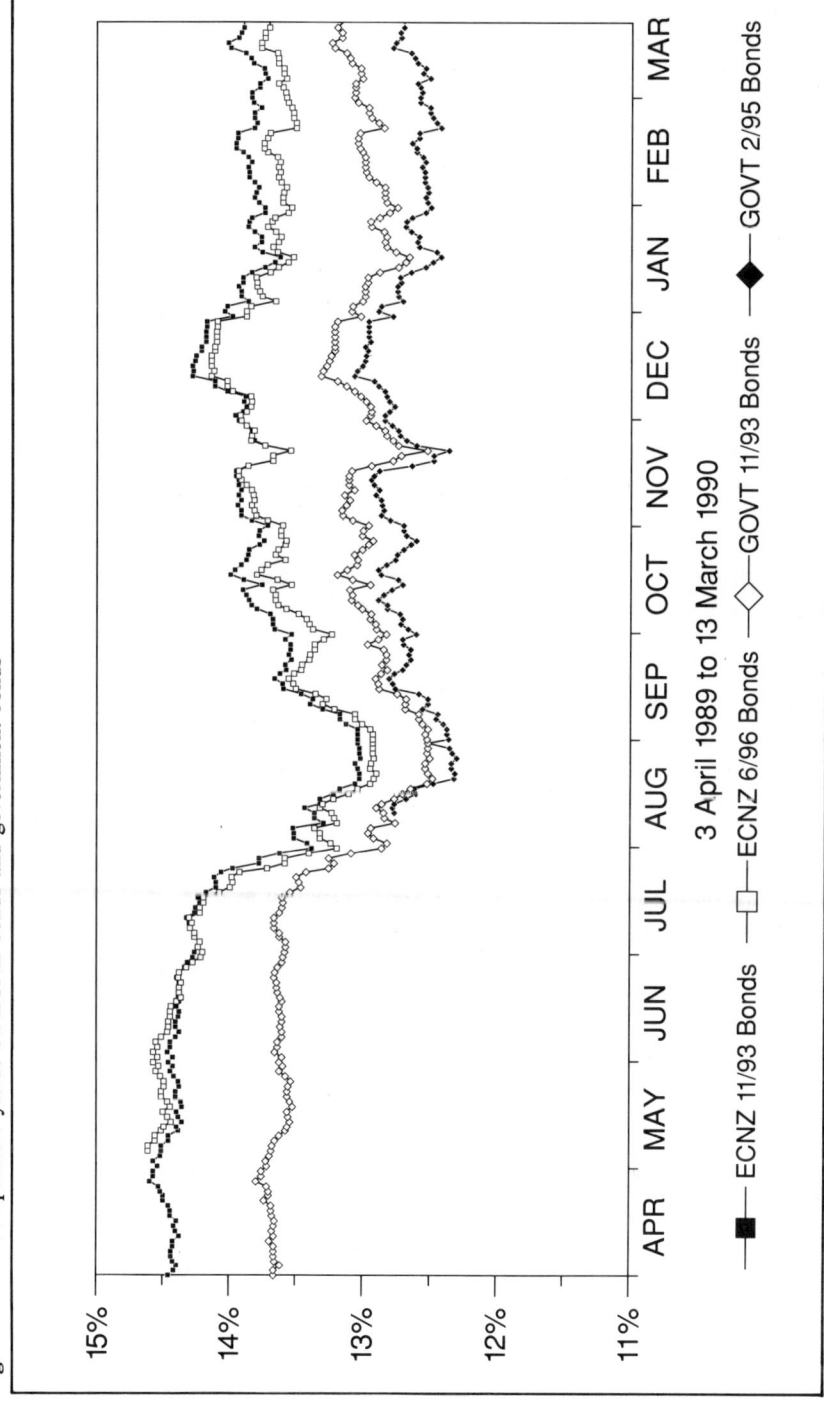

In our own quiet way we've been doing a lot of pioneering work in New Zealand financial markets and after this borrowing programme is finished they will never be the same again. I'm really pleased about that. I feel that the way ECNZ has done this has made a genuine contribution.

The magnitude of the changes that the operation of ECNZ's new treasury function has brought to the New Zealand capital market for debt should not be underestimated. ECNZ has created new markets in debt instruments in New Zealand, markets which were essential not only to interest potential investors in ECNZ's debt but also as a basis for pricing swap transactions undertaken to manage foreign currency exposure.

The treasury function is an area where the large size of ECNZ introduces substantial economies of scale. With the separation of Trans Power and the possible later division of generation into competing corporations, all treasury functions will presumably have to be duplicated. As the risk profiles of the individual companies will have changed, it is possible that the basis point spread will widen. To illustrate: if the spread increases to 120 basis points (from its present 70 basis points), the interest bill will increase by $15 million. The duplication of treasury functions will add substantial costs. Only time will tell whether they will be outweighed by the potential benefits from efficiency gains that some commentators believe will result from breaking up ECNZ.

Fuel supply markets
Although fuel costs are not as large as interest costs, they are still one of the major components of ECNZ's cost structure. Availability and pricing of fuel is therefore critical to the long-term financial performance of ECNZ. Because of the historic volatility of world fuel markets, and the extreme difficulty of predicting future availabilities and prices of fuels, ECNZ has adopted a multi-fuel strategy to minimize its risk exposure. Implementation of this strategy involves two things: development of the flexibility to switch between fuels in order to avoid overreliance on one particular fuel or supplier, and promotion of competition amongst fuel suppliers.

ECNZ with its mix of hydro, gas, coal, and geothermal plants already has the ability to switch between fuels to some degree. Moreover, some of its thermal generating plants such as Huntly Power Station are capable of operating by burning coal or gas. ECNZ's multi-fuel strategy calls for Production to maintain this flexibility in the future. In an internal strategy document entitled *Electricorp Production 1989/90 Capital Investment Strategic Directions* (hereafter *Strategic Directions Report*), the implications of the multi-fuels strategy for planning are spelt out:

> In planning for new generation Production is in a position to choose between hydro, gas, coal or geothermal and it aims to have one or two schemes based on each of these fuel types available at any time. The actual commitment to one of the schemes will then depend only on capital and cost.

ECNZ has made good use of its ability to switch generation between fuel types to inject elements of competition into fuel markets and to drive down the price of coal and gas. When ECNZ acquired the generating assets of NZED, it was not required to abide by the agreements NZED had with other parts of the Crown for supplies of coal and gas. Instead these contracts were to be negotiated afresh. ECNZ's new managers believed the supply price schedules in these agreements were much too high and set about driving prices down. Indeed, the view was held that the price schedule for coal had been set by the Government at these high levels in order to subsidize the operations of the State Coal Mines.

In 1987 ECNZ was buying coal from Coalcorp (the SOE formed out of State Coal) for a price in excess of $100 per tonne. Coalcorp sought to enter a long-term agreement with ECNZ for the supply and purchase of coal at slightly below their current supply price. ECNZ rebuffed Coalcorp's offer, stating they would be prepared to talk again when the price was approximately halved. Coalcorp refused. ECNZ's managers believe that at this time Coalcorp thought it had considerable negotiating power over the price of coal to ECNZ. One reason was the physical layout of Huntly Power Station, which was one of the main users of coal. David Frow, the General Manager of Electricorp Production, tells of the problem:

> Coalcorp have a mine which was built to supply Huntly Power Station. There is a conveyer which goes a couple of kilometers to the Station. The conveyer was the only real route for getting coal into the Station. There was no rail link or anything else. And the loading point of the conveyer is on Coalcorp land. And so they thought they had us.

But as it was also possible to operate Huntly on gas, ECNZ simply switched its operation to gas and did not take any coal for months. In the interim they developed an alternative receiving depot which allowed coal to be delivered by truck. They then developed some other smaller competitors who, although they could not deliver the tonnage necessary to operate the station full-time, were able to deliver enough to power the station one day a week so as to maintain skills and equipment and to keep up stockpiles for emergency use. In this way ECNZ was able to demonstrate to Coalcorp that they were able to operate without Coalcorp's coal. In the end Coalcorp, who by this time were having to lay off staff and close down facilities, capitulated and the price of coal fell dramatically. David Frow comments:

> The current situation on coal is quite healthy. Coalcorp is still making a profit. However the private suppliers are now tight and I am concerned that we don't drive them too hard right now because I don't want them to go out of business. I particularly want those private suppliers to survive because I don't want Coalcorp to get into a monopoly situation again.

ECNZ managers also believe that driving the price of coal down to more competitive levels strengthened their position in negotiations with the Government for the Crown's interest in the Maui gas field. ECNZ has now signed a long-term contract for the supply of the residual gas from the Maui gas fields at what it considers to be a favourable price, resulting in savings to the Corporation of over

$1 billion measured in net present value terms against NZED's gas supply arrangements for the term of the Maui contract. Obtaining this gas was also important to ECNZ because it was the only significant source of unallocated gas available in New Zealand until (and if) future discoveries are made. One consequence of locking up the Maui gas contracts is that the possibility of new entry into generation is significantly reduced, at least in the near future.

However, because the Maui field is expected to be depleted shortly after the turn of the century, maintenance of a competitive coal market in New Zealand is seen to be in the long-run interests of the Corporation. For this reason, too, the economics and technical requirements of other fuel sources are also under investigation. One option is to import coal from Australia. ECNZ believes that, given competitive freight rates and port charges and the quality of Australian coal, there is considerable potential for imported coal to compete with New Zealand coal. Another option is a type of pitch called orimulsion which could be imported from Venezuela in large quantities.

Labour markets
Another large component of ECNZ's cost structure is labour. ECNZ has reduced its labour costs through rationalization of the labour force and deep cuts in staffing. It has also had some success in injecting elements of competitiveness into labour markets. One success has been freeing the top 400 managers in the Corporation from union coverage, thereby making at least this small segment of the market for managers more competitive. Another relates to the way in which ECNZ was able to remove union restrictions on contracting out. This means that external firms employing private sector labour are now able to compete for jobs inside Electricorp.

Even with these successes, the Corporation is still suffering from continuing problems that stem firstly from coverage disputes between public and private sector unions and secondly from union award structures and other pay scales within the Corporation. The Corporation is seeking to eliminate the disputes over coverage and to address the problems associated with award structures and pay scales. By doing so, the Corporation aims to improve its ability to compete for work outside the Corporation.

(1) Disputes over coverage
Given its origins as a government department, union coverage of workers in ECNZ is held primarily by the Public Service Association and the New Zealand Workers' Union. On the other hand, union coverage for the private sector is held by a multitude of craft unions. This has caused problems for the Corporation as its two contracting arms, PowerDesignBuild and EMEC, attempt to compete more vigorously in the private sector for work. Doug Dell, the Manager of EMEC, explains:

> In the situation we are in the PSA coverage of our employees is not acceptable to electrical workers outside the Corporation. This means that when we seek outside

work the outside unions threatened their managers with industrial action should we get the work because our workers are not covered by the Electrical Workers' Union. We have a number of strategies for trying to overcome this problem but none of them is the complete answer.

Strategies for breaking down union obstructionism include (1) lodging papers with the Labour Court seeking to compel the registrar of unions to resolve the matter of overlapping union coverage; (2) taking on jobs, e.g. Commonwealth Games Village electricity reticulation, where outside unions would be shown up in an extremely poor light if they objected, and (3) where possible, taking repair or refurbishment work off-site to be done on ECNZ premises.

(2) Award structures and pay scales
Award structures and other pay scales controlled by the PSA do not allow for easy implementation of some aspects of 'pay for performance' that the Corporation would like to introduce more widely throughout the organization. At present, bonuses which are tied to incentive contracts are limited to the upper layers of management. Union membership in the PSA by professional engineers in PDB, for example, inhibits the introduction of some aspects of pay for performance into the remuneration packages of engineers in what is now a consulting operation. Freeing professional engineers from union coverage by the PSA would help make these markets more competitive.

With the benefit of hindsight, some Board members and top managers in ECNZ are strongly of the view that if they had to do it over again they would handle the whole issue of union coverage differently. A representative statement of this view was made by one senior manager:

> The decision on union coverage was quite a significant one. There was agreement between the Corporation and the PSA that the PSA would continue to be the recognized union. While it is easy to be wise after the event I think that was wrong. At the time it may have avoided a massive upsurge in industrial action but our fears about that may have been overstated in terms of the minimal disruptions we have had. So that was avoided, but at a cost. And the cost has been that we are part of a union which is not really in line with our business. It's a union which, in terms of its very nature, is concerned more with office workers and bureaucrats than it is with the cold-hearted business of getting out there and competing for work.

Markets for managers
ECNZ provides a case study of how markets for managers have been enhanced by the SOE programme. This improvement is a consequence of (1) making all management positions contestable, (2) changing the nature of managerial work within the organization, (3) introducing clear promotion ladders within the Corporation, and (4) changing perceptions about management positions within ECNZ.

(1) All positions made contestable
Job security was considered important in NZED, as in the New Zealand public service generally. When ECNZ was being established, it announced that all

positions would be contestable, regardless of the perceived or implied security of positions within NZED. All positions in the new Corporation were to be applied for. Applications from those who had been employed in a similar position for one or two decades were to be assessed against other external and internal applications. At the management level the objective was to appoint the best individual applicant to each new position. Apart from having the needed technical skills for the new position, attributes looked for were a willingness to question old practices and an ability to learn new management skills quickly. The old system which allowed appointments to be 'appealed' no longer existed.

As a result, significant changes took place in the top management of the Corporation. A Board member described the change:

> In Electricorp, if you count the top ten people there, there are probably only two that were appointed from the old Electricity Division. What happened was that those that were internal were pushed up by about ten years relative to where they would have been in a normal career curve [in the Electricity Division].

In other cases, people who considered themselves, or were considered to be, likely to have difficulty in adapting to the new organization were either encouraged to seek employment elsewhere or were offered positions well below their current levels of responsibility. In addition, outside managers and professionals were hired for the specialized functions which were added, such as treasury, finance, personnel, industrial relations, and marketing. For example, there are now many more accounting personnel than there were prior to incorporation, since the need for management information and financial control is considerably greater in ECNZ than it was in NZED. One senior manager who had been with NZED notes:

> There have been a number of new people introduced in such specialized areas as accounting. I can recall the Electricity Division when we had a budget of $1 billion and three qualified accountants. God knows how many we've got now.

(2) Changing the nature of managerial work

The nature of managerial work has been changed in ECNZ, as it has been in all areas of commerce in New Zealand as a result of economic restructuring. The skills required of managers are different, now that they have been given the power to manage and are held responsible and accountable for a bottom-line profit figure. Roger Kerr, who is an ECNZ Director and Executive Director of the New Zealand Business Roundtable, offers the following assessment:

> I guess the average age of Chief Executives of major companies has dropped about ten years. I would say that the skills that are required now are very, very different. They are skills that have to do with people, organisational culture, marketing, finance, etc. as opposed to lobbying Government, learning how to evade regulations and getting the best tax breaks you can. A generation of human capital has been just about obliterated. People who were able to adapt to the changes were delighted that for the first time in their lives they were able to develop and apply their commercial skills.

(3) Introduction of clear promotion ladders

Reorganizing the Corporation along decentralized lines and delegating management decision-making responsibilities to the lowest possible levels has resulted in an organizational structure in which there are clearer promotion ladders and career pathways in the organization. Managers are now strongly encouraged by Corporate Personnel to plan for their succession, because having a succession plan or candidate improves the possibility of advancement.

The addition of the new functions such as finance, treasury, personnel, industrial relations and marketing has also created new career paths for these professionals.

(4) Changing perceptions about management positions within ECNZ

ECNZ's ability to attract high quality managers was constrained initially by a number of factors. Among these factors were the perception that this was a government department, that the new Corporation lacked a track record and faced an uncertain future, and that the Corporation lacked visibility both domestically and internationally. As a result some top positions were hard to fill and in particular this is true of the Chief Executive position. John Fernyhough, ECNZ's Board Chairman, comments:

> We had been advertising extensively here and overseas and it was very, very hard to get anybody to take the job. 'Who wants to work for the Electricity Department?' was the attitude. It wasn't a job seen as a prestige job at that point in time. Of course it is now but it was not seen that way at all. I personally talked to a number of top managers of one of New Zealand's major companies about the job. There was no way I could prise them out. They were all locked up with share deals. While I couldn't offer that I could offer a lot of money and some pretty good transfer inducements. But it was hard, jolly hard. The short list was not good at all when we got down to it. When I heard from Roger Kerr that Roderick Deane might be interested that was quite an opportunity for me.

All of the negative factors mentioned above have now been overcome or substantially reduced. As a result the pool of management expertise from which ECNZ is able to draw both within New Zealand and internationally is considerably improved. However, there are still constraining factors at upper levels. A major constraint is the inability to offer an equity component in the remuneration package.

Market for maintenance services

Trans Power, which has responsibility for the operation and maintenance of the national grid, was set up without a maintenance staff. This was done deliberately with the objective of controlling costs by forcing Trans Power to contract out for these services. Trans Power was free to contract externally as well as internally for this work.

Construction and maintenance of high voltage, direct current lines is specialized work that, prior to the establishment of ECNZ, was performed almost entirely by work crews employed by NZED. As a result there were very few people or organizations outside of ECNZ with the ability to undertake this specialized work, and almost all of it is still awarded internally to EMEC, PDB, and Production. Work in less specialized areas such as building and grounds maintenance has been easier to contract out. As noted in Chapter 4, about 10% of routine operations and maintenance work is now let to external contractors and this proportion of work is expected to rise significantly in the future. Trans Power has written into its business plan that they expect to see at least 25% of its work going to external contractors.

Trans Power is attempting to strengthen outside competition for its maintenance work by awarding work wherever possible to competent external contractors and Power Boards. This has required awarding work, in some cases, to organizations which have not submitted the lowest tender. It has also involved Trans Power rejecting tenders which are well below what Trans Power estimated the job to cost, where they judge that the contractor may be driven out of business by the low tender price. It has also encouraged outside contractors to develop the expertise necessary to handle high voltage work. Trans Power now advertises for contractors both in New Zealand and Australia. Having outside contractors also provides Trans Power with a way of measuring the efficiency of its internal contractors.

Business units within the Corporation, which compete for Trans Power work, are treated formally by Trans Power in the same way as outside contractors. Trans Power has clearly signalled to internal contractors that the provision of maintenance services is to be competitive and that continued work is not assured unless they could provide a high quality service at lower prices than external competitors. When Trans Power separates, what are now internal contractors competing against each other will become one external contractor. For this reason, ECNZ has now eliminated this competition by amalgamating EMEC into PDB. However, ECNZ will still have an interest in the cost-efficient operation of Trans Power.

Market for capital works

ECNZ is both a seller and a purchaser in the market for capital works. Our interest here is with ECNZ as a purchaser.

Initially, PowerDesignBuild was partially protected from external competition through the operation of a transition agreement. However, since April 1989, ECNZ's other business units (in particular Production and Trans Power) have been able to buy their capital works either inside or outside the organization. PDB has thus been exposed to competitive pressure from external contractors. What impact this will have on the market for capital works remains to be seen. PDB may have an information advantage over the external contractors because of the highly specialized knowledge in heavy power engineering its managers and engineers have developed over the years from their involvement in designing and constructing the New Zealand electricity system.

Competition in electricity generation

At the same time as ECNZ was formed, the generation side of the electricity industry was deregulated. Although the Government decided that ECNZ would not be subject to price controls, it did intend that ECNZ should face the prospect of competition in generation. Chapter 3 described the threat of competition in generation and ECNZ's strategic responses to this and other pressures. One crucial strategic response was a Board decision to reduce electricity prices in real terms. This pricing policy had two interrelated objectives: (1) to reduce the threat of entry into generation and (2) to build volume against competing fuels.

It was also noted in Chapter 3 that we had encountered scepticism outside the Corporation about the reasoning behind ECNZ's pricing strategy, at least insofar as it was based on the need to deter new entry into generation. Several outside observers expressed the opinion to us that the threat of entry had been consistently overstated by ECNZ.

The dynamics of the competitive environment in generation in New Zealand, and ECNZ's response to, and influence on, this environment are important issues. We therefore decided to spend additional time on this matter. We discussed the topic further with the Chief Executive in person and in correspondence, and we had further discussions with other senior managers, including the Acting Corporate Development Manager, and Board members. We also reviewed additional strategy documents which had been completed during the period our study was taking place so that we could more fully describe and discuss (1) ECNZ's past, current and future views on the prospects for new entry into generation, (2) its strategies for dealing with the perceived threat of new entry, and (3) the central role of pricing policy.

Our purpose here is to provide a more complete picture of how ECNZ's managers have viewed and reacted to changes in the competitive environment in electricity generation over time. It provides our understanding of the views of the dominant player in electricity generation in New Zealand.

The threat of new entry shortly after incorporation

To summarize the discussion in Chapter 3, the generating assets ECNZ took over from NZED were far in excess of what was needed to meet current demands for electricity. At that time *The Task Force Report* predicted that 'no extra generating capacity would be required for some time' and that it was 'unlikely a major thermal station will be required in this century'. The fact that ECNZ found itself with excess capacity has strongly influenced its strategy. Completion of the Clyde Dam will add to its excess capacity.

A series of strategic planning papers were prepared for the Board in 1988 which focused on the prospect of several new generating proposals and strategies for dealing with them. A major conclusion drawn from these analyses was that ECNZ's delivered price of electricity was too high when compared with the long run marginal cost (LRMC) for new competitors, particularly those like Auckland Electric Power Board and Hutt Valley Energy Board who were considering building gas-fired combined-cycle stations. This gap between ECNZ's delivered price and the LRMC of new competitors provided a considerable inducement to new entrants. Chief Executive, Roderick Deane, believes that this 'was mainly because the market believed that ECNZ would be forced to price above LRMC because of its high asset value and operating expenses'.

Strategic responses

ECNZ's strategic response to the perceived threat of entry has had four parts: (1) minimizing cost by closing down or mothballing excess generating plant, (2) raising barriers to entry through pricing, (3) other strategic actions, and (4) entering into joint ventures.

(1) Minimizing the cost of generation

With excess capacity in the system, ECNZ's cost structure is determined by the technological constraints of the existing mix of generating facilities. However, it has acted to minimize the cost of existing operations by rationalizing assets to reduce surplus capacity. Analysis of the economics of marginal (high cost) generating stations in 1988/89 which weighed short-term disinvestment against long-term profitability resulted in the mothballing or phasing out of many hundreds of megawatts of capacity. David Frow explains:

> We shut down a unit at Marsden A on a semi-permanent basis. The remaining unit at Marsden is only available 7 months of the year. We've shut down 180 megawatts of capacity at Otahuhu and we converted the generators to provide reactive support for the system but without generating megawatts. We have shut down a 30 megawatt unit at Meremere and we've also changed the operating pattern so instead of having the remaining 130 megawatts available 7 days a week, 365 days a year, they are only available 5 days a week. We have done all these things to reduce surplus capacity and pull down our costs accordingly. For example, Marsden used to have a budget of $8 million per annum. We have reduced the budget there for the last couple of years to $4 million per annum.

Plant that the analyses indicated was economic to retain was mothballed for future use. As a result of plant closures and the growing demand for electricity, the current surplus of installed plant is forecast to exist for only five to ten years before mothballed plant will be brought back into service. Electricorp Production now believes that the present level of commissioned plant is optimal, and the marginal cost of recommissioning mothballed plant is such that recommissioning will occur before new stations are built. On this point Production believes that ECNZ now has a competitive advantage as to the timing of future capital investment because it has not discarded all its surplus generating plant. As the *Strategic Directions Report* states:

> . . . the low marginal cost of recommissioning existing plant gives a financial advantage to the Corporation and a timing advantage as it can make capital investments closer in time to when capacity is needed.

(2) Raising barriers to entry through pricing

The heart of ECNZ's strategy to deal with the threat of new entry is adoption of a pricing policy to lower its electricity prices in real terms towards the LRMC faced by new entrants. There are several reasons why ECNZ decided to adopt such a pricing policy. However, it is best understood in signalling terms. ECNZ

Figure 5.3

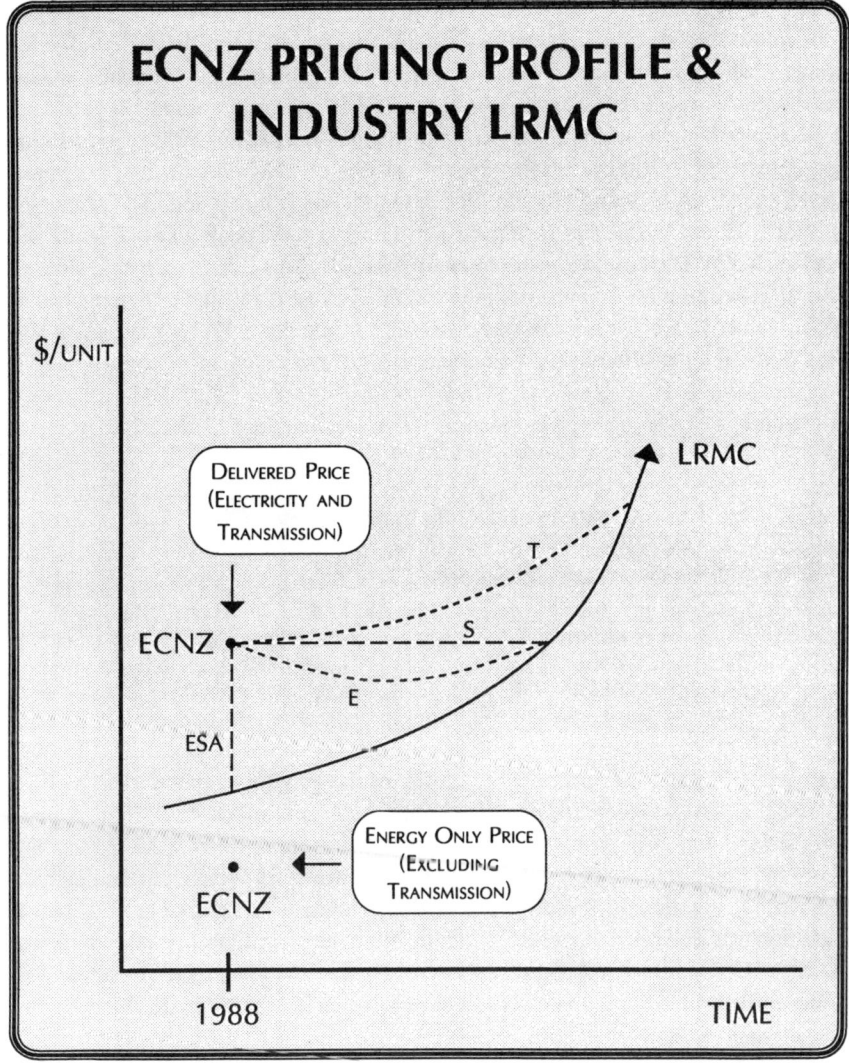

ECNZ PRICING PROFILE & INDUSTRY LRMC

$/UNIT

DELIVERED PRICE
(ELECTRICITY AND
TRANSMISSION)

LRMC

T

ECNZ

S

E

ESA

ENERGY ONLY PRICE
(EXCLUDING
TRANSMISSION)

ECNZ

1988   TIME

wanted to send a clear signal to prospective entrants about the future trend of electricity prices.

The situation faced by ECNZ is best described with the help of a highly simplified diagram. Figure 5.3 provides a general representation of ECNZ's top managers' view of the long-term direction in the movement of LRMC of new power plants. It also shows the general shape of ECNZ's price profile marked E in relation to it.[2] It also shows three other 'alternative' pricing profiles marked T, S and ESA, which we will discuss.

It should first be noted that ECNZ's managers believed that ECNZ's delivered price of electricity (which includes energy and transmission components) around the time of its establishment was above the LRMC of a new entrant, in particular those considering gas-fired combined-cycle plants. In a paper entitled 'Competition and Electricity Pricing Strategy' sent to the ECNZ Board by Corporate Development on 21 May 1990, the 1988 situation was summarized. The price paid by North Island customers (averaged across all supply, peak and off peak) was 6.3c per kWh. The baseload component of this price was 5.0c per kWh. Estimated cost of generating for a new gas-fired combined-cycle plant (including annuitized capital costs at a 7% discount rate) was 4.5 to 5.0c per kWh. Such a plant was thus potentially profitable for competitors. The paper states:

> We concluded that competition was likely if the perceived gap between ECNZ prices and the cost of new plant continued to exist.

ECNZ needed a strategy for deterring new entry. As ECNZ's Chief Executive notes:

> We had to develop a pricing strategy. We've had to think about how to utilise our excess assets. We've had to think about whether new generators are going to get into the business, and whether its actually worth pricing up, letting them come in, or whether we should price down. We've done a lot of comparisons of these alternatives on a net present value basis for the company under different scenarios.

The decision was to adopt the price profile of the general shape marked as E on Figure 5.3. The longer-term prediction on which this line is based is that price will move down towards LRMC of new entry, be held at a lower level for a few years and then, in time, start moving up towards LRMC as depicted in the diagram.

ECNZ's intention in trending prices down towards LRMC of new gas-fired capacity was to create uncertainty about the future profitability of new power stations. Competitor expectations are the target of this strategy. If competitors believed that ECNZ's delivered price was to be held stable (as depicted by line S), or would actually trend up over time (as depicted by line T), then entry would be more likely putting ECNZ's profitability at risk. ECNZ's Chief Executive explains this line of reasoning:

> My view is that proposals for building new generating facilities are sitting around out there. That if people like CRA did not believe our pricing strategy they'd go

---

2. These curves are overprecise. Movements in LRMC come in steps as capacity is usually added in sizable increments so this curve would more properly be drawn as a step function over time. Nor does the diagram portray the considerable uncertainty involved in the determination of the rate at which LRMC might rise. Nonetheless, the diagram does capture the general upwards direction of the future movement in LRMC as new capacity is added into the system. This is sufficient for our purposes.

ahead and build their station. If we don't price it right then the CRA's of the world will proceed. If we didn't believe the threat of competition we could easily jack up our rate of return to Government by upping our prices. Our average price is unchanged this year from last year. You could clearly get more than that.

The speed at which ECNZ has been able to move its prices downwards has been constrained by requirements for a reasonable level of profitability in the short term. ECNZ's stated objective is to achieve an appropriate balance between electricity prices on the one hand, and rate of return on shareholder's funds on the other. The emphasis is on maximizing the shareholder's long-term interest in ECNZ, which has put great pressure on the need to build market share and volume and to contain costs. To quote again from the Board paper 'Competition and Electricity Pricing Strategy':

> The alternative strategy involving prices rising with inflation was likely to lead to competition in the short to medium term and an extension of the current surplus capacity which would lead to loss of market share and thus to depressed market prices and lower profitability for ECNZ in the longer run. It was argued that some moderation in short term rates of return was justified if this promoted higher rates of return in the longer run which more than compensated for the short term sacrifice and maximized the net present value of the business.

Outside commentators have suggested that, from a new entrant's perspective, it is ECNZ's *ability* to reduce price that is important in deterring entry, rather than the actual price level. This line of argument suggests that ECNZ could continue to price above the LRMC of new entry (choosing price trend S or T) and simply rely on competitors' perceptions of ECNZ's ability to reduce its price rapidly towards SRMC as a barrier to entry. In our view this argument overlooks the risk of a competitor misreading the situation and building a station. Once it was built, high exit costs would trap the investment of the competitor who would generate electricity provided that price is greater than SRMC. Such competition could clearly be harmful to both ECNZ and the competitor.

We also put the argument suggested by outside commentators to ECNZ's Chief Executive in writing. Dr Deane replied as follows:

> The gap between current prices and SRMC does provide ECNZ with an ability to reduce price while still making some contribution to profit. However, we do not agree that this implies that ECNZ could price above LRMC and still deter entry. Electricity generation is a capital intensive business and typical thermal power stations have variable costs amounting to only 50% of the overall price required to make a profit from the investment. If a competitor does build a new base load thermal power station, that competitor will have a similar ability to price down towards SRMC. Neither would benefit from such a price war. New stations, once built and costs are sunk, will operate and reduce ECNZ market share irrespective of market price levels.

There are two other issues of interest that can be discussed with the help of Figure 5.3. The first has to do with the initial valuation placed on ECNZ assets.

Both Treasury and ECNZ agree that electricity should be priced at LRMC. However, there are divergent views about how ECNZ should move its price towards LRMC. ECNZ managers consider that the asset valuation discussion with Treasury incorporated a 'ramping up' of price towards LRMC, adopting a pricing profile like that represented by line T in Figure 5.3. Provided price effects outstrip volume effects, the discounted cash flow of the revenue stream implied by the unit prices along line T would be significantly higher than that implied by line E. This difference may well account for the different positions of Treasury and ECNZ in their debates over valuation.

The second issue has to do with the position taken by the Electricity Supply Association with respect to ECNZ prices. In an interview with ESA officials the following view was put to us:

> . . . it is now possible for new entrants to construct power stations which could produce electricity at a lower marginal cost in real terms than the current average price charged by ECNZ. This poses a real question: Is the current price charged by ECNZ a competitive price? An American consulting firm showed that the ECNZ price of electricity was high and could be cut by at least 25%.

This implies a movement towards LRMC as depicted by the line marked ESA in Figure 5.3. There does not appear to be any commercial incentive for ECNZ to choose such a pricing profile.

(3) Other strategic actions
In addition to pricing, ECNZ has made a series of other strategic moves to respond to the threat of new entry. These include (1) the acquisition of long-term contracts for the residual gas from the Maui gas fields, (2) acquisition of other strategic resources such as land, and (3) restructuring of electricity prices by separating energy and transmission charges.

As ECNZ analyses show gas to be the cheapest of the fossil fuels, the Corporation wanted an assured supply of gas to run its gas-fired plants. As discussed above, ECNZ was, for this reason alone, vitally interested in negotiating for the residual supply of gas from the Maui gas fields at the best price it could obtain. But it was not alone in its interest in this gas. AEPB had also expressed interest. ECNZ managers were well aware that, if the Corporation was successful in obtaining a contract for the residual gas, then it would be difficult for AEPB to proceed with its stated intention of building a gas-fired combined-cycle plant. Access to New Zealand's limited gas supply thereby took on a strategic dimension.

ECNZ negotiated vigorously for the gas, well aware of its competition, and was successful in acquiring the remaining reserves of the Maui fields. This left AEPB in a position where it was unable to proceed. We interviewed Peter Cebalo, General Manager of AEPB. He identified access to gas supplies as the critical constraint to going ahead with their proposal:

> The only new entrants that you'll get into the market in the short term are those using gas as a fuel. Now if you haven't got any gas you can forget about short term

entry . . . Now our project. We've purchased a site; we've been through all the town planning issues; we've called tenders; we've analysed the tenders on some very sophisticated computers in Houston, Texas; we've issued an environmental impact assessment report; we've got town planning approval; we've got the Clean Air Act provisional approval. All the design has been done. All we need is the gas supply and we can't get it.

What is surprising is that we were informed by a Treasury offical with knowledge of the Crown's interest in the Maui gas field that, while AEPB had indicated an interest in a portion of the residual gas, they did not actually make a formal bid for the parcel of gas that Electricorp ultimately succeeded in acquiring. This raises a question about what AEPB's strategy was with respect to its proposed power station.

With a long term contract for the residual flow of Maui gas signed by the Corporation, ECNZ managers now readily concede that the threat of entry has declined, at least for the time being, from gas-fired plant.

In addition to fuel supplies, ECNZ has moved to acquire potential hydro sites and plant sites. Strategic acquisitions of this type are important for two reasons. One is to avoid being required to pay exorbitant prices to investors who moved to acquire potential sites ahead of ECNZ. To avoid this problem, at least partially, Electricorp Production has publicly stated its strategy of pursuing a number of potential investments concurrently and has taken care not to indicate a preference for any particular scheme. The second reason is to obtain sites before competitors. There are a number of good investment opportunities which are very site-specific, where early purchases of land can secure the investment for ECNZ. For example, the owner of land above a geothermal resource will play a major role in the development of the field.

One other important issue associated with the threat of entry is the separation of energy and transmission prices. Separation of these revenue streams by Electricorp is a consequence of three factors. First, it is a logical extension of the Corporation's 'ring-fencing' of the national grid by establishing Trans Power as a separate business unit. Second, it was recommended in the deliberations of a government taskforce on electricity industry restructuring. Third, it made strategic sense for ECNZ to separate energy and transmission prices to remove the incentive for grid bypass schemes such as AEPB's proposal to build its own gas-fired combined-cycle plant. By building a station embedded in its own distribution network, a potential competitor such as AEPB could potentially avoid the transmission component of the delivered price of power and compete solely on the energy price. As a result, ECNZ would receive no return on its investment in that part of the transmission network bypassed by the new generating station.

In October 1989, ECNZ announced a fourth pricing option which separated energy and transmission prices. Under this option the energy component was to be priced in a way that closely reflected the SRMC of generation. ECNZ's analysts believed that this would yield a price for the energy component which, as shown in Figure 5.3, would be below the LRMC of new entry.

ECNZ would clearly prefer to compete directly on the basis of energy prices rather than on delivered prices which include prices for both energy and transmission. However, transmission charges must also be recovered. The fourth pricing option was designed to fix transmission charges in the short term through the use of a ten-year moving average mechanism. Such a mechanism allocates a share of the largely fixed transmission costs to each distributor as a fixed access charge related to previous levels of demand. The ten-year moving average allows these charges to be reduced over time and, ultimately, avoided altogether. It also provides for these charges to be reallocated over time to other users of the national grid if a distributor invests in local generation.

Trans Power has continued to develop a transmission pricing methodology in consultation with the supply industry since the introduction of the fourth pricing option. The concept of a ten-year rolling average, or a similar concept, is likely to survive and be a significant component of total transmission charges when Trans Power becomes independent of ECNZ. The supply industry accepts that a separate Trans Power must recover its costs and that, if one distributor avoids the transmission charge by adding new generation, then the cost would have to be borne by all other grid users. There is agreement that this is unfair and therefore the industry recognizes the need for access charges to be avoidable only in the longer term.

Separation of energy and transmission charges, which will now be made necessary by the total separation of Trans Power, will enable ECNZ to compete directly on energy charges with distributors who own generation facilities as well as potential entrants such as CRA.

(4) Entering into joint ventures
As a final line of defence against competitors ECNZ has adopted a policy of 'If you can't beat them, join them'. If a competitor has secured a resource or has gained some other competitive advantage, ECNZ may seek to enter into a joint venture in order to limit the potential impact on the Corporation. For example, Electricorp Marketing has been actively talking to potential cogenerators to persuade them either to defer their investments or to enter into some form of joint venture.

Future competition
ECNZ's strategies for reducing the short-term threat of new entry seem to have been successful. Wholesale price levels over the last three years, the Corporation's signalling of reductions in real prices, and its signing of long-term contracts for the Crown's interests in the residual flow from the Maui gas fields: these have significantly reduced the threat of new entry in the near future. In the opinion of ECNZ's Chief Executive, their pricing policies and their success in obtaining the gas supply contracts are interconnected. In a letter to us Dr Deane stated:

> The Corporation's success in achieving natural gas supply contracts for its existing thermal power stations, in competition with prospective entrants to generation, at such favourable prices, is also a function of pricing strategy. The uncertainty created by this strategy about the future profitability of new power stations made them less

credible projects and lowered the prices which they could afford to bid in competition with ECNZ. The strategy has been so successful that the threat of entry has diminished significantly since 1988, leading to some commentators suggesting that we have overstated it.

ECNZ now believes that future competition will be met by development of resources other than natural gas. Dr Deane again:

> In the short/medium term, we identified gas-fired plant as the main competition (combined cycle for base load and gas turbines for peaking). Although there is some surplus natural gas available over the next few years, the development of new natural gas resources would be required to sustain this. It is our view, and most commentators would agree, natural gas supply to the electricity industry will be limited and expanding demand for electricity will ultimately be met by the development of resources other than natural gas. Whether this is coal, geothermal or hydro, it will be more expensive than natural gas leading to a rise in LRMC. Uncertainty surrounds the rate of rise and the level to which LRMC will rise. Comprehensive estimates of the possible alternatives have been prepared by ECNZ and this range of estimates underpins our pricing strategy. [Outside commentators] seem to think of competitive generation in very narrow terms (mainly as gas-fired combined-cycle plant).

The long-range planning studies to which Dr Deane refers to in his letter were described in Chapter 4 under the heading 'Long-range planning'. Based on the financial analysis of alternative futures simulated out to thirty years, they corroborate Dr Deane's views. In the Board paper entitled 'Competition and Electricity Pricing Strategy' referred to above, the following evaluation of the competitive situation is offered:

> The analysis indicates that new coal fired capacity is unlikely to be competitive until prices rise when new capacity is required towards the turn of the century. CRA now appear to recognize this and recently (March 1990) announced their plans for Marsden Point power station have been deferred. This decision coincided with the completion of a feasibility study to see whether the station would be profitable.

ECNZ continues to monitor its potential competitors closely in order to be in a position to take action ahead of them. As pointed out in the *Strategic Directions Report*, this information is also 'a useful check on Production's own assumptions about specific investments'.

The Corporation is also seeking to retain its competitive advantage through the adoption of a multi-fuel strategy. By having one or two schemes based on each fuel type (hydro, gas, coal or geothermal) available at any time, ECNZ is in a position to make a quick commitment to one of these schemes, based only on capital and fuel costs.

Electricorp also recognizes the need to retain a technological edge. The following statement is taken from the *Strategic Directions Report*:

> By pursuing new technologies at an early stage of their development not only will Production keep in contact with any new developments but it may be in a position

to secure the technology for its own advantage and keep ahead of competitors. Currently this strategy is being pursued with regard to underground coal gasification, where Production has undertaken a comprehensive pre-feasibility study and is currently pursuing the establishment of a joint venture company to pursue the technology further. Wind and wave generation are also being pursued, with wind opportunities looking quite attractive.

Markets for outputs

We focus here primarily on ECNZ's attempts to build new wholesale pricing structures and their flow-on effects to retail customers. We also discuss ECNZ's entry into other markets such as retail services and engineering and works contracting.

Wholesale electricity supply and competition from substitutes

ECNZ's pricing policy to the present time has had two major objectives. The first has been to deter entry by reducing the average price of electricity in real terms. The second and closely related objective is to build market share against competing fuels. Both of these objectives are related to the Corporation's goal of utilizing the excess capacity ECNZ had available in its existing electricity system.

It is important to understand that electricity is only one part of the non-transport, wholesale energy market in New Zealand. Competition from substitutes is real and ECNZ's managers argue that the degree of this competition is much greater than is popularly assumed. Their analyses show that ECNZ has only about 45% of the non-transport energy market and that approximately 70% of the final use market is contestable by other fuels. (Some idea of the market share threat from competing substitutes can be seen by referring back to Figure 3.2.) Moreover, in many cases, large electricity users are competing in international commodity markets. A number of these large users have the ability to locate new facilities either in New Zealand or in other countries. For these reasons, it is important that ECNZ price electricity competitively in both domestic and international markets. This is recognized in a discussion paper on pricing prepared by Electricorp Marketing in April 1990:

> Of particular note for a country such as New Zealand which is remote from the Northern Hemisphere markets, but whose economy is based on significant exports of primary based resources, is that around one-third of New Zealand's electricity is exported in forest products such as pulp and paper, metallic products such as aluminium and steel and agricultural products such as meat, dairy, wool and horticulture. For these products to be competitive, the electricity component must also be competitive on an international basis. The lowering of tariff protection against the importing of goods into New Zealand has had similar implications for firms supplying the domestic market. Electricity supplied to these firms must again be internationally competitive so they can supply their own markets in preference to goods (and in effect, electricity) imported from foreign countries.

The manner in which electricity prices are set, the structure of prices for energy and transmission components of the delivered price of wholesale electricity, and the nature of contracts for supply have changed considerably. Prior to the establishment of Electricorp in 1987, a four-part supply tariff known as the Bulk Supply Tariff (BST) was used. Historically, this tariff was set by the government of the day and bore little relation to movements in the cost of generation and delivery. Little attention was given to the demands of customers or the need to be competitive.

Getting greater clarity in its pricing structure has not been easy for ECNZ. There are at least two reasons for this. The first involves the complexity of the generation and transmission system, in which the costs of the delivered product change with the time of day, season of the year, level of storage reservoirs, and the mix of hydro and thermal generating system operating at any particular time. A second reason involves the continuing restructuring within Electricorp, such as the transfer of local transmission assets from Marketing to Trans Power and the announced move of the Government to make Trans Power an independent corporation.

However, Electricorp Marketing has introduced a series of pricing options (of varied complexity) with the objective of more accurately reflecting the Corporation's changing costs of supply, so that end use customers could respond to prices in an economically efficient way. In an internal pricing document dated January 1988, Marketing recognized the need to

> . . . change from a production oriented structure set up to recover revenue requirements to a market oriented structure which will influence and be influenced by the energy market.

As a first step in their attempt to achieve this objective, three new pricing options were introduced by Marketing in May 1988. These options are now being phased out in favour of a fourth pricing option which was introduced in October 1989. Option 4, as it is known, separates the delivered price of electricity into its two main components: energy and transmission. As a subsidiary of ECNZ Trans Power had proposed to carry this separation still further with the development of its own pricing structure and the establishment of separate transmission service contracts. This further separation is consistent with ECNZ's strategy of 'ring-fencing' the national grid and making its operation and pricing structure transparent. It also furthers ECNZ's strategy of being able to compete with a prospective new generator embedded in a distribution network head to head on the basis of the energy charge alone rather than on a delivered price basis (which includes a charge for transmission cost recovery).

(1) Pricing of the energy component
Pricing of the energy component by Electricorp Marketing includes some innovative elements. The objective is to increase pricing flexibility, thus making it easier to market electricity and improve industry efficiency. Energy elements include:
(a) *Time-of-use prices* quoted at the beginning of the annual contract period. Wholesale customers can use these prices to enter into annual contracts for the delivery of specified quantities of energy during each half hour of the year.

By contrast, the old BST included one day-rate energy charge and one night-rate energy charge.

(b) *Weekly 'spot' market prices* based on half-hourly short-run marginal costs of production quoted throughout the contract period two weeks in advance based on reservoir levels, expected rainfall, and other factors. Wholesale customers can contract to obtain a small part of their energy needs at these prices. The use of a weekly pricing system is claimed by Electricorp Marketing to be at the forefront of international practice for the 'spot' pricing of electricity. The objective is to share risk with direct supply customers and supply authorities by giving them better information on incremental consumption costs with which they can evaluate their own demand-side programmes. However, the success of this pricing innovation will depend on Electricorp's ability to develop customer confidence in the mechanism used to establish short-term market prices. It will also depend on how successfully distributors are able to pass these 'spot' prices on into the retail market place. This will require an improved ability to meter usage. This ability should improve as the cost of individual user metering devices declines. Marketing is investigating this metering technology and its costs.

(c) *A generation service fee* which is a fixed monthly capacity charge to each customer based on the average of the previous five years' annual daytime energy consumption updated on a rolling average basis. The objective of this fee is to have overall energy-related prices which are in excess of those based on SRMC-based prices.

The structure of the price of the energy component provides considerable scope and incentive for customers to shift demand from periods of high cost (peaking) to lower cost times of the day or week. Shifting demand in this way also enables ECNZ to make better use of its existing assets, thereby deferring the need for the construction of additional generating plant.

(2) Pricing of the transmission component

Pricing of the transmission component is a complex undertaking because of the large fixed investment in the grid, variable usage, and the need for Trans Power to recover its costs and make a return on its investment. Option 4 introduced the notion of a transmission service fee based on an allocation of the fixed cost of the grid and an incremental usage cost.

Rather than recover its costs from customers through Electricorp Marketing, Trans Power is now proposing to enter directly into separate transmission contracts with both generators and customers for the use each makes of the grid. The stated objectives of the new pricing system are to

(a) cover Trans Power's costs, including a return on capital;

(b) encourage efficient utilization of existing assets;

(c) encourage efficient investment in new assets;

(d) provide transparency and reasonable price stability; and

(e) treat existing users fairly, and provide access to the grid in a fair and reasonable basis to new users.

Transmission charges will be of two types: access charges and service charges.

(a) *Access charges* are designed to largely recover the approximately 90% of the costs associated with the grid which are fixed: i.e. capital, operations, and maintenance of the grid. Both generators and customers will pay a charge to be connected to the grid to recover the costs associated with the equipment which connects them to the grid. Connection costs will be determined in part by the additional investment, if any, required to enable connection at the connection point. Where there is excess transmission capacity, organizations which choose to connect at that point will not pay high connection costs. Connection costs will become substantial where a location decision requires additional development of the transmission link. Customers taking supply from the grid will also be charged for the use of the 'transmission network' based on their 'use' of individual 'links' of the system, using their previous year's energy consumption patterns.

(b) *Service charges* are designed to recover variable costs associated with the operation of the grid. These include a charge to cover the cost of transmission losses which will be paid by generators and distributors based on loss factors at points of connection. There will also be a charge to recover the cost of spinning reserve and out-of-merit generation from the grid user causing these costs to be incurred (and conversely credit will be given for interruptible supply which economizes on the need for spinning reserve). Finally, there will be a 'deliverability charge' which is based on the peak demand at the point of supply. This charge is included primarily as an inducement for distributors to retain their load control equipment. The charge also covers the cost of providing reactive support to the system.

This proposed transmission pricing structure moves strongly away from the concept of an average price towards the concept of 'user pays'. The pricing proposal has regional effects. Loads close to notional centres of generation will pay less than the average for transmission services while remote loads will pay more. Trans Power's pricing managers compare it to the current transmission charges:

> Under our proposed pricing scheme the Bay of Islands Power Board ends up paying more than the average for fixed transmission services, as does Buller. Buller ends up paying a fair proportion above the average. Whereas those supply authorities end up paying more than the average, supply authorities around Taupo and the Waikato end up paying less than the average. So it certainly is distance related; a regional component does enter the price.

This regional cost effect may modify the manner in which electricity is used. It clearly signals to those who are deciding on the location of facilities what the costs of connection to the grid will be at different points. Heavy users of electricity will clearly take this into consideration in their location decisions. The future location of generation facilities may also affect transmission charges. For example, location of a new generating facility north of Auckland could have the effect of reducing these charges for some customers. This would reduce their use of 'links' on the grid and reduce the load on the constrained Auckland isthmus transmission link.

This raises the closely related issue of 'stranded investment'. For example, were a distributor such as AEPB to install its own generating station within its own local distribution network, it would leave under-utilized the investment in the grid built to supply its original load. Trans Power has taken the position that, if this occurs, the grid user must continue to make payments on these assets. A working party of the Electricity Supply Association who have been consulting with Trans Power on the proposed pricing scheme agree that this type of action by a grid user would result in an unfair shifting of charges to the remaining grid users and be economically inefficient. Trans Power will therefore insert a term in its transmission contracts which requires a user to compensate Trans Power for any existing equipment rendered under-utilized by any action of the user.

To conclude, new structures have been developed by Electricorp Marketing for the pricing of both the energy and the transmission components. Trans Power has now proposed further changes to the pricing of the transmission component.

Overall, these changes significantly reduce the amount of averaging in the wholesale prices of electricity. The introduction of more refined time-of-use prices and 'spot' market prices provide considerable scope for customers to make informed decisions about their energy usage. The ultimate success of such energy pricing innovations, however, will be determined by the extent to which the retail supply industry incorporates such pricing mechanisms into their own price structures and moves to promote electricity against substitute fuels. Whether retailers will take full advantage of this opportunity remains to be seen. Similarly, the introduction of strong 'user pay' concepts into transmission pricing further reduces the degree of averaging in the delivered price of electricity and provides more refined and economically sensible pricing signals to users of the national grid.

Other services
Electricorp Marketing has two business units that are actively involved in selling services into the retail market place. These are Appliance Wholesaling and Retail Services. Both of these operations are important to ECNZ's attempts to enliven the downstream market for electricity.

(1) Appliance Wholesaling
Appliance Wholesaling operates the Brightspot Appliance Group which is a franchise retail electrical appliance operation and acts to stimulate the downstream market for electricity sales through the use of quality, efficient electrical products. The Brightspot Group now has over 60 shops throughout the country and is profitable. Appliance Wholesaling has also successfully introduced Unidaire Night Store Heaters, Climatisers (Heat Pump) and is to market a new hot water cylinder with updated technology.

(2) Retail Services
Electricorp Marketing has also set up a new unit to sell services into the retail market place through a business unit called Retail Services. Two distinct types of services are offered. The first is a strategic planning consultancy service to

electricity retailers to assist them with maximizing sales volume and market share of electricity. The second is a resource marketing service to assist with the promotion of electricity.

The need for such services is noted in the *Electricorp Marketing Business Plan 1990/91*:

> The non-transport energy market has been highly contestable in the last few years. While some retailers have responded to this challenge in a positive manner, others have stagnated and as a consequence, with the exception of last year, market share fell. The recent upward trend in market share is conclusive evidence that electricity will respond to aggressive marketing. There is potential for continued growth if we can 'persuade' retailers to change to a commercial mode and produce superior performance. Retail Services is an integral part of the mechanism for inducing this change.

Retail Services expects to face competition from several management consultancy groups for its strategic consultancy services but it has been successful in helping several retailers develop marketing plans.

The resource marketing service plan offers a number of programmes to help retailers. Examples of these programmes include (a) the Premier Electricity Retailers Marketing Award designed to reward excellence in marketing performance, and (b) a Medallion Home Award which is awarded to those homes which meet a set of specifications aimed at promoting the efficient use of electricity.

Contracting

With the announced separation of Trans Power, ECNZ's two contracting arms PowerDesignBuild and Electricorp Marketing Electricity Contracting were brought together under the control of PDB in September 1990. Both of these business units were actively engaged in seeking to sell their services in markets outside the Corporation.

(1) PowerDesignBuild

The PowerDesignBuild Group Limited was formed from the design and construction section of NZED. The design section was formed into DesignPower New Zealand Limited and the construction section became PowerBuild New Zealand. With little likelihood that new generation facilities would be built by ECNZ in this century, there was a pressing need to develop markets for their services outside the Corporation. As Steven Blanch, the Managing Director of PDB, put it recently: 'We need to diversify our client base. Ninety percent comes from one client. If they sneeze, we leap out the window.'

Serious effort is being put into developing markets offshore and domestically. The development of overseas markets for heavy power engineering is critical if PDB is to retain it capabilities in this area. However, attempts to penetrate highly competitive offshore markets have had problems. They have been constrained by the reluctance of ECNZ's Board and its shareholders to take on the many economic and political risks that can attend major projects in developing countries. PDB is also hampered by a lack of experience in working overseas and anonymity in world markets.

As part of a strategy to become established internationally, PDB has registered with the Asian Development Bank and the World Bank. Its proposals have been declined, usually by a narrow margin, because of their lack of overseas experience. To overcome this problem, PDB has attempted to 'piggyback' by forming associations with other engineering and construction firms already doing work overseas. Also, instead of simply submitting tenders on work that has already been identified, PDB is taking the lead by identifying opportunities and presenting proposals that indicated they can do the work. PDB is slowly developing a track record. As the Managing Director of PDB told us:

> When I write down the list of overseas jobs we've done I'm now onto page two. We've started to get there. It's a stepping stone. I think we've done very well in building that up in the short time PDB has been going.

PDB's entry into the engineering market in New Zealand has had difficulties over union coverage. It has also suffered from disagreements with Treasury's advice to Ministers over what its core business should be. Steven Blanch:

> Treasury has viewed our [PDB's] core business as just building power stations. I have tried to point out to them that our core business is engineering. When you build a power station you actually add sewers and roads and all sorts of things. Our skills are very wide based. There isn't anything we don't do. The only way we can survive is by doing business in whatever area our skills are available.

One non-traditional area in which PDB is seeking work in is energy management. It has now undertaken energy management audits for a number of clients. This area of work is likely to grow in importance in the future.

(2) Electricorp Marketing Electrical Contracting

Like PDB, most of EMEC's work has come from internal contracts, primarily Trans Power. EMEC is now actively competing, primarily in domestic markets, for electrical-based contracting work outside the Corporation.

Two of its most notable outside contracts were the Commonwealth Games Village Contract (the work included reticulation of underground cables, lighting, and supply and installation of switching stations and distribution transformers) and, in association with the Airways Corporation, the installation of an antenna at the Seagrove Receiving Station.

The deregulation of the electricity distribution market and the separation of distribution costs and energy charges by retail distributors may open up distribution-line maintenance work to competition. This would provide EMEC with an opportunity to compete vigorously for this work. Other areas in which EMEC is seeking to compete for work include: (a) electrical construction work for large commercial and industrial institutions; (b) refurbishment of large electrical equipment in industrial establishments, (c) communication system installation and maintenance, and (d) training of overseas personnel in operations and maintenance work.

Of concern to EMEC is the generally difficult economic environment in the contracting industry. EMEC's assessment is contained in the *Electricorp Marketing Business Plan 1990/91*:

> The generally difficult economic environment . . . has resulted in a significant number of contracting firms bidding for a limited number of jobs, possibly undercutting each other's charge-out rates to the point of diminished profitability. Contractors may be adopting this strategy from purely a short-term survival perspective. The impact of this on the contracting market and Contracting in the medium term, however, might be quite detrimental.

Like PDB, EMEC's ability to compete externally has also been hindered by problems of union coverage. The manager of EMEC commented on the effect of this on the ability to operate in external markets:

> Most of our work is still internal to the Corporation so we are in a vulnerable position if Trans Power decides to award more work to other inside and outside contractors. But one of our targets this year is to get 10 - 15% of that work outside and there appears to be no reason why we can't achieve that except for one thing and that is the union problem.

With the limited amount of outside work available, EMEC has also expressed concern that it could be tendering against PDB for the same work outside the Corporation. With the internal amalgamation of EMEC and PDB this will now be a thing of the past.

6

Social and Political Pressures upon ECNZ

The Electricity Corporation has had to respond not only to commercial but to social and political pressures. As with any organization, these overlap and interact with each other. For example, ECNZ's relationship with its customers gives rise to political as well as the usual commercial pressures. Like the commercial pressures identified in Chapter 3, the key social and political pressures identified in the present chapter include some that were a direct result of the SOE process and others that already existed but became more keenly focused. Another area of overlap is the issue of regulation. Chapter 3 dealt with the commercial aspects of the threat of regulation and this chapter addresses the political aspects. As with commercial pressures, social and political pressures have cost and organizational implications.

Sources of pressures

Figure 6.1 identifies a number of social or political entities that give rise to pressures upon ECNZ:

- *Unions* give rise to the issue of *industrial relations.*
- *Public perception* could be said to drive all the social and political issues. In particular, it gives rise to the issues loosely categorized as *corporate relations.* Public perception also contributes to the political issues relating to the *implications of commercial pricing policies.*
- *Māori* contribute to the political issues relating to *land ownership, water and geothermal rights,* and general *environmental issues.*
- *Employees* form part of many social and political pressures as they are likely to be part of the other groups that have an impact on ECNZ. For example, employees may be members of conservation groups or a union. However, one social issue that is largely derived from the interests of employees is the issue of safety. Other *personnel issues* relate to the attractiveness of ECNZ as an employer.
- *Conservation groups* give rise to the pressures of *environmental issues* and *water rights.*
- *Local government* has given rise to political issues related to the payment by ECNZ of *local body rates.*
- *Rural interests* exert pressures relating to the *implications of commercial pricing policies.*
- While *customers* are generally seen as a commercial pressure, they also exert political pressures.

Figure 6.1

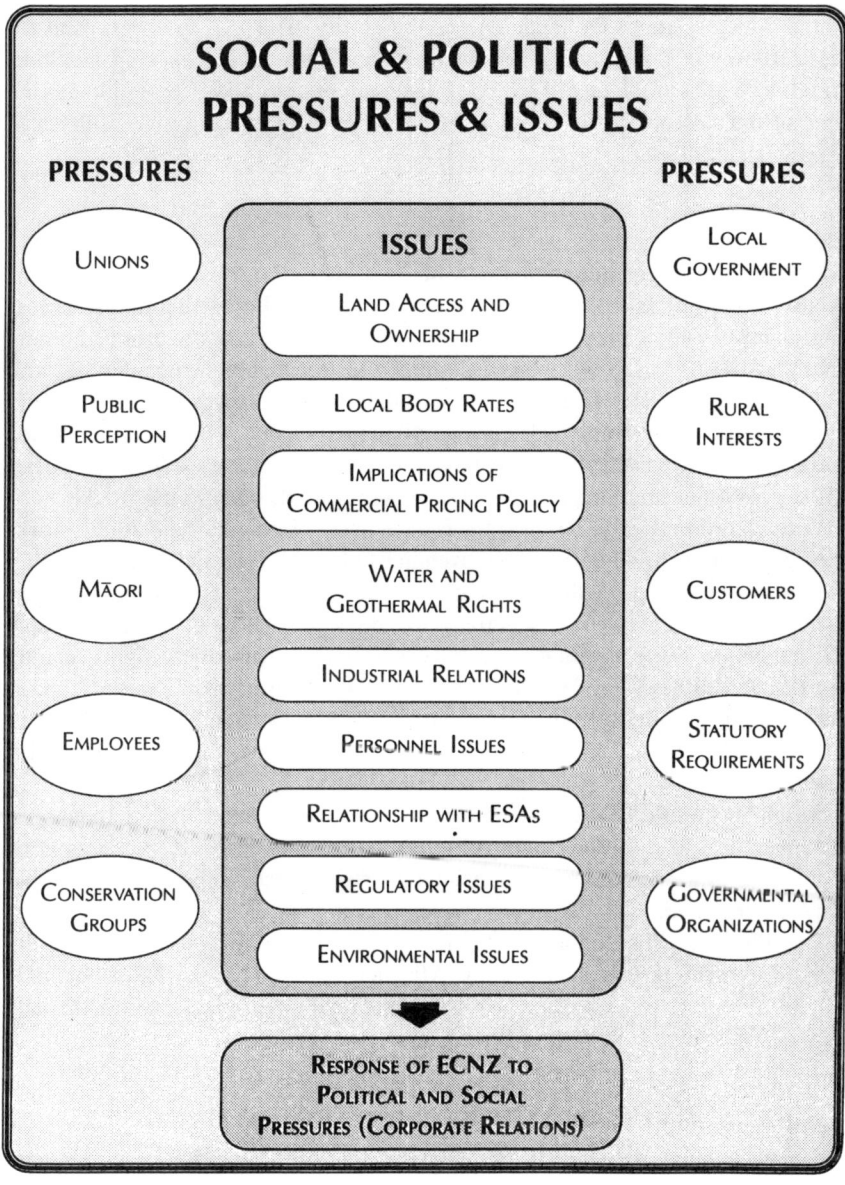

SOCIAL & POLITICAL
PRESSURES & ISSUES

PRESSURES

UNIONS

PUBLIC PERCEPTION

MĀORI

EMPLOYEES

CONSERVATION GROUPS

ISSUES

LAND ACCESS AND OWNERSHIP

LOCAL BODY RATES

IMPLICATIONS OF COMMERCIAL PRICING POLICY

WATER AND GEOTHERMAL RIGHTS

INDUSTRIAL RELATIONS

PERSONNEL ISSUES

RELATIONSHIP WITH ESAs

REGULATORY ISSUES

ENVIRONMENTAL ISSUES

PRESSURES

LOCAL GOVERNMENT

RURAL INTERESTS

CUSTOMERS

STATUTORY REQUIREMENTS

GOVERNMENTAL ORGANIZATIONS

RESPONSE OF ECNZ TO POLITICAL AND SOCIAL PRESSURES (CORPORATE RELATIONS)

- *Statutory requirements* such as those contained in the SOE Act, the Companies Act, and the Official Information Act exert a number of political pressures on ECNZ. Examples are the issues relating to *industrial relations, corporate relations, regulatory issues, pricing* and *environmental issues.*
- *Government organizations* such as Treasury and the Commerce Commission give rise to the pressures of *regulatory issues* and *pricing.*

Land access and ownership

Three issues relate to the land. One is the ability of ECNZ to access land for the purposes of constructing new facilities and maintaining existing facilities. Another relates to the identification of land essential to power generation at the time of the sale of NZED assets to ECNZ. The third relates to land subject to Māori land claims.

Land access

To operate power generation and transmission systems in New Zealand requires access to land so as to enable maintenance checks and construction. To access land owned by the Corporation, it is necessary in some cases to cross adjoining land. NZED had the right to access land under the Public Works Act, as well as specific rights under the Electricity Act 1968. Even before incorporation, NZED along with other government departments had their rights to access land curtailed and more clearly specified. This required the access to be for a specific task, notice to be given, and that the workers should wear clearly identifying markings.

With incorporation, ECNZ lost the right to access land under the Public Works Act and no compensating right was given in its place. Access under the Electricity Act 1968 was retained by the Corporation with respect to existing work. However, land access relating to any new activity will be negotiated by ECNZ on the same footing as any other corporation in New Zealand. Because these rights relating to existing facilities were given to ECNZ, when Trans Power New Zealand Limited was formed as a wholly owned subsidiary of ECNZ, Section 2 of the Electricity Operators Act 1987 had to be amended so that the definition of Corporation included subsidiaries.

Easements would have to be purchased through negotiation. Where there is an easement over land for the passing of transmission lines across it, it is a common legal concept for the easement to include the right to access the easement across surrounding land.

The Resource Management Bill contains the concept of a 'network user' who may, if everything else fails, ask the Minister to allow access. After obtaining planning approval for a particular route, if the land or easements across the land cannot be obtained, then the Minister may intervene.

Land ownership

When negotiations over the sale of the assets of NZED to ECNZ were proceeding, the issue arose of what land was to be transferred to the new Corporation. The method by which these land assets were to be identified was outlined in the sale and purchase agreement. Officers of the Corporation and the Treasury were to discuss land held by NZED on a site-by-site basis. The criterion for transfer was to be that the land was reasonably required for the generation of electricity. Once the land had been identified, the interest in land was to be addressed (i.e. freehold, leasehold, or some lesser legal interest).

Land held by NZED was not necessarily the minimum required to operate effectively. Land held for the generation and transmission of electricity was mixed with land held for other uses, e.g. environmental and recreational uses. While NZED was a government department, this was not a major difficulty. The objectives of NZED were such as to permit the holding of land for a variety of purposes other than the 'productive' use of generating electricity. However, ECNZ had to show a commercial return on the assets employed, including land. Land held for other purposes and for historical reasons was not to be owned by the new Corporation.

Nevertheless, ECNZ considered that some land, not directly used in the generation or transmission of electricity, was strategically important. An example of this strategic use is the holding of land adjacent to a geothermal steam field so as to exclude or control activities on the land that may affect the ability of ECNZ to continue to use the geothermal resource. Other examples of indirect or infrequent use, justifying transfer, are geologically unstable land that may in future need to be repaired so as to maintain the level of a lake, and land very occasionally used as a spillway.

The land surrounding lakes associated with hydro power stations has high recreational value. Where ECNZ owns all or part of this land, there is the issue of who is responsible for the upkeep of recreational facilities. Closely aligned with this issue is the issue of local body rates. Rateable land may in some cases be providing a service to the community, just as much as providing for the generation of electricity.

Māori land claims

The Treaty of Waitangi (State Enterprises) Act 1988 amends Section 27 of the SOE Act 1986, which outlines the procedure to be followed in the transferring of Crown land to SOEs where the land is subject to Māori land claims made under the Treaty of Waitangi Act 1975. Land subject to a claim can still pass to the SOE, but remains subject to the claim. The SOE is then able to sell the land. However, a caveat is registered on the title to the land, the wording of which is as follows:

> Subject to Section 27B of the State-Owned Enterprises Act 1986 (which provides for the resumption of land on the recommendation of the Waitangi Tribunal and which does not provide for third parties, such as the owner of the land, to be heard in relation to the making of any such recommendation).

If the claim is upheld by the Waitangi Tribunal and return of the land to Māori ownership is recommended, then the Act requires that the land be returned, regardless of the subsequent passing of ownership. The mechanism for return of the land is resumption by the Crown under the Public Works Act 1981.

Local body rates

Rates are now levied by local authorities on land owned by ECNZ. Prior to corporatization, NZED had paid local body rates on office buildings and grants in lieu of rates on residential sections. Specific service charges such as water pipe connections were also paid by NZED. ECNZ identifies local body rates as a major cost over which it does not have control. Rates demands, if they were accepted, would account for approximately 2% of the Corporation's costs, excluding financing.

ECNZ believes that local bodies have used rating differentials on electricity generating facilities to target ECNZ for their own funding requirements. Some councils have also moved to assess rates on the capital value of improvements, rather than on land value alone. The issue is whether a power station is 'machinery' and therefore excluded from rateable value, or whether generating facilities form part of the rateable value of land. Because of the capital-intensive nature of electricity generation, this effectively creates a further differential between ECNZ and other ratepayers.

On 25 July 1989, Dr Roderick Deane wrote to the Minister of Finance:

> The reaction of a number of local authorities to the fact that the Corporation is now rateable has become a source of major concern to the Corporation. The degree to which local authorities have attempted to demand excessive payments from the Corporation has exposed serious deficiencies in the present rating legislation.

To demonstrate the effect of these differentials, ECNZ has calculated the rates demands as a percentage of the land value. The rates demand of Waimate County Council amounts to 137% of the land value, and the rates demand of Waitaki County Council amounts to 108%. An example of a local body that has moved to the rating of capital improvements is the McKenzie County Council, where the rates demand of $3.2 million accounts for 60% of the total rates revenue of the county. ECNZ assesses that the cost of services provided to the Corporation would not exceed $20,000. Because of the remote areas in which many ECNZ facilities are situated, the Corporation provides its own services such as roading, water and sewage. Therefore, ECNZ considers that the local body rates bear no relation to services provided.

Extensive lobbying and considerable discussion has resulted in reductions in rates demands by several local authorities. Payments to local bodies over the last five years are as follows:

1985/86	1986/87	1987/88	1988/89	1989/90
$0.9m	$1.1m	$1.4m	$1.7m	$5.5m

Part of the payment in the last financial year would have related to past years. Rates demands were expected to be $15 million in July 1989, but have been approximately $12 million. The difference between the rates demands and the amount actually paid is accounted for by negotiated reductions and demands under dispute.

Implications of commercial pricing policy

Historically, electricity has been sold in New Zealand as the bundled product of energy and its transmission to the consumer, priced at the average cost of both these components. In the commercial environment in which the new Corporation finds itself, it has become important to price electricity in a manner that reflects the actual costs of these two components. Furthermore, the Government has worked towards the separation of line and energy charges at all levels of the electricity industry.

Reflecting the cost of these two components of the product in the price of electricity has two effects. Firstly, reflecting the differing electricity transmission cost to various geographic locations will mean that the price of electricity as a final product will vary across New Zealand. Secondly, reflecting the differing electricity production cost at various times of the day will mean that the price of electricity will vary accordingly.

Modifying charges for the first of these components will have clear implications for remote and rural areas of New Zealand, giving rise to social and political pressures. The second modification also has political implications because of the resistance of electricity supply authorities to new pricing structures. It is important to note that ESA Boards are currently made up of elected members rather than commercial managers. However, this is currently changing. ESAs will become Electric Power Companies, with directors appointed by elected trustees[1]. Local authority power boards will become Electricity Trading Enterprises, with directors appointed by the local authorities.

Rural pricing implications
Up until the present time, transmission charges have been allocated on the basis of the volume of electricity purchased. Trans Power is presently moving to price transmission services on the basis of peak winter load and the distance from notional centres of generation, as discussed in Chapter 5. Combined with this move on the part of Trans Power, restructuring of the electricity industry is expected to result in electricity pricing to the end user which reflects the costs and investment required to provide the consumer with power. This will significantly reduce the present cross-subsidization from commercial and industrial to residential consumers, as well as from urban to rural consumers.

Removal of cross-subsidization would create political and social pressures. An example is the opposition by Auckland Electric Power Board to the separation of line and energy charges. They cite the example of Waiheke Island. If line and energy charges are separated, the 3,500 customers on Waiheke would pay considerably more for electricity than the current charge. Waiheke Island customers are 25km from the closest point of supply, linked by a very expensive submarine cable. According to AEPB, the revenue from Waiheke does not even cover the cost of capital employed.

---

1. Both trustees and directors will be appointed initially by the Minister of State-owned Enterprises, and then subsequently trustees will be elected in local body elections, and appoint directors.

Treasury provided comments, dated 4 December 1987, to the Minister of Finance on the proposal to cabinet by the Minister of Energy that the Chatham's system be subsidized:

> Continued subsidisation of the Chathams electricity supply will result in consumers demanding more electricity than if they faced the true cost of having power supplied. In turn, this means additional generation and transmission assets have to be built in order to meet demand; investment that in the absence of a subsidy would not be commercially or economically justified. Subsidisation of electricity tariffs therefore imposes inefficiencies.

While the Chatham Islands electricity system does not come under the control of ECNZ, these comments can also relate to the provision of power to any remote or isolated consumer.

In an interview with the Minister of Energy, David Butcher, published in *Marketing Matters*, issue 2, 1990, the following comments are made relating to rural pricing implications:

> I believe that electricity retailers will find, like telecommunication retailers, that it will pay them to equalize charges to some extent in order to simplify administration. I also believe that a system will need to be devised to ensure that those people who have installed supplies in good faith are not faced with untenable cost increases.
>
> I have seen and opened efficient, cheap, stand-alone units that represent another economically viable option for some electricity consumers. Where it is economically viable for these to be installed, they should be. It may even pay the community to underwrite a portion of the cost. The bottom line is that our tariff structures and capital charges should encourage remote consumers to make an intelligent choice.

Time-of-day pricing implications

Cross-subsidization from commercial and industrial users to domestic consumers is partly related to the time of day in which these groups demand electricity. Demand by domestic consumers is greatest during the morning and evening, when the cost of producing electricity is greatest. Demand by commercial and industrial consumers is far more constant, with most usage occurring during the day, between the two demand peaks.

To pass on time-of-day charging to the consumer requires the use of costly meters, which a number of electricity supply authorities consider to be uneconomic. This is one source of pressure against such changes in pricing structures. Another source of the pressure seems to be the inertia of the electricity industry. Electricity in New Zealand has been priced according to a government-imposed flat bulk tariff rate for decades, and it appears difficult to change this.

Another point is that cross-subsidization from industrial and commercial users to domestic users is politically advantageous. All end users of electricity are domestic users, and only a few of those are also industrial or commercial users. The residents of an area or city are the people who elect the power boards. There would be potential political costs if the board of an ESA were to remove a cross-subsidy that is in favour of the people who elected them.

Water and geothermal rights

As a consequence of the SOE process, the perpetual Crown rights held by NZED as a government department were lost, although it is by no means clear that rights in perpetuity would have continued. Even before incorporation of ECNZ, there were moves within Government towards placing a cap on these perpetual rights. As a result, ECNZ must obtain rights to use water and geothermal resources directly or indirectly in the generation of electricity on the same basis as any other entity.[2] All existing water rights held by NZED were assumed by ECNZ, with the understanding that they would be progressively reapplied for over a period of fifteen years. Also, rights in perpetuity were limited to a period of 35 years as part of an agreement between the Government and the Maori Council.

Paragraph 11 of this agreement concerning the transfer of Crown land to state-owned enterprises reads as follows:

> The Government agrees that it will not transfer to any State-owned Enterprise water rights that have been issued in perpetuity. The Government will seek a variation of such water rights so as to ensure that they are for periods no longer than 35 years.

While ECNZ accepted this agreement, they were concerned about the practical difficulties of renegotiating each water right before it could be transferred to the Corporation, particularly as such negotiations were likely to be protracted. As ECNZ pointed out at the time, the Corporation would be unable to use any of its stations without water rights. Also, variation of water rights that limited the use of generating facilities would substantially affect the value of the facilities being transferred to the Corporation.

A solution was proposed by ECNZ in a letter dated 16 February 1988 from Geraldine Baumann, Company Secretary, to the Treasury:

> The Corporation accepts the risk that some stations may end up with water rights that constrain their operations more than is the case at present; generally these constraints will have a significant cost penalty for which some compensation may be needed. However, the acceptance of the risk must be qualified by the following two caveats.
> - There is sufficient time to allow the orderly processing of the several hundred new water right applications that will be required as a consequence.
> - We are permitted the free, unencumbered right to prosecute the application ourselves [Compare Treaty of Waitangi (State Enterprises) Bill which prevents SOEs from presenting evidence.]
> The proposals outlined in this letter therefore are that the rights should be transferred to the Corporation and that after transfer, the Corporation initiates a programme of water right renewals so that over a set period of time those water rights held in perpetuity are gradually converted to ordinary water rights.

---

2. Water rights also include geothermal rights. The Report from the Chairman in the 1989/90 ECNZ Annual Report states: '. . . the hot fluid used to drive our geothermal stations is classified as water'.

The Resource Management Bill would have terminated by statute the concept of Crown perpetual water rights, regardless of contractual agreements.

Water rights are a complex political and environmental issue. ECNZ sees the water rights issue as a balancing of regional and national interests, as well as a balancing of interregional interests. Such a balance is discussed below, under 'Environmental issues'.

The issue of water and geothermal rights is closely related to the issue of Māori rights. In a letter to Jane Kelsey, Senior Lecturer in the University of Auckland Law School, from Geraldine Baumann, Company Secretary, dated 2 August 1988, the uncertainties relating to Crown resource ownership are outlined:

> The Treaty of Waitangi goes beyond land claims . . . For the Electricity Corporation this could have major implications in the area of water and geothermal steam. For both these resources ownership is vested in the Crown . . . This appropriation could be regarded as contravening the Treaty of Waitangi. For example geothermal steam could regarded as a taonga, a prized possession, under article 2 of the Treaty. Claims are already before the Waitangi Tribunal on this basis.

Tradeability of water rights has been advocated by ECNZ. However, the difficulties involved in defining property rights over water, the effects on third parties of the trading of the rights, the initial allocation of the rights, and the non-exclusivity of some of the rights, mean that a regulatory allocation system is likely to prevail. ECNZ considers that trading of water rights should be allowed where third parties are not affected.

Recently the Commerce Commission has suggested a resource royalty or rental be placed on the use of water for hydro generation. The following comment was made in the Report From the Chief Executive in the 1989/90 ECNZ Annual Report:

> The Corporation made a substantial submission on hydro royalties in February 1990. It is our view that if users of water should be charged then this should encompass all users; that the Crown, through its ownership of the Corporation which has 96 per cent control of the generation market, is effectively already gaining any economic rent that exists on hydro developments; and that any application of hydro royalties should be integrated with the mechanisms for allocating water. It should be noted that the Corporation's Sale and Purchase Agreement with the Crown protects the Company from any adverse impacts of water royalties.

Industrial relations

Although ECNZ's endeavours to decentralize industrial relations created considerable political pressures in the Corporation's first few years (as we discussed in Chapter 4), these pressures seem to have abated. However, other pressures still exist. One example is the PowerDesignBuild union coverage issue. All of PDB's workers are members of one of two unions, rather than members of the multitude of craft unions that would normally cover employees.

Within NZED, design and construction engineers worked only on projects internal to the Division. Since incorporation ECNZ still has the construction organization and capability, but no longer has a need for it in the near future. So as to maintain this skills resource within the Corporation, and also to put existing skills to productive use, PDB has been actively seeking projects outside the New Zealand electricity generation industry. This creates a union coverage conflict between the unions covering PDB's employees, the PSA and the New Zealand Workers' Union, and the unions covering employees of other contractors, with similar skills, working on the same site.

In a November 1989 paper to the Board, PowerDesignBuild outlined this political pressure and their response to it:

> The problem of gaining private sector union acceptance of PDB working in the private sector has been progressing steadily. Papers have been lodged with the Labour Court seeking to compel the registrar of unions to resolve the matter of overlapping union coverage, by amending union rules. Letters have also been sent to the Chief Mediator and the Arbitration Commission stating that we will challenge or object to the registration of industrial awards which do not specify our exclusion from their coverage. There are good legal grounds for taking this position and the result has been to make other parties realize that the issue can have real problems for them.

There is a corresponding problem for EMEC, the contracting arm of Electricorp Marketing.

Personnel issues

Political pressures relating to personnel issues are minimized by the Corporation being, and being seen to be, an employer that looks after its employees. The State-owned Enterprises Act 1986 requires ECNZ to be a 'good employer'. This means providing a safe environment and also making employment with ECNZ attractive. This also has a commercial result in that it reduces staff turnover. Two examples of measures taken to make employment with ECNZ attractive are superannuation plans and a health care plan.

In Section 4 (2) of the SOE Act 1986, the requirement to be a good employer is defined as

> an employer who operates a personnel policy containing provisions generally accepted as necessary for the fair and proper treatment of employees in all aspects of their employment, including provisions requiring –
> (a) Good and safe working conditions
> (b) An equal opportunities employment programme
> (c) The impartial selection of suitably qualified persons for employment
> (d) Opportunities for the enhancement of the abilities of individual employees.

The issue discussed here is the safety of the workplace environment. A way of measuring effectiveness in safety control has been introduced, called the International Safety Rating Scheme. Safety performance can be compared between business units. Business unit safety measurements are then consolidated to give overall safety measures every six months or at the year end. In this way, safety can also be compared over time. Safety has become a more important issue since incorporation because of the opportunity for outsiders to suggest that the new commercial emphasis jeopardizes safety through inadequate training and maintenance.

ECNZ has a Safety, Health and Loss Control Policy which is displayed widely. It reads as follows:

> The health and safety of our employees is fundamental to the Electricorp management philosophy. In fulfilling this commitment to our people, we undertake to provide a safe and healthy work environment and also to protect the property of the Corporation from theft, fire and other damage.
>
> We will promote these objectives through strict adherence to industry standards and the requirements of the law, coupled with constant vigilance to eliminate potential hazards.
>
> Maintaining a safe working environment requires an equal commitment from all employees – a commitment to follow the job practices and procedures spelt out in the Corporation's safety booklets and manuals.
>
> We want to protect your health and safety and, through loss control, to protect our business. I trust you will join me in a co-operative effort to help make this philosophy work.

Two examples of how ECNZ endeavours to make employment with the Corporation competitive and attractive are the recent modifications of the health care programme to provide enhanced benefits to employees and the setting up of a Corporation retirement plan. Half of the total staff are now members of the health care plan.

Membership of the ECNZ Retirement Savings Plan, combined with the membership of the Government Superannuation Fund, means that 42% of staff are members of a superannuation plan. At incorporation, an agreement was reached that employees already in the Government Superannuation Fund could stay in that fund, while ECNZ was free to set up their own fund for employees not already in the Government scheme. The scheme has an employer contribution of $2 for every $1 contributed by an employee. Such a high membership rate in the superannuation schemes means that planning of career paths within the Corporation becomes very important. This is because of the high cost of passing up the cumulative benefits of years in the superannuation scheme to pursue a career path outside the Corporation.

Relationship with ESAs

Prior to corporatization, the relationship between NZED and the ESAs[3] was very simple. Commercial interaction was limited because the Government set bulk tariff rates for electricity. Interaction was limited largely to the technical area. After incorporation, ECNZ was given a very clear commercial objective. The ESAs were still part of local government and had not undergone a similar change in emphasis.

---

3. 'ESA' is used to refer to the retailers of electricity, in whatever organizational or ownership form.

As Electricorp Marketing (EM) began to undertake commercial initiatives, particularly in the area of pricing, a tension emerged between ECNZ as a commercial organization and the ESAs as primarily social and political organizations.

EM considers that it has a good working relationship with the majority of retailers. However, in its view, a small number of vocal retailers continue to make relations difficult. EM sought to ascertain the basis of this animosity. Four areas of concern which were expressed by the ESAs involved:

(1) Concern over possible entry by EM into the retail market. EM's focus on co-operation with ESAs toward end use customers was perceived as providing a 'springboard' for EM to enter the retail marketplace.

(2) Belief that ECNZ generation should be split up. ESAs consider that by taking a hard line and not co-operating they are making a stand against the Corporation's 'monopoly position'.

(3) Dissatisfaction with the strong stance taken by EM over inclusion of a CPI provision in all contract renewals, invoked if the contract is not renewed by the expiry date.

(4) Rejection of the philosophy that the electricity industry should conduct its business in a commercial manner. They believe that electricity is a social service and should be distributed accordingly.

ECNZ suggests that these problems are being fuelled by the Electricity Supply Association executive for broader political reasons, and perhaps even for self preservation.

As discussed below, the ESAs are concerned that ECNZ will vertically integrate forwards into the retailing of electricity. Such an intention has consistently been denied. John Fernyhough, ECNZ Board Chairman, commented on the prospect of vertical integration:

> I told them it didn't make commercial sense for Electricorp to get into retailing. Its like getting into competition with your customers. . . The only time we would consider going direct with a retail customer would be if you [the ESAs] were screwing them. That doesn't do our business any good and be on notice that if a sawmill rings me up and gives me a pricing structure that you are using to rip him off to subsidize domestic customers, then we will supply. But short of that, no! That's what I've said from day one and that has been the position of the Corporation.

Perceptions vary as to the effect of the organizational change on 'quality of service'. A representative of New Zealand Steel, a customer with electricity demand slightly greater than the city of Wellington, considered that while any disruption is costly and therefore unacceptable, there is no indication that reliability has changed from NZED to ECNZ. When asked whether he was satisfied with reliability, he replied:

> Reliability, probably not. Whether the change to the new structure will help significantly is probably not yet proven, because system disturbances don't normally happen very often anyway. But one is too many.

On the other hand, AEPB contends that there has been an increase in outages over the last couple of years, which they consider is a consequence of declining quality of maintenance. Concerns over the state of some transmission facilities have received public attention recently. However, it is difficult to know whether to attribute their current state to post-incorporation maintenance policies or to past inadequacies whose consequences are only now being felt.

As to the orientation of ECNZ towards its customers, the creation of Electricorp Marketing (EM) would appear to demonstrate the importance ECNZ attaches to them. However, because of its advertising thrust, EM has been perceived as directing its efforts to the end consumer rather than its own customers, the ESAs. EM sees its advertising as a response to competition from alternative energy sources and as a means of the stimulating demand to use excess capacity. ESAs view it with the suspicion that EM is attempting to circumvent the retailer's position in the industry.

A number of the ESAs are in a position to take advantage of the opportunity to enter the generation market. Therefore, competition in generation is an important issue in the matter of assessing the relationship of ECNZ with some ESAs. There is concern that the Government is not serious about creating true competition since as shareholders they receive the 'monopoly profits'. As long as there is no competition in generation, the ESAs consider that profitability cannot be used to measure the performance of the Corporation. In its comment on the 1988/89 ECNZ Annual Report, the Electricity Supply Association of New Zealand (ESA NZ) state:

> If managerial and financial efficiencies are to be used only to achieve the maximum rate of return for the Government, then there will always be profit and no regard for the consumer.

Another concern of the ESAs is that return on investment pressure from shareholders results in consumers being made to pay for unused capacity. The reasonableness of such a concern depends on how one judges the valuation applied to the assets transferred from NZED to ECNZ.

ESA NZ believe that ECNZ favours competition, except where it affects its own business. From an interview with the ESA NZ:

> ECNZ continues to oppose any major breakup of its generation, likes to retain Trans Power under its exclusive control, and favours deregulation and privatization of the ESAs.

Regulatory issues

Political pressures relating to regulatory issues can be loosely identified under the following categories: (1) natural monopoly, (2) vertical integration, (3) supplier of last resort, and (4) pricing.

Natural monopoly

The issue of natural monopoly gives rise to the political pressure for the split up of the assets of ECNZ. It also has the potential for price control.

It was suggested by Dr Jan Acton of Rand Corporation that as long as there is a central despatcher, there is no reason why individual generating units could not be under separate ownership. Examples of such ownership in the electricity industry are cited as existing in Sweden and the US. Thus, it is argued that the system for generation of electricity is not a natural monopoly.

Although it may be possible to divide the New Zealand electricity generation system into a number of units and place them under different ownership, ECNZ points out the benefits of retaining the majority of the system under the one common ownership. In particular, they point to the benefits of common ownership of both hydro and thermal plant. One of the main reasons for this is that hydro plant managers would have difficulty in knowing with sufficient certainty what the opportunity cost of running their plant is at any one time.

The transmission and distribution networks are what is considered to be a natural monopoly. Of major concern is that there should be non-discriminatory access to transmission services. This issue led ECNZ to establish the National Grid Division as a subsidiary company, Trans Power. In a letter written by ECNZ to the Minister of Finance, dated 14 January 1988, the reason for the establishment of Trans Power is outlined:

> The principal reason for the establishment of a subsidiary company is to ensure the independence of the National Grid Division by creating a main electricity transmission system in New Zealand which is open to any party's use for the transmission of electrical energy and has a transparent cost structure. This is seen to be an important factor in establishing competition in the electricity industry in New Zealand.

Earlier, the Cabinet Policy Committee had considered the question of whether access to the transmission system required regulation. Treasury's comments were given in a letter dated 7 January 1987:

> . . . officials consider, and Ministers have agreed that this sort of problem is best handled through general competition policies and rules including the provisions within the Commerce Act. We would not agree with the contention that special legislation governing access may be required. The introduction of legislation would imply an ad-hoc approach to regulation of the Electricity Corporation and electricity industry that is inconsistent with the general thrust of policies agreed to for SOEs. In particular, corporation or industry specific legislation can, as history has demonstrated, create major distortions in the economy which result in the inefficient use of resources.

Concerns about monopolistic behaviour will be dealt with by allowing the Corporation to be subject to the Commerce Act in the normal way. The regular efficiency audits required of the Corporation can also be seen as part of the regulatory environment, providing a check on whether a dominant market position is being abused.

Vertical integration
Vertical integration is an issue which covers entry by the Corporation into both resource development and retail sales. Political pressure is generated by this issue

because of the concern that vertical integration would increase the likelihood of predatory pricing. ECNZ's 1990 Statement of Corporate Intent includes a statement on 'Nature and Scope of Activity', with which any extension of its activities should be consistent:

> The Corporation's business will primarily be the generation, marketing, servicing and supply of electricity. It will also undertake consultancy services and the design and construction of electricity related facilities in New Zealand and overseas.
> Consistent with these principal activities the Corporation will also pursue activities designed to ensure the efficient utilization of its existing capital assets and human resources.
> Any major expansion of its activities into new business areas will be subject to consultation with the Shareholding Ministers.

ECNZ considers that vertical integration backwards into resource development has not been an issue, as it has been possible to meet the objectives of the Corporation without ownership of fuel resources (see Chapter 5). Had ECNZ wished to enter the gas or coal industry, they would probably have encountered political resistance.

In previous years the Statement of Corporate Intent stated that ECNZ were suppliers of 'bulk electricity to the retail industry and major industrial and commercial electricity users'. The current Statement of Corporate Intent says that ECNZ are suppliers of electricity, without restriction as to who may be supplied.

Possible forward vertical integration by ECNZ into the retail electricity market is of major concern to the electricity supply authorities. For this reason, ECNZ currently has an informal agreement with the Government and the ESAs that they will not enter the retail electricity market, except where the ESA tariff structure is unfair to a customer. This exception creates an incentive for supply authorities to modify their tariff structures so as to reflect actual costs; in other words, to reduce averaging across both time and geographical location.

Electricorp Marketing provides functions such as the Brightspot franchise, Retail Services and Appliance Wholesale as services to the retailers. These services are seen by some supply authorities as a threat, and consequently they resist these ECNZ initiatives. An example was the response of some ESAs to Brightspot.

Treasury was initially concerned that the involvement of ECNZ in Brightspot was not consistent with their Statement of Corporate Intent.

In late 1989, ECNZ announced that Brightspot franchises could be operated by Electricorp Marketing. According to ECNZ, all members supported EM's involvement in the downstream market. However, they also noted that a small number of electricity retailers, including one who has resigned from Brightspot, see involvement of EM as a threat to their own operations in a deregulated market.

Supplier of last resort
Electricity is subject to political and social pressures that few other products bear because of the concern that electricity may not always be available. If General Foods withdraws one of their products from the market, consumers restructure

their food requirements with little difficulty. However, if ECNZ were to cease supply of electricity, it would be difficult and costly for consumers to restructure their energy requirements. Also, many users identify the 'ability to rely on continued supply' as a major product attribute.

Among other things, the Electricity Act 1968 imposed upon the Electricity Division the duty to supply all electricity needs. When ECNZ took over many rights and responsibilities of the Division, this particular responsibility was not placed upon the Corporation. In the June 1986 Provisional Report of the Advisory Board, 'Reforming the Electricity Division as a Commercial Entity', the following statement was made:

> The Board's view is that the special characteristics of the electricity industry make a 'voluntary' approach to supply inappropriate. It would be more practicable to create a formal responsibility for the Corporation to provide supply to every consumer able to pay for the cost of that supply. [4]

This view of the Advisory Board was supported by the Ministry of Energy, but opposed by the Treasury. In January 1987 Treasury wrote:

> Officials strongly disagree with this conclusion for two reasons. First, we are not convinced that electricity is an essential commodity any more than many food products. The Government does not ensure the supply of these products and officials can see no reason why an exception should be made in the case of electricity. In a commercial environment, the Electricity Corporation, just like any other business organisation, will have an incentive to meet the needs of its customers. In the event that it is uneconomic to supply a particular group of consumers or region, Ministers will have the option of providing an explicit subsidy to the Corporation . . .

Political and social pressures alone would make it difficult, if not impossible, for ECNZ to cease the supply of electricity to a customer.

Pricing

Regulation of pricing has not been actively proposed by any organizations. However, if the pricing of electricity by ECNZ could not be demonstrated to be fair, then pressure would mount for the political setting of electricity prices, and the efforts of the last few years to price electricity commercially would be lost.

In a Marketing paper on the new pricing Option 4, dated April 1990, the following statement was made:

> The present industry structure is designed to provide incentives for the ECNZ to ensure effective cost control and to encourage marketing efforts through the normal profit motives of the owners. Price itself is constrained by effective even access to both capital and the market place for any prospective generation entrant. Potential

---

4. Section 3 (b), Page 5.

abuse by ECNZ of its dominant position is constrained by normal commercial practice statutes and also the threat of regulatory intervention. This is the reality of a dominant SOE in New Zealand.

Pricing regulation would be likely to stifle competition. This is because, if a regulated price was below the cost of supply or there was a perceived likelihood that it would be so in the future, then building a power station would be an unattractive proposition. Also, pricing regulation would be likely to limit the ability to develop pricing options that suit individual customers. One such pricing option is the acceptance of a lower standard of reliability or continuity of power by some industrial users in return for a lower price.

In Treasury letter's of January 1987, the following opinion on pricing is expressed:

> Officials recommend against political intervention in setting electricity prices. History has demonstrated that the process of establishing electricity prices through ministerial intervention has resulted in prices which do not reflect the cost of supply. The Bulk Supply Tariff has been characterized by periods of steadily declining real prices with prices significantly below the cost of supply followed by sudden sharp increases. This has tended to encourage greater consumption of state supplied electricity and excessive investment in power station construction.

Removal of averaging in the pricing of electricity across geographic location would result in large electricity price increases for some consumers. This could increase political and social pressure for electricity price regulation. In the same letter, Treasury submit their viewpoint:

> With respect to the concerns over the social implications of revised electricity tariffs, we would note that Ministers will have the option of paying an explicit subsidy to the Electricity Corporation in order to enable it to deliver electricity at a price below the cost of supply. We would caution however, that social equity objectives may be more efficiently met through the tax and social welfare systems.

Environmental issues

The previous sections, 'Water and geothermal rights' and 'Personnel issues', have alluded to environmental issues. Perception of the Corporation is very important in reducing the political and social pressure associated with environmental issues.

New Zealand has the advantage, when compared to other countries, of being able to meet four-fifths of its electricity needs largely through renewable resources that produce no pollution. Over the last two financial years combined, 74.7% of electricity generation was by hydro power stations, with another 5.3% generated by geothermal plants.

One difficulty in this area is in balancing local and national interests. Local interest may require a free-flowing river for fishing, birdlife, and its inherent beauty. Farmers may want water to flow for irrigation purposes. This local interest might not be the same as the national interest. There is a similar difficulty in balancing interregional interests. Because ECNZ operates a national network of generating facilities, constraints on the use of water in one region can mean that greater use must be placed on water resources in another region. Ecological 'costs' are also transferred from one region to another. Where the ability to utilize hydro electricity generating facilities is limited, greater use must be placed on thermal electricity generating facilities to meet the same demand. Consequential increase in the use of fossil fuels creates additional ecological 'costs'.

The same applies to the complex issue of water rights. Constraints on the use of water in one region may produce benefits for that region, and at the same time impose a burden on the nation overall. This is because the cost of those constraints is borne by all consumers through an increase in the price of electricity. ECNZ is critical of the Resource Management Bill because it believes that it does not provide an adequate mechanism for the weighing of regional and national interests. They point to the recent Wanganui water right hearings, where the Central Districts Catchment Board decided to substantially increase the minimum water flow in the Wanganui River, thus affecting the Tokaanu station, the eight Waikato stations and the Huntly power station in the Waikato Catchment Board's area.

To minimize the political and social pressure created by environmental issues, ECNZ must demonstrate that it can be entrusted with the natural resources of New Zealand, and that constraining their use of water resources will result in increased burning of fossil fuels and will therefore be more detrimental to the environment.

The interests of Electricorp Marketing and Electricorp Production are not identical in the matter of environmental issues. Surplus generating capacity is useful to Electricorp Marketing since it is able to argue that, while this surplus exists, ECNZ is the most rational source of non-transport energy for New Zealand. However, Electricorp Production have no desire to portray the Corporation as being in search of ways to use up excess electricity; they need to be seen as efficient custodians of New Zealand's natural resources. When the time comes to build another power station, public acceptance will be adversely affected if the need for the station is perceived to be a consequence of imprudent promotion of demand on the basis of a short-term excess in capacity. Therefore, Electricorp Marketing's stimulation of demand is likely to come into conflict with Electricorp Production's image of environmental concern.

Some responses of ECNZ to political and social pressures

One of the more visible responses of the Corporation to social and political pressures has been the explicit recognition of corporate relations as part of the business of generating and selling electricity. Public perception and the goodwill between the public and ECNZ will affect the ability to develop and operate power stations in the future. Therefore, ECNZ's Corporate Relations are important in the reduction of current and future political costs.

Section 4 of the State-owned Enterprises Act 1986 places upon ECNZ the requirement to show social responsibility by having regard to the interests of the community in which it operates. Since the vast majority of the New Zealand public have to use its product, the public relations image of the Electricity Corporation must relate to all New Zealanders, rather than to a specific client market.

ECNZ follows a sponsorship policy that would largely match other major commercial organizations. Electricorp Marketing directs sponsorship towards occasions to which they can take their customers. An example of this was their contribution to the Commonwealth Games. Electricorp Marketing also sponsors the arts, also with the intention of inviting their customers to performances.

Electricorp Production sponsors a number of water-related activities, recognizing its reliance on the natural environment, particularly rivers and lakes. They also provide research funds for Universities, recognizing the reliance of the industry on engineering technical skills.

It could be argued that because the users of electricity are the same group as the people of New Zealand, then the best gift to the people of New Zealand would be cheap electricity. This would imply that ECNZ should not spend anything on sponsorship. However, it could be argued equally well that ECNZ has a responsibility, just like any other large corporation, to run a sponsorship programme.

ECNZ looked for an appropriate way to 'acknowledge a duty to creative New Zealanders' and decided on building up the Rutherford House collection of New Zealand art. To be considered for inclusion in the collection, a work must be an original and by an exhibited New Zealand artist. Juliet Hensley, Corporate Relations Manager, outlines the objectives of the collection:

> [It] will really give an outline of the progression of New Zealand art since New Zealand was established in more or less its present form 150 years ago and would particularly concentrate on works by present day young artists and Maori artists and would really reflect what the arts were doing in New Zealand about the time our Corporation was set up.

Sponsorship programmes of the magnitude that are entered into by ECNZ would not have been undertaken by NZED. Funding of such programmes was likely to have been difficult within the government department structure. Also, as a government department, NZED would have been perceived as having the national interest at heart. ECNZ with its commercial objective is likely to have a different public image. Thus, sponsorship signals to the public that ECNZ does still act in the national interest.

Acting in the national interest is also the perception that ECNZ wish the public to have of its environmental record. State Hydro and NZED engineers were early environmentalists. Now, ECNZ must demonstrate that they also have a sensitivity to the environment that would make them fit to manage the natural resources and environment of New Zealand.

An area of social pressure is the safety of the public who may live or work near ECNZ facilities. Perception of the safety of generation is assisted by the absence of nuclear powered generating facilities. The major safety concern of the general public relating to the generation of electricity would be the possibility of the failure of a dam. This issue has been addressed in recent studies.

Another area where Corporate Relations are important is the public perception of how ECNZ is fulfilling its obligations to the Treaty of Waitangi. This is particularly important because Section 9 of the State-owned Enterprises Act 1986 imposes an obligation to act in accordance with the principles in the Treaty of Waitangi. As Juliet Hensley, ECNZ Corporate Relations Manager, comments:

> The old organisation had very good relationships with many of the tribal authorities in the area it was building and they just took it for granted that they would continue. In the new climate, we've had to redefine some of those relationships and work, if not harder, a bit differently on them because we've lost our Crown rights to water and land. So, it's not going to be a relationship that you can ever say is settled, but I have to say that we have found enormous goodwill from the Tainui and Ngai Tahu which have been the two where we've been most closely involved in the 18 months I've been here.

An example of how ECNZ have worked together with the Māori people has been in the building of the Ohaaki geothermal power station. This is outlined in the Report from the Chief Executive in the 1989/90 ECNZ Annual Report:

> During the construction period the Corporation assisted the Ngai Tahu trustees with the refurbishment of their historic marae. The Corporation is also restoring and maintaining the legendary hot pool, the Ngawa, which is part of the history of the area. The Corporation believes that the restoration of the tribal heritage and the building of the award winning Ohaaki station is proof that the sensitive issue of development of natural resources on land owned by the tangata whenua can be managed harmoniously for the overall benefit of New Zealand.

In all these areas of public perception, a factor that affects them is openness. If ECNZ is perceived as withholding information, then corporate relations will be damaged. An openness with the public will generate trust. Both the Chief Executive and the Chairman of the Board expressed willingness to provide information to opponents of the Corporation, which they believe would remove the points of opposition.

ECNZ remains subject to the Official Information Act. According to Geraldine Baumann, Company Secretary, this does not greatly affect the Corporation. She stated, 'This organisation has been a contestable monopoly and it is in its own interests to be open about some of its activities.' The Official Information Act prompts the release of information that should be released by Electricorp of its own accord for commercial reasons. However, the Official Information Act is used by some people to involve ECNZ in providing information for curiosity's sake, or for the purposes of those who wish to criticize large corporations. Examples are requests for disclosure of remuneration and bonuses of people in the organization. Requests for commercially sensitive information have been declined; a decision that has been upheld when challenged.

The same issues of public perception existed before and after incorporation. However, responsibilities to the public are now defined by Statute and the commercial need to operate freely in the future.

7

Appraisal of Financial Performance

In this chapter we summarize the financial performance of Electricorp and its predecessor organization, the Electricity Division of the Ministry of Energy. The analysis covers the years ending 31 March 1980 through to 31 March 1990. Because ECNZ shares are not traded, an analysis based on share market performance is not possible. For this reason the analysis is based entirely on accounting reports. The focus of the appraisal of financial performance is on the return on shareholder's funds. The aggregate of shareholder's funds reflects the Crown's investment in ECNZ. A primary objective of the entire corporatization programme has been to improve efficiency and to earn an appropriate return on the Crown's investment.

The appraisal is structured in the following way. First, we discuss the accounting adjustments we had to make to generate a usable time series of accounting data from 31 March 1980 to 31 March 1990, a period which spans both sides of the intervention (ECNZ was incorporated on 1 April 1987). Next, we present the basic part of our analysis, using our 'adjusted' time series of data. We use an equation to break down the rate of return on shareholder's funds into its component parts. In the following sections we present three additional analyses. First, we generate a new time series of data to deal with changing price levels by deflating appropriate data streams to their 1987 equivalents, and then we discuss operating performance over time making use of both the 'adjusted' time series and the deflated 'adjusted' time series. Second, we discuss ECNZ's performance, using data taken directly from its annual reports for the three years of its existence, i.e. 1988-1990. Third, we provide some cross-sectional comparisons of ECNZ's results to those of other companies. Lastly, we offer some concluding remarks. The tables and figures referred to appear in Appendix C, which starts on page 158.

Generating a usable time series of financial data

The accounting adjustments discussed here are necessary for two reasons: (1) the interruption in the time series caused by the substantial change in valuation of assets that took place on ECNZ's incorporation, and (2) changes in accounting policy made by ECNZ. We discuss each of these in turn.

Change in valuation of assets
At 31 March 1987 the aggregate total assets on the balance sheet of the Electricity Division of the Ministry of Energy totalled $4.3b. The agreed final valuation of the assets transferred to ECNZ was $6.3b. The impact of the increase on the post-

corporatization performance of ECNZ will be major, particularly given our focus on returns relative to shareholder's funds. In terms of the annual impact on the profit of ECNZ, it is clear that the revaluation will have a large effect on depreciation and interest. As the major part of the asset value increase relates to long-lived assets which are being depreciated at a rate of about 1.5-2% per annum, the impact on depreciation will be of the order of $40m per annum. Further, given that the desired debt/equity ratio of ECNZ is approximately 1:1, the impact on interest will be substantial. This is exacerbated for ECNZ (particularly in the year ended 31 March 1988) as the debt had a short-term structure, attracting very high initial interest rates. It is more difficult to estimate the impact of this change as two things are happening concurrently: the establishment of quite a different capital structure, combined with a higher level of debt generated by the asset revaluation. If we assume that the asset revaluation generated an additional $1b of debt than otherwise would have been the case, then the impact on the 1988 profit statement would be of the order of $190m given a short-term borrowing rate of 19%. However, it is noted that ECNZ has developed a policy of capitalizing interest on development work in progress, something which was not done by the Electricity Division. In 1988 and 1989, interest capitalization has been around $100m, with 1990 being $78m, so the final impact of interest on accounting profit, at least in 1988, is approximately $90m before tax.

The following procedures have been adopted to generate the time series of results through the period of the intervention.

(1) Eleven-year time series, 1980-1990
Where the analysis spans the entire eleven-year time period and the aim is to draw some comparisons between the pre-SOE and SOE periods, the asset revaluation and associated accumulated depreciation totals (a total value of about $2b) have been eliminated, as has the impact of interest capitalization. Total interest is unaltered, so the major part of the 1980-1990 analysis is done at the pre-interest level (that is, relating earnings before interest to assets, etc.). Depreciation expense has been adjusted to the NZED basis, as indicated below.

Some performance assessment is also based on a measure we call ROCI − Return on the Crown's Investment. For that measure, interest on New Zealand government loans to NZED is added back to 'profit', and the New Zealand government liability figure is added to 'equity'.

(2) Three-year time series, 1988-1990
Where the analysis is limited to the 1988-1990 period (that is, ECNZ's accounts only), the numerical analysis is based on the reported ECNZ figures. Hence all analyses are based on the 'revalued' figures. We return to this topic below.

Changes in accounting policy
ECNZ, as a new entity, was able to determine its own accounting policies. Four issues deserve particular attention here: depreciation, capitalization of interest, taxation (including deferred taxation), and foreign exchange accounting. In part

these items relate to activities that are new for the Corporation, and in part they relate to decisions to measure expenses in a different manner.

(1) Depreciation
Apart from the larger asset base which will clearly have a direct impact on the reported results of ECNZ, the Corporation has adopted different depreciation policies for most major fixed asset items, which would appear to shorten the implied useful lives of several major asset classes, and hence increase the depreciation relative to the amounts previously being charged by NZED. Further changes were made in the 1990 year, which also impact negatively on that year's result. We have however adjusted all depreciation to the 'old' NZED basis and eliminated the impact of the revaluation to produce consistent time series data for the analysis.

(2) Interest
As indicated above, ECNZ now capitalizes interest on uncompleted major capital works at its weighted average interest rate. The NZED did not capitalize interest and so in order to generate meaningful time series comparisons we have eliminated the interest capitalization from the asset base, and added it back into the income statement as an expense. This is not a commentary on ECNZ's choice of accounting policy as we would believe it is appropriate to capitalize interest. It is performed in this case simply to produce a more comparable time series.

(3) Taxation
ECNZ is subject to taxation, and applies appropriate accounting principles including those relating to deferred taxation. The major timing differences that generate deferred tax appear to be depreciation and the interest capitalization procedures described above. Because taxation becomes an issue only for the 1988-1990 years, almost all the analysis has been undertaken at the pre-tax level. However management of taxable income, within the confines of the relevant statutes with regard to taxation, would clearly be a central strategic activity of any profit-oriented corporation. We note that two of the performance measures in the Statement of Corporate Intent are expressed in 'after tax' terms. These are discussed below. We also note some potential problems in this area in Chapter 8.

(4) Foreign exchange accounting
A central feature of the new Corporation is that it has responsibility to manage any foreign currency exposures. Two changes stand out when compared with the NZED. The first is that a fixed exchange-rate regime existed during the early part of the analysis. This was inevitably accompanied by substantial regulation of international financial flows. The second is that during the later part of the period, as it affects NZED, any exchange exposure management would have been undertaken by the New Zealand Treasury and hence would not impact on the accounts of NZED.

As a result of the SOE process, ECNZ and other corporations have established treasury sections within their organizations, with clear objectives associated with financial risk management. This includes interest rate and foreign currency exposure risk management. To the extent that NZED was affected by currency realignments, etc., and had borrowed through the Treasury from off shore, in most years currency realignment expenses (or revenues) were shown in the income statement. In those years where reserves were used, we have adjusted NZED's reported income numbers. On the other hand ECNZ, through its treasury management activities, attempts to match monetary assets and liabilities denominated in foreign currencies, and/or match foreign currency assets or liabilities against foreign currency expense or revenue streams. The consequence is that realized gains and losses are taken to the income statement, but gains and losses on designated hedge transactions are deferred and released to the income statement on maturity of the hedge. The impact of these new procedures on profitability when seen in a time series context is impossible to measure.

Table 7.1 provides the data used in this part of the analysis. The table consists of six panels covering profit and loss statements (Panel A), balance sheets (Panel B), common size profit and loss statement data (Panel C), ratio analysis (Panel D), operating ratios measured in cents per kWh (Panel E), and a reconciliation of the asset values between NZED and ECNZ (Panel F).

Analysis of the return on shareholders' funds

Here we present the basic part of our analysis using the 'adjusted' time series of data previously discussed.

The basic equations and measures used

The focus of the appraisal of ECNZ's financial performance is on the return on shareholders' funds. The aggregate of shareholders' funds reflects the Crown's investment in ECNZ. ECNZ contracts with its Shareholding Ministers across three dimensions:

(1) Profit less tax and preference dividend to average ordinary shareholders' funds
(2) Profit before interest and tax to average net funds employed
(3) Increase in the value of the shareholders' investment at a rate similar to that of the market value increases of comparable large private sector companies.

It is not possible to generate these measures for the entire time series. During the NZED era in the time series (1980-1987), the notion of capital structure was unimportant. The Crown's investment in NZED consisted of a limited amount of 'equity' and a large amount of 'debt'. There was no preference capital. To overcome these problems in this part of the analysis, we will focus attention on three major performance measures:

(1) Return on assets
(2) Return on shareholders' funds
(3) Return on Crown's investment

The first two are commonly used measures of financial performance. The third is a new measure.

At this point we will confine our analysis to a discussion of these performance measures. However, later in the chapter, we will also discuss ECNZ's performance with respect to contracted measures, but only for the period 1988-1990.

Return on assets (ROA) can be expressed as:

$$ROA \ = \ \frac{EBIT}{SALES} \ \times \ \frac{SALES}{ASSETS} \ = \ \frac{EBIT}{ASSETS}$$

(The terms are defined below.) The advantage of this measure is that it abstracts from leverage effects. As mentioned above, this turns out to be desirable as far as the NZED analysis is concerned, as there is no clear focus on leverage as a policy variable during the 1980-1987 period.

Return on shareholders' funds (RSHF) can be expressed in the following way:

$$RSHF \ = \ \frac{NPBT}{EBIT} \ \times \ \frac{EBIT}{SALES} \ \times \ \frac{SALES}{ASSETS} \ \times \ \frac{ASSETS}{SHF} \ \times \ (1\text{-}T_c)$$

EBIT   =   Sales − Operating Costs − Depreciation
          =   Earnings Before Interest and Tax

NPBT   =   EBIT − Interest + Other Income
          =   Net Profit Before Tax

T_c =   Effective Corporate Tax Rate

Return on the Crown's Investment (ROCI) can be expressed as:

$$ROCI \ = \ \frac{NPBT + CI}{SHF + CD}$$

CI   =   Interest Expense on New Zealand Government Debt
CD   =   New Zealand Government Debt

Presentation of results
Here we present a brief overview of the results, and preliminary interpretative statements. The overview follows the structure of the RSHF formula above. More detailed comments are provided later in the chapter.

(1) NPBT/EBIT
Figure 7.1 shows the ratio of net profit before tax to earnings before interest and taxes. This ratio indicates what percentage of ECNZ's earnings flow through to owners. Strategically, the aim of the Corporation should be to minimize the difference between NPBT and EBIT conditional on the established level of leverage. This simply means that the Corporation should endeavour to ensure that all debt raisings are done at the minimum possible cost. The ratios for 1989 and 1990 indicate that ECNZ has been successful in improving the percentage of earnings

flowing through to owners. The 1990 ratio is the highest of the eleven years that are examined.

(2) EBIT/SALES
Figure 7.2 shows the ratio of earnings before interest and taxes to sales revenue. This ratio indicates the level of operating income relative to revenue generated. It is popularly regarded as a measure of 'margin' with the level depending on the operating cost characteristics of the business involved. Margins vary dramatically across industries. For example, supermarkets typically have extremely low margins and luxury item vendors and capital-intensive industries require high margins. Margins are very strongly negatively correlated with asset turnover measures. NZED's margins have declined steadily from 1980 to 1986. This must be due to the sum of operating expenses and depreciation rising at a faster rate than sales revenue. Since 1988, however, this trend has been reversed.

(3) SALES/ASSETS
Figure 7.3 shows the ratio of sales to assets. This ratio is referred to as the 'asset turnover' ratio and provides an indication, in dollar terms, of how hard the assets of the Corporation are working. As indicated above, there is a strong relationship between the asset turnover ratio and the margin. Strategically, ECNZ's objective should be to maximize asset turnover conditional on some given level of margin. From Figure 7.2 we see that ECNZ's margins are relatively high. This is not surprising given that the industry is capital-intensive with the low asset turnover ratios shown in Figure 7.3. The trend of this ratio over time is strongly increasing.

(4) EBIT/ASSETS
Figure 7.4 shows the ratio of earnings before interest and taxes to assets (ROA). This ratio provides a measure of performance which is not directly affected by the Corporation's leverage. From this figure it can be seen that there is a clear and dramatic distinction between the NZED era (1980-1987) and the ECNZ era (1988 -1990). While there was some increase in the ROA just prior to incorporation in 1986 and 1987, the big jumps are in 1989 and 1990 where the ROA is around 20%. From 1980 to 1985, ROA was about 13%.

(5) ASSETS/SHF
Figure 7.5 shows the ratio of assets to shareholder's funds. This ratio provides a measure of the leverage of the Corporation. The higher this ratio, the higher the reliance on debt in the capital structure. There is a direct negative relationship between leverage and NPBT/EBIT which measures the percentage of earnings which flow through to shareholders. Increasing leverage will cause interest expense to increase and hence will reduce the percentage of EBIT flowing through into NPBT. If leverage increases faster than NPBT/EBIT decreases, then the return on shareholder's funds will increase.

The graph in Figure 7.5 attempts to capture the effects of leverage over the entire time series 1980-1990. As can be seen, this is a less than satisfactory aspect of our analysis. The problem is that in the NZED era (1980-1987) the division between equity and government loans seems somewhat arbitrary and this directly affects the ratio. The problem is further complicated as we have removed the impact of the revaluation of assets in 1987 from the final three years of data in order to generate some useful time series. In particular, this makes the final leverage ratios appear higher than they are in reality. Hence not much can be made of Figure 7.5.

(6) NPBT/SHF

Figure 7.6 shows the ratio of net profit before tax to shareholders' funds. This provides a measure of return on shareholders' funds. This ratio suffers from the same difficulties as the leverage ratio discussed above. The meaning of shareholders' funds in the NZED period is rather arbitrary and numbers appear extremely high because of the removal of the effects of the asset revaluation and increased depreciation.

The advantage of the return on assets measure (EBIT/ASSETS) is that it abstracts from leverage effects measured by ASSETS/SHF and the associated problem of the meaning of shareholders' funds. As our objective is to get the cleanest possible comparison of performance before and after incorporation, return on assets is a much more satisfactory measure.

(7) NPBT/CROWN INVESTMENT

Figure 7.7 shows the ratio of net profit before tax to Crown investment. This ratio provides a measure of return on crown investment (ROCI). To get a better focus on the return on shareholders' funds around the period of the intervention, we reclassified all New Zealand government loans held by NZED (1980-1987) as part of the Crown's investment. Interest on these loans was then added back into net profit before taxes, as described above. For the ECNZ period (1988-1990), any Crown liability is treated as debt and not added into Crown investment, as the explicit intention from the point of incorporation was that ECNZ would refinance this debt. The adjusted time series are shown in Table 7.2.

The results of the ROCI calculation can be seen in Figure 7.7. From 1980 to 1987 ROCI is in the range of 12% to 18% with the highest returns in 1986 and 1987. This is consistent with the ROA results shown in Figure 7.4 and discussed above. This is not surprising given the reliance of NZED on Crown financing. In 1988, the first year of results for ECNZ, ROCI is lower, the result of transitory expense items and a much higher interest expense as discussed above. However in 1989 and 1990 ROCI is above 40%, around three times the former level.

Analysis based on time series adjusted for changing price levels

The analysis presented above was based on an 'adjusted' time series of financial data. Adjustments were made to remove the effects of the revaluation of assets in the post-incorporation part of the time series (1988-1990), and to adjust ECNZ's depreciation and interest accounting policies to NZED equivalent policies. These and other minor adjustments are described at the beginning of Appendix C (pages 158–9).

We took the 'adjusted' time series in the profit and loss statements (Table 7.1, Panel A) and deflated them for the entire 1980-1990 period to their equivalents in March 1987 dollars. We chose the March 1987 dollar value as the base simply because it marks the start of the SOE era. Table 7.3, Panels A and B, present the data used for this part of the analysis.

We also used these deflated 'adjusted' time series to calculate a series of operating ratios in cents per kWh and dollars per employee. The results are shown in Table 7.3, Panel C.

The adjustment for depreciation in this part of the analysis is as follows:

$$\text{Historical Cost} \atop \text{Depreciation} \times \frac{\text{CPI March 1987}}{\text{CPI Average Purchase Date}}$$

Note that this is more than just a scaling of numbers into units of common purchasing power. The depreciation adjustment can turn a 'nominal' profit into a 'real' loss.

(1) Performance measurements

Sales
Figures 7.8 to 7.10 present sales information. Figure 7.8 gives volume data, Figure 7.9 gives 'real' and 'nominal' sales revenue per kWh, and Figure 7.10 gives total dollar value revenue in both 'real' and 'nominal' terms.[1]

In nominal terms, sales have grown at approximately 12% per annum over the 1980-1990 period. The real growth rate has been less than 1% per annum. Since corporatization, the growth in sales volume has been approximately 2% per annum, offset by a decrease in unit prices, so that sales have remained constant in real dollar-value terms.

Sales per kilowatt hour expressed in 1987 dollars decreased fairly steadily through the period of analysis, with the three lowest observations being for 1988, 1989 and 1990. These results are consistent with the ECNZ objective of lowering the real cost of power. ECNZ indicates that a North Island competitive price of power appears to be about 4.45c/kWh for bulk electricity (presumably in 1987/1988 dollars). If this estimate is reliable, it is clear that ECNZ faces potential competition, as its overall sales per kWh in 1987 dollars is above this figure, although not by much. There still appear to be some incentives for ECNZ to lower its unit real cost of power to keep competitive generators from entering the market, assuming that competitors can secure a fuel supply to make the 4.45 c/kWh price realistic.

---

1. All 'reals' are expressed using 31 March 1987 units of purchasing power, measured by the CPI. Sales and all expenses, excluding depreciation, are adjusted using mid-year CPI figures. Hence for 1987 the 'real' sales, for example, will be greater than the 'nominal' sales.

Pricing policy has been a central and overt aspect of ECNZ's activities since corporatization. Clearly it is part of a more general marketing strategy which is required given an emphasis on return on shareholders' funds. 'Market share' is a notion that simply was not present in the NZED era. An emphasis on sales (rather than production) arises as a direct consequence of an emphasis on 'return' measures.

In summary, therefore, the results are consistent with ECNZ's explicit dual objective of lowering the real price of power and expanding sales volumes.

Operating expenses
For our purposes operating expenses include all ECNZ's costs with the exception of depreciation, interest and tax. There is a change in classification of items between NZED's reporting and ECNZ's, which restricts our ability to say much about the performance of individual items. Some comments will be made about fuel costs.

From Figure 7.11 it is clear that the real operating cost of power, expressed as cents per kWh, has been rising over time to 1986. The year 1988 shows a higher operating cost per kWh than 1987, but includes a substantial set of new costs that the NZED would not have incurred. In particular, redundancy costs impacted on the 1988 result. In addition, both marketing and administrative costs would have risen. To illustrate: ECNZ now has to maintain its own treasury function, and is responsible for all financial evaluations. ECNZ also now has to manage its personnel function, part of which would previously have been the responsibility of the State Services Commission. It was also free to pay market-based salaries to attract staff in certain strategic areas.

With regard to 1989, the real cost of operating, expressed in cents per kWh, has decreased by about 8%, with a further 8% reduction achieved in 1990. The real operating cost of power production, excluding depreciation, is at a level last achieved in 1982, although ECNZ must now maintain a set of marketing, financial and administrative overheads that its predecessor body, NZED, did not have to contemplate.

Two major internal factors which help to explain the reduction in real operating costs are the lower overall staffing levels, and the renegotiation of the contract for the supply of coal. Fuel expense per unit of production using fossil fuels decreased from approximately 2.5 cents per kWh in 1988 to 2.0 cents per kWh in 1990. (See Figure 7.12).

Interest
The remaining expense item is interest. Given the debt/equity ratio that ECNZ now maintains at approximately 1:1, interest is the major expense that ECNZ faces. There are two driving factors associated with ECNZ's debt management programme. The first is that the duration of the debt portfolio should be as long as possible, to match the very long-lived nature of the asset structure. The second is that the debt needs to be denominated in New Zealand dollars, as the entire cost structure, and revenue, is New Zealand denominated.

Figure 7.13 shows net finance costs as a percentage of sales over the 1988-1990 period. The highest percentage was reached in 1988, when the Corporation was first established, and where the debt structure was all essentially short-term, attracting extremely high interest rates, at least by historical standards. Not surprisingly, ECNZ is devoting substantial effort to addressing ways of minimizing interest cost. Prior to corporatization, this activity was largely irrelevant. Further, there was no strategic emphasis given to capital structure management, and as we have already seen the division between equity and government loans was essentially arbitrary for NZED. For these reasons it is impossible to make anything of the 1980-1987 time series with regard to this item.

For the 1988-1990 period there is a clear downward trend in net finance costs as a percentage of revenue. (Details of net finance costs are given in Table 7.4, Panel B). Interest expense is lower in 1989 and 1990 as nominal interest rates declined. Further, the inverted yield curve, combined with the strategic aim of lengthening the duration of ECNZ's debt, will lead to a lower reported interest expense item as the interest captured by the accounting system and reported in the income statement will be based on the coupon on the debt, and not on the one-year spot rate.

Profits

Figures 7.14 and 7.15 show operating earnings and EBIT, as we have defined them, in both 'real' and 'nominal' terms, per kWh of output. Figure 7.16 shows NPBT, both in 'real' and 'nominal' terms. The clear feature of all these graphs is the trend of increasing profitability per unit of output since corporatization. As is illustrated in Figure 7.16, real NPBT is at the highest level of the 1980-1990 period, as is real EBIT (see Table 7.3, Panel A).

(2) Employee productivity

Figures 7.17 to 7.20 give details of employee numbers, and measures of output, expenses and profitability per employee. Numbers of employees are substantially lower for ECNZ than during the NZED era. Further, numbers have decreased from 1988 to 1990, reversing the trend of increasing numbers during 1980 to 1987. Not surprisingly, measures expressed on a per employee basis emphasize this trend.

(3) Operating efficiency

Reference has been made above to the capital-intensive nature of ECNZ's activities. A measure of this is the asset turnover ratio, which is expressed here in the form SALES/ASSETS. As can be seen from Figure 7.3, the SALES/ASSETS ratio has increased substantially over time. In 1980 it was marginally less than 19% and in 1990 the SALES/ASSETS ratio is approximately 32%, with the impact of the revaluation removed from the analysis. While this measure is a commonly used way of assessing asset utilization, it suffers some defects in this context because of the very long-lived nature of the asset base, given that accounting techniques rely on historical cost methods.

The extent to which the accounting measurement methodology impacts on this analysis is difficult to assess. Further the dollar value of sales clearly reflects both price and quantity decisions, and in many respects asset utilization is probably better assessed in terms of quantitative measures of output relative to some total generating capability that might be available. An appropriate measure is plant (or circuit) availability. The data for link availability are for calendar years and for circuit and plant availability they are for financial years ended 31 March. Plant availability is the weighted average of availability to megawatt capacity, across all power stations. Circuit and link availability measures relate hours of availability to total hours in a year.

Summary data are as follows:

	1981	1982	1983	1984	1985	1986	1987	1988	1989	1990
Plant availability (%)										
Hydro	85.6	84.6	84.0	87.4	88.2	87.3	87.4	90.0	91.9	90.9
Thermal	72.2	69.9	73.4	66.7	70.1	64.8	73.2	76.4	82.5	80.8
Trans Power (%)										
HVDC Link	98.1	94.7	95.8	92.6	95.0	96.3	96.5	90.6	96.6	94.2*
HVAC Circuit	97.2	97.6	98.2	97.6	97.0	97.6	97.0	97.7	98.0	98.2

(* Estimate)

As indicated in Chapter 1, we provide these data as a means of controlling for 'quality' while emphasizing the financial performance aspects. It seems reasonably clear that plant availability is greater since 1988, circuit availability is unchanged, and the HVDC link availability is at roughly the same level as it was during the NZED era, except for calendar year 1988 when it was markedly lower.

Analysis based on data drawn from ECNZ's Annual Reports 1988-1990

Figures 7.4, 7.6 and 7.7 report returns relative to assets (Figure 7.4), shareholder's funds (Figure 7.6), and Crown's investment (Figure 7.7). All graphs have the impact of the revaluation removed, as indicated at the beginning of this chapter. Figure 7.4, EBIT/ASSETS, also abstracts from problems associated with interest expense due to the large asset revaluation at the intervention and the higher debt levels that resulted.

Return on assets, and return on shareholder's funds, as reported by ECNZ for 1988-1990, are shown in Table 7.4, Panel B. Data on which these calculations are based are shown in Table 7.4, Panel A.

Return on Assets (EBIT/ASSETS) shows the general trend of increasing profitability of ECNZ over the 1988-1990 period. A similar increase is shown in Return on Shareholder's Funds (NPBT/SHF). Return on Net Funds (EBIT/NF) is greatest in 1989, caused simply by the high level of current debt in that year. Current liabilities were $600m ($500m) higher in 1989 than in 1990 (1988). Further, the after-tax measures are affected by the increase in the effective tax rate in 1990.

Note that all measures are based on year-end balance sheet aggregates, and taken directly from ECNZ's accounts.

The general improvement from 1988 to 1990 in these ratios is also clear. Attempts have been made to lower reported interest expense by extending the period of the debt. Further, nominal interest rates were generally lower in 1989 than in 1988 so this impact on the larger amounts of debt that appear on ECNZ's balance sheet will be substantial. However the reduction in interest rates is partly a reflection of lower expectations with regard to inflation in the New Zealand economy. With lower inflation rates will come lower nominal sales growth. So the criticism of ECNZ from some quarters, namely that the improved performance shown by ECNZ is largely due to a 'windfall gain' as a result of reducing interest rates, appears to us to be invalid.

The 1988 profit after taxation for ECNZ was $141m, and for 1989 it was $353m. The major items explaining this change, as recorded, are (1) increased income $130m, (2) reduced finance costs $151m, and (3) increased taxation $79m. In 1989 ECNZ, for the first time in history, had a liability for taxation of $75m. (This excludes the $63m of deferred taxation.)

In 1990, profit after tax was $339m, after adjustment to asset lives which effectively reduced reported profit by $44m (pre-tax). The major items explaining the 1989/1990 change, as recorded, are (1) increased income $77m, (2) increased operating costs including depreciation $62m, (3) reduced net finance costs $10m, and (4) increased taxation $39m. Part of the increase in taxation is attributable to a higher statutory tax rate (33%, compared with 28% previously).

Net finance costs report substantial interest income (see Table 7.4, Panel B), particularly in 1989 and 1990. While it is difficult to predict future levels of this income item, it reflects an important activity associated with treasury management.

The most likely scenario is that interest from other investments will decrease, probably substantially, if (1) interest rates fall, (2) the yield curve flattens, and (3) as the duration of the debt is lengthened with the repayment of the Loans from the Crown.

Comparing ECNZ's results with those of other companies

The unique aspects of New Zealand electricity generation and transmission make any comparisons with other electric utilities extremely tentative. These unique aspects include the absence of nuclear, the heavy reliance on hydro relative to thermal, and the distance between the major generation sources and the major load. Accounting policy issues also impinge on the analysis. For example, US utilities in their construction phases account for AFUDC — Allowance for Funds Used During Construction. This is a more general version of interest capitalization, designed to include an overall cost of capital element in the asset base, the major aim of which is to ensure appropriate pricing by the rate regulators.

In the United Kingdom, electricity generators report on a current cost basis, with 'trading profit' including depreciation (on current cost) and a cost of sales adjustment but excluding interest and a monetary working capital adjustment. This larger asset base, relative to historical costs, will clearly result in lower levels of profitability, in exactly the same way as 'real' rates are less than 'nominal' ones. Given ECNZ's recent revaluation on corporatization, we would expect its results to be somewhere in between those reported in the USA and the UK.

Median five-year average return on equity measure, across eighty US electric utilities, to 1988, is 13%. For the UK Generating Board, the median return throughout the 1980s (except for the 1984/85 coal strike) has been about 2.8% (before interest).

ECNZ's 1991 Statement of Corporate Intent includes the following 'Commercial Performance Target':

> (a) to increase the value of the shareholder's investment at a rate similar to the increase in the market value of comparable large private sector companies . . .

This target is problematic for a number of reasons. The first is that the only measure of 'the value of the shareholder's investment' is book value. Second, an increase in book value of the shareholder's investment is constrained by ECNZ's dividend policy, which involves payouts of about 75% of profits available to the ordinary shareholder, whereas the average payout of comparable companies would be about 40%. Third, although investors expect market values to rise, they sometimes fall. For example, for the year ended 31 March 1988, almost all New Zealand companies' change in market value was negative. Finally, our perception is that the risk of ECNZ is less than its comparators. One would expect, therefore, that its predicted (required) return would be less, and that on average its realized return would also be less, regardless of how measured.

The only meaningful thing that can be done over the post-incorporation period is to compare ECNZ's return (measured as return on equity) with (say) the top fifty New Zealand companies' ROEs. If our perception of ECNZ's risk characteristics is correct, we would expect ECNZ to appear at about the lower quartile of the distribution. Judging by an analysis of forty large New Zealand companies, ECNZ's return of 9.68% on shareholder's funds would place it at the median. This analysis is supported by data prepared by Jarden Morgan New Zealand Limited. Their analysis of fifty companies would place ECNZ just below the median (22nd out of 50) on its 1990 result, and at the median (25th out of 50) on its 1989 result.

Concluding remarks

The entire analysis is based on accounting reports. In this respect, the analysis will inevitably compare unfavourably, from a methodological perspective, with those analyses that are based on share market performance, which have the following advantages:

(1) Share prices can be thought of as including both historical information and future prospects. In this sense they capture a much wider information set than that included in traditional financial reports.

(2) Share-price analyses are typically not affected by the particular accounting policies chosen by the entity. In the analysis that follows, the changing accounting policies, combined with the large increase in asset valuation when ECNZ was established, create major problems in trying to identify and present a meaningful time series of data.

(3) Performance appraisal based on the share market enables the analyst to explicitly factor risk into the analysis. The methods of analysis attributed to Treynor, Sharpe and Jensen all generate percentage excess rates of return per unit of risk. Excess returns are typically measured by calculating the return on the capital asset being evaluated and subtracting the risk-free rate. Risk can either be variance of return or market co-variance. This means that much of the analysis is developed within a partial equilibrium framework that is accepted by financial economists. Financial accounting measures cannot be developed within the same kind of framework.

From an overall perspective the following results show through:

(1) ECNZ has experienced a decrease in real sales, consistent with a strategic aim of reducing real prices and increasing volumes.

(2) In 1988 there was a substantial increase in costs, arising from redundancy payments and the establishment of new procedures and activities. Real operating costs, expressed in 1987 dollars, are about 1.7c per kWh, excluding depreciation. ECNZ's explicit policy is for cost containment, and costs are now at a lower level than they have been for the last three years.

(3) The asset revaluation, and new emphasis on capital structure, has resulted in substantial increases in depreciation and interest. Interest is now the major cost that ECNZ faces, so it is hardly surprising to find substantial emphasis placed on efficient treasury management. With a downward sloping interest rate term structure, and the yield curve moving down in total, we find that the reported interest cost of ECNZ in 1989 and 1990 was substantially less than that in 1988. Already there is clear evidence of ECNZ's aim to increase the term of the debt.

(4) The net effect of these changes has been for ECNZ to report a return on shareholders' funds close to that contracted for through the Statement of Corporate Intent.

(5) We have also presented a substantial number of figures using number of employees as a base. Not surprisingly, any aggregate using employees has shown dramatic change when comparing 1988, 1989, and 1990, with 1987 and prior periods. A feature of ECNZ's activities has been the creation of internal and external competition through the development of markets. This was discussed in detail in Chapter 5. To the extent that contracting out, for example, for maintenance in Trans Power, is a lower cost alternative compared with the previous systems, efficiency gains will accrue. These will flow through into improved profit results. However a large number of changes have occurred at once and based on this aggregate analysis it is difficult to assess the efficacy of such a change.

In summary, we would regard the financial performance of ECNZ as being markedly superior to that of NZED, both in rate of return and levels of profitability. Output per employee is also substantially higher in 1988-1990 than it was previously. While a number of assumptions have been made in developing a time series to span the entire period of analysis, we do not believe that our results are dependent on them. This improved performance does not appear to us to have been at the expense of quality as measured by plant and link availability.

8

Reflections on the Electricorp Experience

In this chapter we reflect and comment on the process of change at Electricorp and attempt to draw some lessons from the experience. One important caveat is that there are obvious hazards in drawing conclusions or making recommendations on the basis of just a single case study, even one so rich in descriptive detail as that of Electricorp. Wider study of the experiences and performances of other SOEs in New Zealand, both successful and unsuccessful, is necessary to isolate key factors which may account for the success or lack of success of these reorganizations.

Reflections on the process of change at Electricorp

In this section we comment on those events, actions and decisions which appear to have played an important role in the performance of Electricorp and to have been instrumental in the process of transforming the organization from a government department to a commercial, profit-oriented corporation within the framework provided by the SOE Act.

The influence of key leaders
The critical influence of key leaders on the direction and process of change at ECNZ is, in our opinion, the major lesson that emerges from our study of the ECNZ experience. Our interviews with senior managers, and our review of documents, convince us that two individuals have played pivotal roles in the establishment and development of ECNZ. These individuals are John Fernyhough, the Chairman of the Establishment Board and subsequently Chairman of the Board of ECNZ, and Roderick Deane, the Chief Executive. We believe that the direction and performance of ECNZ is due, in large part, to the vision and the complementary leadership and management skills of these two top executives. They have been backed up and supported by an interested and committed Board.

(1) The Chairman of the Board
The appointment of the Chairman of the Board is of vital importance to the successful transformation of a public organization into a profit-oriented SOE. Considerable thought should be given to the business acumen and leadership qualities of the person who is appointed to this position. The appointment of John Fernyhough as Chairman of ECNZ was important because it provided ECNZ with a chairman with the necessary combination of business experience, leadership

qualities and mental toughness necessary to make the hard choices needed to bring about radical change in the organization.

What marks the early days of the establishment of ECNZ are his initial challenges to the status quo. He accepted no management structure, decision, or past practice in the organization without challenge. This approach led him to the conclusion that the organization should start again 'with a clean sheet of paper'. This one conclusion was to have a profound impact on the structure of the Corporation, its management, and its organizational culture. Important decisions that flowed from it included decisions to go for revolutionary rather than evolutionary change, to use a small Task Force working behind the scenes to develop a blueprint for the new organization, and to throw open all positions in the organization to reappointment. These decisions will be discussed in detail below because they provide important insights into the way radical change was effected at ECNZ in a very short space of time.

The one story which best captures the way in which John Fernyhough challenged and changed the old Electricity Division concerns his treatment of the centralized computer facility which was being developed at the time he became Chairman of the Establishment Board. This story is important for three reasons. First, it clearly demonstrates the nature of the challenge he made to the status quo. Second, it sent powerful messages to everybody in the organization that (1) a new page had been started in the history of the organization, (2) the heavily centralized nature of the organization was about to change, and (3) the new organization was going to be managed in a radically different way. Third, this story has now become part of the 'folklore' of the new Corporation. Many people mentioned it to us in interviews as an example of change from the old to the new organization.

John Fernyhough tells the story:

THE WIND OF CHANGE: CLOSURE OF THE CENTRALIZED COMPUTER FACILITY

Not long after I had been appointed as Chairman of the Establishment Board, the Minister started sending me over any papers involving large capital expenditures. I remember getting this one for computer equipment. It had a typical government cover-page with boxes that had to be ticked off for approval. Everyone had ticked it, including all the people in the organisation and over at Treasury. The Minister was being asked to add his tick when he sent it to me. I had a look at it, I think it was for $16M. I said, 'that's a lot of money to be spending on computers' so I started asking questions. I was told: 'it is for a new centralised data processing facility in Paraparaumu. We have a big airconditioned building and we have hired a lot of people in England who are downtown living in a hotel. Sign here'.

I said 'I want to know what the sense of this is'. I was inherently suspicious of anything as large and cumbersome as this seemed to be. From a business point of view it didn't seem right. I had a hell of a time finding out about it. I'd ask a couple of questions and they'd say 'glad you asked that, we've got a report on that'. Well I waded through it and then I had another set of questions and I'd go back and say that I was still concerned. They'd say 'very good questions, glad you asked that, we'll bring in Bill'. So Bill would come in with a team and they would set up a whiteboard and try to explain it to me. I still wasn't convinced!

I was at a Management Conference that they'd organised and started talking to some of the younger fellows in the organisation. I remember talking to Keith Turner [now Corporate Development Manager] who was doing a lot of modelling work. I thought, if anybody's using computer horsepower, he will. I said what do you want? You have this big facility going in — is that what you want? He said 'No that's not what I want. I don't want to wait in endless queues to get work done, I want something that is dedicated to me'. So he told me what he needed and it seemed very modest. I then started talking to some of the key accounting people outside of the main office. Everybody said they wanted a decentralised, distributed computer system. Not everybody of course, but enough to know that I was on to something.

I had to go overseas and I left it with the Establishment Board and I told them I thought it was all wrong and would they have a good look at it while I was away. They spent a whole afternoon on it and listened to a presentation by the chap who was head of EDP — a very talented individual who persuaded them it was the thing to do.

However, it still didn't seem right to me and so when the order form came to me to sign for this $16M, I said 'no I am not going to sign it'. To make a long story short, I kept chipping away, chipping away at it until I got the Board to see the problems. I knew I was on a winner when the Chief of IBM came to see me and bit by bit it came out that the overall cost wasn't $16M. The actual all up cost was more like $80M! I didn't know that as they had actually got it through on a capital expenditure approval that didn't tell you that. So I canned it and we redid the whole financial information system right throughout the organisation in a decentralised way. I know that the final costs were certainly under $20M.

That's the way it was in the old organisation. Everything was centralised.

(2) The Chief Executive

The Establishment Board found the Chief Executive position a difficult one to fill. Although they advertised extensively in New Zealand and overseas, they found it hard to convince individuals with the appropriate qualifications to take the job. Part of the problem seems to have been that, at that time, it was not seen as a prestige job because Electricorp was still closely identified with the NZED. It was not perceived as a corporation with substantial autonomy in its operations. That this position is no longer viewed this way but rather as one of the top jobs in the country is testimony to the changes that have taken place in this organization.

Not having a Chief Executive on board from the beginning put additional demands and pressures on the Chairman and the Establishment Board. As a result, the organization had to manage without an administrative head for part of its transition and the Chairman and Committees of the Board became involved in trying to operate the firm. This turned out to be a necessary but inefficient way to run the organization and created difficulties in the short run. As one member of the Establishment Board put it:

As an Establishment Board, without a Chief Executive appointed, we noticed that there were a number of things we were fumbling with. It didn't start to go right until Roderick Deane was on board as Chief Executive and had a grip of it. A good example of that was industrial relations which we were taking over from the State Services Commission. We didn't exactly cover ourselves with glory in the early stages of that.

Another difficulty was that the Board had to go ahead with a Task Force which developed the blueprint for the new organization structure without the new Chief Executive because they did not have time to wait. (The role of this Task Force is discussed below.) The Board clearly would have liked to have had the new Chief Executive heavily involved in this process of setting up a business structure.

It was only later that the Board Chairman found out that Roderick Deane might be interested in the job of Chief Executive. This opportunity was seized by the Chairman and the Board and Roderick Deane was appointed as Chief Executive at the end of June 1987, but he actually became involved in decision making on new appointments at the end of May. He immediately became a key individual in the further development of Electricorp, bringing unique strengths to the job. Roger Kerr, a Board member, commented as follows:

> Roderick Deane has a lot of strengths but the one that stands out is his ability to turn an organization around in terms of its culture, attitudes, general philosophy and so forth. One strength is his financial experience as a banker which has allowed him to exercise good oversight of the treasury function. The Board is happy with this because of the importance of dollars involved in the treasury function of this organization.

More generally Deane is acknowledged by Board members and senior managers to be an excellent administrator and manager who is extremely skilled at operating in and dealing with the political external environment in Wellington.

(3) Complementary leadership and management skills of the Chairman of the Board and the Chief Executive
Both the Chief Executive and the Chairman as individuals have made very significant contributions to the reorganization and subsequent success of ECNZ. But there is also leadership and management synergy between these two men which is important to an understanding of the successful transformation of ECNZ. The interesting thing is that while they appear to share an underlying management philosophy they differ in terms of their skills and orientation. The closest simple analogy to their relationship is that which exists between architect and builder. John Fernyhough has been the architect at ECNZ, whereas Roderick Deane has been the builder — the manager who made it work.

The complementary skills of these two executives are best described in their own words.

Roderick Deane:

> The Chairman provided the intellectual leadership but not the delivery of that. He had the right ideas and the right framework but he didn't have enough time and its just not his style. So the actual assignments for people, making sure things got done and so on was more my style. But intellectually and analytically we are very compatible. Lots of vigorous interchange intellectually but never with friction. I like working with him and I think he likes working with me. He is a very strong Chairman in terms of intellectual input. I sometimes say to my managers he is the best consultant we have.

John Fernyhough:

> I really didn't want the job of the Chief Executive. My theory of a Chief Executive is that they eat, sleep and breathe the job and do nothing else. If they are not doing that they are not doing their job. I'm far too eclectic for that by temperament, background, outside interests, and other business investments.

The importance of getting these two appointments right is a key lesson that emerges from the ECNZ experience. Although this is not a startling revelation, top appointments have not always worked out as well in other SOEs.

Another potential lesson involves timing. Difficulties encountered in the search process explained the late appointment of ECNZ's Chief Executive. The late appointment hampered the new corporation in its early days and resulted in Board members having to get involved in day-to-day operations of the firm on a part-time basis. This created some short-term difficulties for the firm.

(4) The Board of Directors

The Board has played an important role in the transition both through its policy making and monitoring role and through some of its members becoming involved in day-to-day management. This involvement in management occurred prior to the appointment of the Chief Executive and the new senior management team.

Although it is not possible for us to make a judgement on the quality of the Board at ECNZ relative to other Boards, it does appear from our interviews that ECNZ has been fortunate in getting a Board that is largely free of philosophical wrangling and is committed to the process of building a profitable commercial operation at ECNZ. Although not all Board members have extensive managerial experience, they do have a diverse set of skills and experiences to contribute. There are sufficient members with strong business backgrounds to provide valuable support to the Chief Executive and the senior managers of the company in their commercial dealings.

It is common practice in private sector corporations for the Chief Executive to have a seat on the Board. However, this has not been the practice with SOEs other than in exceptional circumstances. The Chief Executive of Electricorp was not appointed to the Board by the Government, even though the Chairman of the Board and Board members supported his appointment.

Our interviews with managers suggest that the Board is viewed as providing clear policy direction to, and strong oversight over, the operations of the Corporation. One manager described his view of the Board's perspective as follows:

> The Board took the approach, which was the right approach I believe, that they expected us to perform to budget. By holding people accountable and expecting them to perform, people invariably did. The normal thing at the beginning might have been to say 'we know you haven't had a chance to budget properly this year because all the systems aren't up and running so we'll worry about that next year'. The Board's attitude was that it wasn't a problem that we had no system; they just expected us to perform as though we did. You get a system in fast as a result. That strong leadership from the Board and the Chief Executive has been very important.

Developing a blueprint for the new organization

John Fernyhough recognized that the process at the beginning of the life of a new organization was critical. When he walked in the door in August 1986, the senior managers of NZED presented him with what they had been doing to reorganize and get ready for corporatization. Two things struck him about the organizational charts he was shown: first, that this was an engineering-dominated organization, and second, that the spans of control of managers were very small, so that the management hierarchy was very deep. As he puts it:

> They had one man reporting to another man reporting to another man (one on two or three at a maximum) instead of the usual management spans of six or seven. There were layers and layers. They told me it was like this because they had to create new positions to get around State Service Sector rules. If they wanted a particular salary level for someone they would have to create another level to put the person in so as to get them the appropriate salary. The organisation looked hopeless.

Having some idea what the organization was like at the centre, he went on a trip to find out what the organization was like in the field. What he says he learnt on this trip was 'that there were some really good individuals in the organization that were just locked in with three or four layers above them'. These were people who were bright and anxious for change and prepared to challenge some of the old ways.

(1) Changing the organization – revolution not evolution.
The early opinions that Fernyhough drew about the inadequacy of the engineering-dominated reorganization that was already under way, his discovery that there were bright, capable individuals in the organization anxious for change, and his initial experience with the central computer system, convinced him that the organization needed to start afresh and that it needed to be done quickly to succeed. As he put it, 'I knew I'd only get one shot at it'.

He decided that any change should take place in a revolutionary rather than an evolutionary way. Fernyhough discusses the advice he was receiving at this time:

> There were people outside the organisation and some within who were counselling care in making the change. The line was that this was a proud organisation going back many, many years and had a lot to be proud of. It had built very considerable engineering works, it had a long tradition, and it had a culture of its own; and if I went in there like a bull in a china shop, I'd put the whole thing at risk. Electricity was too important to the nation. The advice was take it gradually. If you want to change it do it little by little, incrementally, turn it slowly. I was left with having to make the choice. You either did it that way or bang, full on. I decided on the latter way but I knew that if it was known generally that we were going to do it this way, the forces against change would marshal rapidly.

(2) The Task Force
The next step was to set up a small Task Force with the objective of developing a blueprint for the new organization. The formation of this Task Force, the manner

in which its work was carried out, and the implementation strategy used to gain approval of its restructuring plan for the organization, are major parts of the ECNZ story. How this Task Force was used should be instructive for others engaged in restructurings of public organizations.

The Task Force was formed by John Fernyhough and the Establishment Board in September, 1986. Its primary members included two individuals from the old organization (David Frow and Bob Thompson), who had impressed him as bright, capable individuals who were anxious for change and willing to challenge some of the old ways, and a management consultant (David Edwards) who was brought in to lead the team. The existing senior management was invited to nominate one individual to the Task Force. (Their nominee was Brian Cox.)

The role of the Task Force was to come up with a sensible business organization structure for the new corporation. To forestall resistance to change, the real work of the Task Force was kept confidential until it was completed. Fernyhough believed that if each proposal had been generally debated before decisions were taken, vested interests would have had a chance to mobilize against specific proposals. Also, he believed that a greater degree of uncertainty for staff would have been generated by a prolonged discussion of different possibilities. The existing senior management was simply told that the team was going to conduct an audit of the organization structure they had developed in anticipation of being reorganized as an SOE. As noted above, they were already in the process of implementing a structure. In reality, the Task Force's terms of reference were far more sweeping in scope.

John Fernyhough explains the charge he gave to the Task Force:

> I said to these young blokes 'you've got a chance to rewrite history, are you interested?'
> I said to them 'you have to swear to me that you will not have any regard whatsoever
> to the existing organisation, structure or way of doing things. You have to be able
> to start with an absolutely clean sheet of paper. Forget everything that has been done
> on reorganisation to date.'

Fernyhough met regularly with the Task Force to discuss underlying principles and the progress of the work. Several basic principles emerged from these meetings and the deliberations of the Task Force and became the foundation of the new organizational structure. One principle was that decision making in the new corporation should be decentralized by isolating different parts of the Corporation's activities. This was important to clarify individual manager's responsibilities and accountabilities and to be able to measure performance. Underlying this approach was the concept of proprietorship. Fernyhough explains: 'What we wanted from managers was for them to behave as if the resources they were managing were their own'.

A second important principle was that internal contestability and competition should be built into the organization. This principle meant that, wherever possible, there should be a separation between those who commissioned and paid for a service and those who carried it out. Competition to provide these services would come from internal and external suppliers. The intention was to create a structure in which, as Fernyhough puts it, costs would be controlled by having 'the monster devour itself'.

The third important principle was that the national grid, which was the natural monopoly part of the organization, should be 'ring-fenced'. That is, it should be separated organizationally from other business units and its operations made transparent.

The plan was completed on 19 December 1986. Copies of the *Task Force Report* went to the Board just before Christmas and a tight timetable was set for the Board to act on it. The Chairman asked for a decision in principle as to whether the plan should be endorsed. With this approval in hand, he was able to to go to the staff and say that the plan had been accepted in principle. The Board then called for discussion and suggestions against the background of what had already been decided in principle. The plan for the organization was then fine-tuned on the basis of these suggestions and was adopted as the plan in February 1987. At this point it was ready to serve as the blueprint for the new organization which was shortly to come into being.

The new Chief Executive who, it will be remembered, came on board after the Task Force report was completed, recognized its importance and set out to implement it. He comments:

> There were some aspects of the Task Force report that I didn't feel comfortable with at the time but basically it seemed to be a good model. It had a lot of sensible management practices built into its underlying philosophy. I had a series of meetings with my senior managers and before they started I said to each of them 'Read the Task Force report, read some of the previous annual reports of the division, and then tell me what you are going to have to get done between now', which was May 1987, 'and April 1, 1988'.

(3) The total reappointment process

The new organization structure was radically different from the structure that was being implemented by NZED in preparation for corporatization. With no correspondence between the structures, it was not possible for managers and personnel to move easily from a slot in one structure to a position in the next. This allowed the Establishment Board to declare all positions open to external as well as internal applicants. All managers were forced to reapply for positions.

This was a major opportunity for the new organization to gain the allegiance of re-employed managers to the new organization, while at the same time clearing out the old, entrenched managerial hierarchy. The objective was to appoint managers from inside and outside the organization who would be effective change agents and who were willing to challenge old practices.

The appointment of new management was not accomplished without significant trauma. It is generally acknowledged by the Board members and the managers we interviewed that this was a terrible time for staff morale. However, as new managers were appointed, their morale improved quickly. They then had to select the managers and people who were to work for and report to them. Although there were high costs for those people who lost their jobs or were unable to get the jobs they aspired to in this process, it did act to switch the culture in the organization very quickly, at least in the ranks of management. It also allowed staff that were not required to run the business to be identified. This allowed staffing and its associated costs to be driven down sharply, with significant reductions achieved throughout the organization.

Perhaps most importantly, the reappointment process allowed the considerable talent that existed in the organization to surface. Ray Meyer, a Board member, summed it up as follows:

> With the exception of the few people at the top of the Corporation, the rest of the people actually came from inside the organisation. Putting them in the correct framework, liberating their energies and their talents was accomplished by the reorganisation. There are some very talented people who in the old organisation would have just disappeared into the grey background of the organisation.

To summarize: dramatic, revolutionary change occurred rapidly at ECNZ because the Board under the leadership of John Fernyhough acted quickly and decisively to bring about swift, radical alteration in the organizational structure and the management of the new company. The principal mechanism used to effect this overhaul was a small Task Force which worked behind the scenes to develop a new structure for the organization. This was followed by a total reappointment process. The objective of the Task Force being disguised and the nature of its work kept confidential until its report on the new organizational structure was completed and approved in principle, existing managers who may have been inclined to oppose change were not given the opportunity to frustrate or delay the sweeping reforms considered necessary to turn the organization around. Although the process had a human cost, it was generally successful in placing the best management candidates available from inside and outside the organization into the new structure, and changing the management culture of the organization extremely quickly.

John Fernyhough believes that the ECNZ experience has lessons for other public sector restructurings:

> My view is that even if you've got what you believe is the perfect organisation structure you should kill it and invent another one in order to provide an opportunity to make new appointments. This provides the opportunity to hand select these appointments and to make them contestable. It is the only way to get commitment to the new concepts and enthusiasm for new management practices. Many organisations ossify over the years. You have to do something like this to get at the talent.

Formation of the top management team

Formation of the top management team was a critical undertaking. Appointing a new management team from scratch is a very high-risk operation. The problems of adverse selection are present and the potential costs associated with mistaken choices are very large because of the high levels of discretion exercised by senior managers in a decentralized organization.

In the Chief Executive's view, it was imperative to get the top management team at least 75% right if they were going to be able to deliver the improved performance that was expected of the new corporation. Although it is freely admitted that some mistakes were made in this process, they were corrected as they became obvious.

The Chairman of the Board, some Board members and the Chief Executive devoted considerable effort to this selection process before the appointment of the Chief Executive. Some members of the top management team had been appointed, and some others had been identified but not appointed. On his arrival the Chief Executive spent a significant amount of time completing this process. The remaining task was to mould them into a management team that would work well together. Roderick Deane explains his approach to team building:

> We spend a lot of time talking. We have a lot of interaction in formal meetings of the top management team which includes the four general managers and the managers of corporate development and finance. I try to get along with people. I try to create a spirit whereby we are a team. I have tried to develop the culture in the sense of people feeling they shared the objectives and that we're all in it together and that it is actually to be enjoyable as well as a lot of hard work.

Our discussions with senior managers revealed enormous respect for Roderick Deane's ability to build trust, mutual respect, and a sense of shared purpose.

The importance of the right incentives, motivation, and culture

With the senior managers appointed, attention was then given to setting up contracts and incentives so as to motivate performance, allow delegation of authority and responsibility, and provide the basis for holding people accountable for their performance. This process in ECNZ is best described as performance contracting tied to achievement of objectives.

Although the process is described in detail in Chapter 4, we summarize it again briefly here. The people process starts with the negotiation and setting of the Chief Executive's objectives by the Board Chairman in consultation with the Remuneration Committee of the Board. A substantial part of the Chief Executive's total remuneration package is in the form of a performance bonus payment which is tied to the achievement of these objectives. The Chief Executive negotiates incentive contracts with each of his senior operating managers, who then do the same thing with the managers reporting directly to them. The same process is followed for corporate managers.

The Chief Executive's view of the importance of the incentive contracting process is as follows:

> We set targets and I expect them to be met. People get paid their bonuses on the basis of whether they achieve them. That is a signal that they are important. There are some things I put a lot of attention on. Cost control is one. I said to senior managers you will get your bonus if you exceed all your targets, but, if at the same time as exceeding all your targets, you actually overshoot your budget, not only will you not get any of the bonus, you are in trouble. To not have financial control over costs in this organisation is the ultimate sin as far as I am concerned.

This doesn't mean that they can't get their budget adjusted if they come and talk to me. What it means is that they are not allowed to run off and exceed it without going through the appropriate steps of bringing it to the attention of myself and the Board. You'll find my letters to General Managers are absolutely explicit on the consequences. Only one business unit in three years has run over budgets on costs for a short period and I came down on them like a ton of hot bricks.

Investment and business planning, incentive contracting tied to bonus payments, and close monitoring by the Chief Executive and the Board provide a triad of motivating and control mechanisms in ECNZ. These mechanisms have been successful in motivating managers to achieve their performance targets, which have been translated into the improvements in bottom-line performance which were analysed and reported in Chapter 7.

Although the incentive contracting process as practised by ECNZ is not perfect,[1] it does seem to have had a major influence on the behaviour and motivation of managers who are subject to it. We believe it is the key mechanism for institutionalizing the major shift in culture that was achieved by the initial radical change in the organization. It is what has forced the change in management culture to be effective in changing performance. It is also likely to be a key mechanism for driving the cultural change deeper into the organization.

There is currently concern among senior managers about how deep into the organization the cultural change at ECNZ has penetrated. Cultural change at this point is uneven throughout the organization. Senior managers are aware of this. We were told that considerable thought is now being given to how a bonus scheme for staff can be designed. This may be particularly important, for example, for individuals engaged in the consulting operations of PowerDesignBuild, where continued viability and future success rests heavily on bringing in new business. However, one strongly inhibiting factor in the wider use of bonuses is the union membership held by many of the professional staff. ECNZ is understandably unwilling to include professionals who retain their union membership in performance bonus schemes.

There is a need for cultural change to be driven through to the lowest levels of the Corporation. One of the big policy issues now being addressed by top managers is how to accomplish this change and how much participation in decision making should be sought. For example, a team briefing system is being used in Production. This involves communication downwards, but limited communication upwards. The issue is to what extent the Corporation can get employees at 'the rock face' to participate through such methods as quality circles and/or by involving them in the writing of their own job specifications. The question is how to get the lowest levels of operating staff to make continual improvements in the way they perform their responsibilities. As John Fernyhough states:

---

1. As pointed out and discussed in Chapter 4, incentive contracting has penalties for not achieving targets but no rewards for exceeding them; a problem that is also present in the Corporation's return on equity objective.

It is a matter of educating your managers. It is a question of how you motivate people. It is question of how you organise them. It is a question of leadership. We have a long way to go. This is our biggest piece of unfinished business. We've knocked off the easy bits but there is so much more to do. It is a big organisation and you can get a heck of a lot more out of it in terms of efficiencies.

Relations with unions

The challenge of dealing with union issues remains a critical one for the Corporation. Union power in the electricity industry had traditionally been regarded as among the strongest in the country and change in this area has been difficult to achieve. Chapter 4 describes some of ECNZ's major successes in reducing union involvement in the management of the company. Two of these successes involved introduction of an enterprise approach to bargaining with separate agreements for each business unit (the first SOE to do so), and doing away with union restrictions on contracting out for services.

However, there is still concern over the extent and form of union involvement of staff. Although the Corporation was able to get freedom from union coverage for the top layers of management, they agreed to roll over the majority of existing conditions of employment for other staff. The Corporation is still struggling with the consequences of this. As pointed out above, one consequence has been to inhibit the development of bonus schemes lower in the organization.

This is one area which the Chairman of the Board states he would handle differently had he the opportunity to do it again. He now believes ECNZ should not have agreed to roll over the majority of existing conditions. Rather they should have accepted the potential costs of disruption that may have been provoked by the refusal to do so. One reason why this stand was not made was pressure of time. Another was because a cohesive senior management team was not yet in place, so that the Chairman and the Establishment Board were left to bear the brunt of this issue.

If there is a lesson to be drawn from this experience, it is the importance of having a cohesive, functioning management team in place before actual incorporation takes place. The timetable set by the Government for carrying out the reorganization was very short and this weakened the position of the Establishment Board in the initial and crucial negotiation with the unions. On the other hand, the tight timetable for completing the reorganization allowed the new organization to avoid capture of the new organization by the old management. If the Board had had more time, the probability of at least partial capture of the new organization by the old management would have been higher.

Electricorp also faces difficulties with external unions. As pointed out in Chapter 5, its contracting arms, PDB and EMEC, have experienced difficulty in competing for outside work because of disputes over the union coverage of Electricorp workers in the PSA.

A major change in Electricorp is that managers now attempt to communicate directly with workers rather than through their unions. The manager of EMEC believed that this had actually improved the relationships with workers, at least in his business unit:

I think the relationship between managers and staff is closer than it was before because we've said to managers, 'look, nobody is going to come in and manage your staff.' So they have developed the right sort of relationships and that has been beneficial.

Reflections on the SOE process based on the Electricorp experience

We turn now to commenting on the SOE process itself on the basis of what we have learned from studying the establishment and operation of Electricorp.

The importance of an appropriate governance framework

The SOE Act 1986 put into place the framework for change in the governance structure of the organization. The Act did this by defining the objectives of SOEs and their relationship to Government and by specifying a monitoring regime. The Act effectively removes an SOE from day-to-day political involvement and places it under the provisions of the Companies Act. Subsequently, the market for the bulk generation of electricity was deregulated and the organization's legislatively protected monopoly removed.

The basic ground rules are competitive neutrality, a charter to operate as a successful commercial business, managerial freedom to make decisions, and a framework for holding managers responsible and accountable for results by requiring a Statement of Corporate Intent and annual reporting.

In our view, the institutional change made possible by the SOE Act played the primary role in the sweeping changes in organization and management that we have described in preceding chapters. First, the possibility of making these massive changes was largely responsible for attracting high quality managers with private sector commercial experience to the organization. Second, the longer-run performance of ECNZ is critically dependent on the form of the new institutional arrangements and an ownership structure which separates ownership and control in much the same way as companies in the private sector.

(1) Recruitment of top managers

We found in our interviews of Board members and senior managers of ECNZ a lot of enthusiasm for the SOE process. This enthusiasm and the challenge of being involved in a major experiment with the ability to influence change played an important role in attracting high-calibre managers to ECNZ. The following quotations capture some of this enthusiasm for the challenge this change presented.

John Fernyhough, Board Chairman:

> When they asked me if I would go on the Board I said I would be interested if I was Chairman but not as an ordinary board member. I wasn't prepared to put in the effort unless I could have a major influence and actually see some results. I was fortunate in being financially independent so that I could take on this challenge.

Roderick Deane, Chief Executive:

> All through the process of creating the SOEs I'd said to my wife, the heads of Telecom and Electricity are going to be two of the most exciting jobs in the country for the

next few years. I was tempted by just the range of issues and the challenge of it. Also I was offered a competitive chief executive salary package but that factor was not overwhelming. The driving force at the end of the day was the challenge. That was why I took the job. I had a really strong wish to demonstrate that the SOE model I had been involved in getting into place could work.

Roger Kerr, Board Member:

I was interested in being involved because I had been quite close to the SOE-privatisation process. I saw a huge scope for improvement in performance through the deregulation of the electricity market, the movement of the organisation into an SOE form, and the eventual privatisation leg of the trip. Getting a major chunk of the economy, namely the electricity industry, running more efficiently fitted in with my prior activities at the Treasury and now at the Business Roundtable.

We asked Roger Kerr, who had been involved in the recruitment of top managers for the new organization, whether they would have been able to attract top-calibre businessmen to the organization had it remained as a government department. His answer was: 'No, not a dog's show!' As it was, they experienced some difficulties in the early days, particularly with the Chief Executive appointment.

(2) Long-run performance
The change in governance structure made possible by the SOE Act is important to the longer-term performance of ECNZ. Although it is probably true to say that government trading organizations can be made more efficient by the introduction of mechanisms borrowed from the private sector (e.g. appointing chief executives, measuring performance in terms of the delivery of outputs rather than inputs, and so forth), without a change in governance structure it would be difficult to have any confidence that performance improvements would last. As one Board member put it:

It is like Helen Clark [then Minister of Health] trying to run the hospitals now under the old kind of system. If you put enough energy into it for a time, fire a few people, put in budgetary disciplines, you'll get a bit more out of the system for a while but I don't think it would go far and I don't think it would last long.

The point is that gains could come from a concentration of effort but they would not be consolidated and institutionalized. Institutional arrangements of the sort allowed by the SOE process are fundamental to long-term change. Although good performance comes when there is a sense of enthusiasm and commitment to objectives, without a major change in governance structure it is likely that there will be a rapid reversion to old structures and practices when initial enthusiasm and commitment fades.

(3) Freedom from central control agencies of Government
As a consequence of incorporation, treasury and finance functions, which had been largely centrally controlled from the Treasury, became the responsibility of

the Corporation. Similarly, control over personnel and human resource issues involving pay rates and working conditions for staff was no longer handled through the State Services Commission but became the direct responsibility of the Corporation. These changes have profound effects on governance. The act of incorporation as an SOE places all necessary functions under the direct control of the Corporation. The Corporation has the clear and relatively unambiguous objective of operating as a commercially successful business operation.

These changes in governance structure are important to understanding the sweeping changes in organizational structure, management, personnel and operations in the new corporation. Martin Holden, who was Chief Accountant in NZED and is now Financial Controller in ECNZ, provided his thoughts on this matter to us in a letter:

> The creation of the SOE, appointment of the Board of Directors and appointment of a Chief Executive with business skills rather than engineering as his primary attribute changed the emphasis of the management of the business. Financial management is now uppermost in managers' minds because the commercial results are now the first measure of performance. This is not to say that cost containment overrules other considerations – they do not, but cost is a more integral part of the equation. In addition, pricing policy is set by Management, adhered to and not manipulated by Government.
>
> Within the Public Service there was a tendency to grow the organisation and within the Electricity Division there was a view that because we were a 24 hour, seven days a week, 365 day a year business, we needed immediate access to all types of facilities and therefore a very self contained business was created. The Electricity Division identified in the early 1980's that the need for depots, workshops and indeed some offices were debatable and possibly very costly but because of the environment at the time it was difficult to close them down. I am of the opinion that without the policy change – taking responsibility away from Ministers, Members of Parliament – the change could not have been made by officials.

Robustness of the SOE model of organization
Although the SOE Act provided a framework for change which had a major impact on the operation and performance of ECNZ, there is still serious concern about the robustness of this model in the longer run. In this context, it is interesting to consider the question of what we can learn about the 'robustness' of the SOE model by reflecting on the ECNZ experience and reporting on some of the concerns of the managers of this SOE.

There are a number of reasons given for concern about the long-term prospects for an organization under Government ownership.

(1) Problems associated with a lack of tradeable equity
The fact that SOEs have no tradeable equity reduces the pool of available managers, weakens incentives, and attenuates the effectiveness of monitoring the organization. One story we were told involved a search by ECNZ for a general manager for one of the business units, using a world-wide executive search firm. They were unable to recruit one particularly attractive candidate because he wanted part of

his remuneration to be equity-related and tied to movements in share value. Since ECNZ was unable to offer him that option, he walked away from the job. Although such an anecdote does not provide evidence that the pool of available managers was seriously depleted, the story does suggest that SOEs such as ECNZ have less flexibility in the type of compensation packages that they can offer prospective senior executives. SOEs are clearly at a disadvantage in competing for managers for whom the inclusion of an equity-related component tied to share value is important. Interestingly, the SOE Act allows for the issuance of equity bonds. To our knowledge these have not yet been utilized.

Similarly, the SOE monitoring process, in general, is not as strong as the monitoring that takes place in capital markets where there is tradeable equity. The problem lies in the leverage that the monitors have over the SOEs. Although accountability is now tighter with the annual budgetary process, the requirements for Statements of Corporate Intent, and the annual reporting introduced by the SOE Act, the monitoring capability of Government is still weak. Politicians as shareholders are subject to the vagaries of the political process and, over the long run, have only weak incentives to bring sustained commercial rigour to the monitoring process. Investors have direct property rights in dividends and the market value of the equity they hold. Shareholding Ministers who hold political office do not. Also, the resources that the Treasury makes available for carrying out the monitoring function are relatively small relative to those of the private sector for a corporation of ECNZ's size.

ECNZ, however, does compete in domestic and international markets for substantial amounts of unsecured debt financing. As noted in Chapter 5, this debt has been rated jointly by Standard & Poor's and Moody's. ECNZ's debt is typically held by large investors such as banks and financial institutions. It is traded and there are market prices which can be observed. The incentives are clear for large investors with interests in ECNZ debt to closely monitor the financial stability and performance of the Corporation. However, with no tradeable equity there is no threat of takeover.

(2) Political vulnerability
Even though there is a view that the monitoring capability of Government is weak, there is still concern over the extent to which SOEs such as ECNZ remain vulnerable to politically motivated interference from politicians and government officials. The concern is over the implications of changes in government with institutions which are essentially creatures of the political process. Although the present Shareholding Ministers are viewed as being remarkably restrained in interfering with the day-to-day operation of the company, there is concern that public sector bodies like ECNZ will, sooner or later, be subject to political interference.

An example of the hands-off policy of the present Government is the manner in which ECNZ was able to drive down the price it paid for coal. In fact, ECNZ's Board Chairman expressed some surprise that the Government maintained a hands-off policy throughout:

The change in coal contracting had huge benefits to the company. The amazing thing was that the Labour Government at the time allowed us to do it. Miners were put out of work because we screwed the heck out of our main costs.

One aspect of political vulnerability has to do with the contestability of advice to Ministers. The formation of an SOE with a Board and a Chief Executive provides another avenue for advice to flow to Shareholding Ministers in addition to the traditional route through Treasury officials. One concern expressed to us was that Treasury officials are in a position to cut SOEs out of the information and decision flows on important decisions which affect the future structure and operation of the SOE.

The continued vulnerability of this form of organization to political and bureaucratic processes of government is the major weakness of the SOE model. One risk is that it could result in the loss of the managerial expertise which has been crucial to the commercial success of the organization. A Board member put this danger to us as follows:

> I've got a long fuse by comparison with some New Zealand businessmen. Some of the nonsense you get out of the political system. Most businessmen haven't got those kinds of fuses. They get bloody frustrated when they find the Government wobbling or interfering. I would guess that if the Board Chairman judges we are starting to get blocked in respect of further developments he sees as important in the Corporation he's got other things he'd rather go off and do.

One aspect of political vulnerability, however, has positive effects on the behaviour of a dominant firm such as ECNZ. This has to do with the Corporation's vulnerability to regulation. Because ECNZ has an extremely dominant position in the market for electricity, we were told, top managers are concerned that they do nothing that could be interpreted as unreasonable because of the danger of provoking price regulation. Their view is that unless they are pricing as if they have another competitor out there ready to turn on the switch on a new power station, ECNZ could conceivably attract the attention of the Commerce Commission and raise the risk of being price regulated. John Fernyhough makes this point as follows:

> Unless we can be confident that what we are doing will stand up to robust scrutiny and price on that basis then what we are doing is just extracting monopoly rents. We'd be proving everyone who says we are just a dirty monopoly, exactly right and we'll end up price regulated. That is the last thing we want.

Although such a comment may be understandably met with scepticism, it is consistent with what can be inferred from a careful analysis of ECNZ's pricing behaviour to date, statements made to us in interviews, and our review of internal documents related to pricing strategy. ECNZ is a highly visible entity which is subject to continued scrutiny from a variety of sources including major industrial users, electricity supply authorities, the press, and other groups. ECNZ managers say they recognize this and understand that it makes the organization vulnerable to political regulation.

There is no doubt that ECNZ has market power, but there are also limits on how it can wield this power. These limits are determined not only by the threat of competition in generation and competition from substitute fuels, but also by the power of major customers to refuse to play ECNZ's game. As discussed in Chapters 3 and 5, ECNZ managers have been genuinely concerned about the threat of entry into electricity generation and have priced to forestall new entry into generation. The inability of ECNZ to effectively discipline Auckland Electric Power Board's refusal to agree to a price increase since 1989 seems to have convinced ECNZ's new managers that there are practical limits to their market power. The ultimate sanction of cutting off the supply of electricity to their single biggest retail customer is simply not an option when they have no other source of supply.

(3) Political constraints

As profit-making entities, SOEs are still subject to political constraints on their range of operations. Of particular concern to the Government are changes in risk caused by SOEs moving into new areas of operations. For example, in ECNZ's case, taking large equity positions in the construction of power stations offshore, or backwards integration into exploration for fuels, could conceivably change the risk profile of the Corporation.

Private sector companies also subject themselves to constraints on the range of operations they undertake (e.g. Fletcher Challenge is currently rationalizing its activities to a defined core of operations). What is different is that these boundaries are established by the firm itself for strategic and commercial reasons and are not mandated by an outside organization. Present Government policy of restricting the diversification of SOEs is not incompatible with ECNZ's present policy of 'sticking to the knitting'. However, in the longer term, being continually subject to external political constraints raises the risk that some potentially profitable opportunities and ventures may be passed by.

Weaknesses in the SOE form provide the SOE Boards and managers with a powerful drive towards full privatization. These weaknesses arise from the lack of tradeable equity, continued political vulnerability, and political constraints. Operating as an SOE certainly provides more autonomy and freedom of action than is possible as a government department. However, the Government still remains as the owner or residual claimant. Given the nature and vagaries of the political process as governments come and go, there remains the possibility of interventions that are motivated by fiscal pressures or political ideology rather than commercial objectives. Privatization in this context is seen as a way of preserving efficiency gains from future dissipation by politicians and government bureaucrats.

Performance appraisal and the SOE Act

Section 4(1) of the SOE Act requires (among other things) each SOE to be 'profitable'. The contracting between the SOE and the Crown is through the

Statement of Corporate Intent, the details of which are specified in Section 14(2) of the Act. These include information about gearing (in the form of shareholders funds/total assets), accounting policies, dividend payout, an estimate of the commercial value of the Crown's investment in the group, and targets and other measures by which the performance of the group may be judged.

The nature of the 'performance targets and other measures' is not specified in the Act. In our view this is appropriate. It gives the opportunity for relevant measures to be developed through the contracting process. In ECNZ's case, the following aggregate financial measures have been employed:

(1) Increase the value of the shareholder's investment at a rate similar to the increase in the market value of comparable large private sector companies.
(2) Net profit after interest, tax and preference dividend to average ordinary shareholder's funds.
(3) Profit before interest and tax to average net funds employed.

Apart from the obvious issues of what are the sanctions for underperforming, and what are the incentives to overperform, there is another set of issues that arise in attempting to apply these performance measures in the SOE setting. Some of these comments will also apply to SOEs other than ECNZ.

As indicated in Chapter 7, performance indicator target (1) above is problematical for the following reasons. First, although we appreciate that the principal objective of the SOE Act is that SOEs should be 'as profitable and efficient as comparable businesses that are not owned by the Crown', it is not clear to us how those comparable businesses are to be selected. It seems critical that the issue of risk be *explicitly* factored in to the assessment process. To illustrate: our perspective is that ECNZ is less risky than the average New Zealand business, primarily because it has highly predictable earnings. This point was recognized by the Advisory Board (for the establishment of ECNZ) in its Preliminary Report:

> . . . The Electricity Corporation should seek to achieve a return on investment, equivalent to the norm in the New Zealand corporate sector on a risk adjusted basis . . . The Corporation should have a somewhat lower profitability target than the average for the sector.

Second, ECNZ's increase in the value of shareholder's investment, particularly if measured by book value, will be constrained by the high dividend payout. ECNZ's payout is contracted at 75% of profits available to the ordinary shareholder. The average for listed companies has been around 40%, although this may increase under a dividend imputation taxation regime.

Finally, while investors *expect* the market value of comparable large private sector companies to increase, and while they also expect the increase in market value to be greater for low payout than for high payout companies (having controlled for risk and other relevant valuation parameters), it is clear that market values sometimes fall.

For these reasons performance target (1) is not operational in that it cannot be used for retrospective evaluation. This is not to deny its use in a predictive setting, since it aligns ECNZ's objectives with appropriate value-maximizing behaviour, but for this purpose a much simpler statement might be appropriate. The problem would be alleviated, perhaps even eliminated, if the SOEs were to issue equity bonds.

The second and third measures are both fairly conventional 'return' measures, with (2) being a return on ordinary equity (ROE) and (3) being a pre-tax return on net funds, defined by ECNZ as total assets less current liabilities (or shareholder's funds plus term debt). This is similar to the ROA (return on assets) measure used in Chapter 7. Both are extremely common assessment measures. The following discussion is designed to highlight some difficulties with their use, without suggesting that the measures themselves are inappropriate.

First, it is clear that the targets have to be interpreted with a clear understanding of the accounting principles being used. Section 14(2)(d) of the SOE Act requires that the accounting policies be included in the Statement of Corporate Intent. This is indeed critical. Presumably such a legislative provision would not stop an SOE from changing policies, but such a change is much more likely to occur before the year starts, rather than after it has finished. Hence the ability of managers to use accounting principles in an opportunistic way to 'reach their targets' is constrained.

Second, once again the return measures must be set (and assessed) conditional on the risk involved. Third, one way of reaching an ROE type of target is to use debt to finance asset expansion, as long as the return on the assets is greater than the interest cost. Such an investment may not be value-increasing, yet it would improve reported ROE. This could be done opportunistically. Having contracted for a particular ROE through the Statement of Corporate Intent, the probability that the ROE could be reached would be increased by the 'excessive' use of debt finance, provided at least some investment opportunities were available. This is precisely why it is so important to factor risk into the analysis, and also why it is so important to include a leverage measure in the Statement of Corporate Intent, as required by Section 14(2) of the Act. We hasten to add that there is no evidence of any such behaviour at ECNZ. Indeed, given excess capacity, ECNZ's investment opportunities are severely constrained currently.

Third, with regard to the ROE measure, we must look at the impact of dividend imputation tax. New Zealand adopted a dividend imputation system as from 1 April 1988. Prior to that date the tax system treated dividends under a regime commonly referred to as the classical tax system, under which the income of a company is taxed twice: first, in the company tax return at the corporate tax rate, and subsequently, upon the payment of dividends, in the shareholder's tax return at the shareholder's tax rate.

The basic principle of the imputation system is that corporate profits should be taxed only once and at the rate of tax applicable to the shareholders. Corporations continue to pay tax on their taxable income and at the corporate tax rate. However, as dividends are paid from after-tax dollars an imputation credit equal to the corporate tax paid on the pre-tax income is passed to the shareholder. The result of the imputation system is that the 'tax' at corporate level is effectively a personal withholding tax. The effective tax payable on receipt of a dividend fully covered by imputation credits is the extent to which the personal rate exceeds the corporate rate.

The imputation system adopted here applies to dividends paid by New Zealand resident companies. Resident individual shareholders receiving dividends are allowed an imputation credit for tax paid at the corporate level. Currently in New Zealand both the individual and corporate tax rates are 33 percent, so the marginal rate on fully imputed dividends is nil at worst, and negative for shareholders whose marginal income tax rate is less than 33 percent. New Zealand resident companies that receive dividends covered by imputation credits are not taxed on the dividends and the credits can be passed through to their shareholders.

Dividend imputation has potentially profound implications for the financing and investing decisions of corporations in New Zealand. Under the classical (double) taxation system, there was a tax shield benefit of debt arising from the tax deductibility of the interest expense. For most companies under the dividend imputation system, there is no tax-induced incentive for debt as opposed to equity. Under the classical taxation system there was a tax disadvantage to paying dividends. For most companies the optimal dividend policy under imputation will be an increase in the level of dividends paid.

There is one implication of dividend imputation of New Zealand companies with New Zealand resident shareholders that is very compelling. Companies normally endeavour to manage their tax liabilities so as to minimize the tax paid and to delay the timing of the payment of tax. The optimal management of their tax will generally necessitate incurring costs. Under the classical tax system, this can be a value-creating effort for the company and its shareholders. However, dividend imputation alters the incentives and value-creating alternatives available through management of tax at the company level.

The critical distinction is whether the level of dividend being paid is in excess of what can be fully covered with imputation credits. To the extent that dividends paid exceed imputation credits, a tax liability is incurred by the shareholder. Clearly there may be activities that a company might undertake which reduce company tax, hence increase ROE, but which generate a tax liability for the shareholders. This is not a value-increasing activity. Indeed, to the extent that a company incurs costs to reduce taxable profit (without affecting reported accounting profit), the activity destroys value.

We note the obvious point that the Crown, as ECNZ's shareholder, does not pay tax, and any tax-reducing activities of ECNZ might be regarded as not being in the Crown's interest. However, we would argue that appropriate financial management principles applied to the ECNZ situation require decision making inside ECNZ to be carried out as if its shareholders are New Zealand resident taxpayers. Judging from material we have read (for example a discussion of an appropriate hurdle rate, given dividend imputation tax), this is precisely the way ECNZ management views its task.

If the investment appraisal techniques are appropriately applied in a post-imputation tax world, then problems associated with the possibility of undertaking value-reducing investments should be alleviated. However, we still have a general concern that an emphasis on ROE, that is an after tax measure, might result in SOEs undertaking certain 'tax-reducing' activities that are not value-increasing. ROE might well be increased, but to the extent that these activities are costly, value is lost. In the private sector this loss of value would find its way into share prices. Indeed most leading firms of share market analysts regularly report imputation credits available and adjust dividend yield and price earnings ratios for imputation credits. Hence the monitoring of returns in after-tax (personal tax) form is much more explicit and focused than it is for the SOEs.

We note that for ECNZ there is also a return requirement expressed in pre-tax form. However this measure is also taken before interest, and managing interest expense is crucial in assessing ECNZ's performance.

We also note that the Audit Office, in a recent report on Statements of Corporate Intent, has recommended both an after-tax ROE, and a pre-tax ROA, in that order.

It is far from clear to us how analysts reviewing ECNZ's performance would weigh the two return measures. One approach to address the concern raised here might be for the SOEs to report, or the Treasury analysts to compute, an equivalent imputation credit account. Once again an issue of equity bonds might reduce this problem, as market prices of an equity instrument would be observable and would presumably reflect these tax considerations.

Measurement issues

The formation of the SOEs involved the establishment of an initial valuation which in many cases bore no resemblance to the previous accounting values reflecting the situation in the government departments. As indicated in Table 7.1, Panel F, the initial value of the assets taken over by ECNZ was put at a figure approximately $2b greater than the book value at 31 March 1987 in NZED's accounts. New accounting policies and estimates were also introduced by ECNZ: shorter asset lives, capitalization of some interest costs, and foreign currency accounting.

The evaluation of performance of these organizations from pre-corporatization government department though to SOE may depend critically on the procedures used to control for these changes. In this project we have attempted to create an as if situation − reporting adjusted ECNZ numbers as if the assets, etc., were still held by NZED. We have also introduced a measure called ROCI, Return On Crown's Investment, which was possible in this case because of the ease of identifying New Zealand Government debt on NZED's balance sheet. We have also supported the financial evaluation with some non-financial measures. However, at the end of the day, the financial measures must prevail as the efficacy of investment must be evaluated using 'return' measures. As indicated at the outset of this study, the non-financial measures are used primarily to control for quality degradation, and to supplement the financial analysis.

Appendices

Contents

Appendix A

The Task Force on Electricity Corporation Organization Structure and Transitions in Organization Structure from NZED to ECNZ

Prior to the formation of ECNZ on 1 April 1987, the Establishment Board set up a small task force made up of several consultants from the firm of W. D. Scott Deloitte Limited and several carefully selected members of the Electricity Division. Their charge, as it is stated in the *Task Force Report*, was to review the major reorganization structure the Electricity Division was then putting into place and to inject more commercial objectives into the Division. The stated Board objective in setting up the Task Force was to confirm that the structure and associated staffing being put into place was appropriate for the deregulated industry structure in which the new Corporation was to operate. Actually, the real charge to the Task Force was more sweeping. They were, in fact, instructed to start afresh to design a new structure for the organization without reference to the restructuring which was already underway. The reasons for this difference between the stated and real charge to the Task Force are discussed in detail in Chapter 8.

The *Task Force Report* is the key document to read to understand the initial design of the new Electricity Corporation and the reasons for particular organizational mechanisms and devices that were chosen to establish responsibilities, accountabilities and incentives in the new management structure.

Prior to 1986, as part of the Ministry of Energy the basic structure of the Electricity Division was:

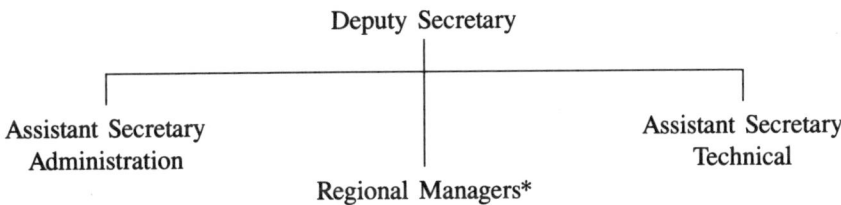

Deputy Secretary

Assistant Secretary Administration

Regional Managers*

Assistant Secretary Technical

* Regional Managers reported directly to the Deputy Secretary

There were a number of problems with this structure. They included: (1) a lack of accountability mechanisms; (2) inadequate management information systems; (3) inadequate management control and decision making; (4) an inability to identify specific production costs and the needs of business; (5) lack of an environment which encouraged efficient commercial behaviour; (6) lack of a management resource with a strong commercial bias; (7) constraints imposed by Treasury instructions; (8) lack of autonomy for managing staff (staff employed by the State Services Commission); and (9) methods by which capital budgeting programmes were developed and approved by the Government.

In 1985 the Division proposed a reorganization of its structure to respond to some of these criticisms and problems. The objective of this reorganization was to put in place a structure that would (1) reflect the change in emphasis that was taking place in the Division's operations away from the development of new generating plant to the operation of existing plant, and (2) adopt a more commercial approach to the management of the Division. The basic structure proposed was as follows:

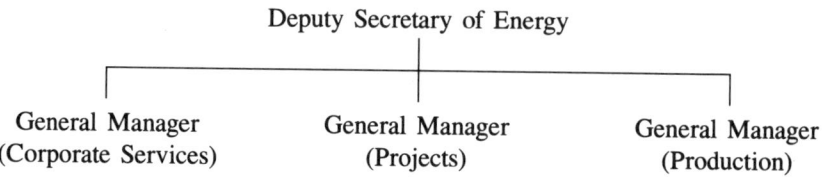

Even though the transition to this new structure was two-thirds complete at the time the Establishment Board was appointed to ECNZ, the Task Force considered it to be deficient in a number of ways for the new Corporation. For example, (1) some functions were missing or poorly performed, including marketing, treasury, personnel and industrial relations, financial management, and corporate planning; (2) the organization structure was considered too centralized and lacked clear delineation of separate business units; (3) Projects (which had responsibility for design and construction) was emphasized as a key business activity when the major need of the new Corporation was to optimize the efficient operation of existing plant; (4) staff numbers were increasing without offsetting increases in the effectiveness of output; (5) there was little incentive in the structure to optimize sales or make improvements in cost effectiveness or efficiency; and (6) there were too many levels of management.

The Task Force believed that major improvements could be made to the operation and management of the organization by the introduction of commercial management principles and concepts in general use in profit-oriented companies. Basic management principles and concepts used to guide the design of the new Corporation were as follows:

(1) The organization structure should facilitate the achievement of objectives and the implementation of strategies by concentrating management attention on key activities.

(2) Performance accountability and associated decision making should be delegated to managers that are as close to the operations concerned as possible. Managers should have access to resources critical to performance.

(3) Accountability must be to individuals not committees.

(4) Managers should have a manageable number of subordinates.

(5) The structure should be sufficiently flexible to provide for future developments.

(6) The design of the organization should allow for the development of management skills.

These management principles led the Task Force to several conclusions that proved to be very important to the design of the new Corporation:

(1) It was desirable to organize around clear, relatively discrete and small business units in the total organization.

(2) Whenever possible business units should be organized as profit centres because profit responsibility was seen as an effective motivator, allowing for easier measurement of performance and effective delegation of responsibility with controls kept to a minimum.

(3) Contracting out should be investigated for handling peaks of work or activities and for routine activities to encourage the growth of internal productivity.

(4) Internal and external competition should be encouraged to drive down costs. This would include competition between internal units doing similar work to keep costs down and competition externally to put pressure on internal costs.

The basic organization structure that emerged from the work of the Task Force is given in Figure 3.4 and the associated discussion. One of the main intentions of the Task Force was to create an organization structure that would provide for some internal competition yet was well positioned to respond to and encourage external competition. The Report states:

> The fundamental philosophy behind the structure is that it creates separate business units that not only are able to compete internally but also allow a significant level of exposure to external competition. (p. 69)

Appendix B

Electricity Corporation of New Zealand Ltd

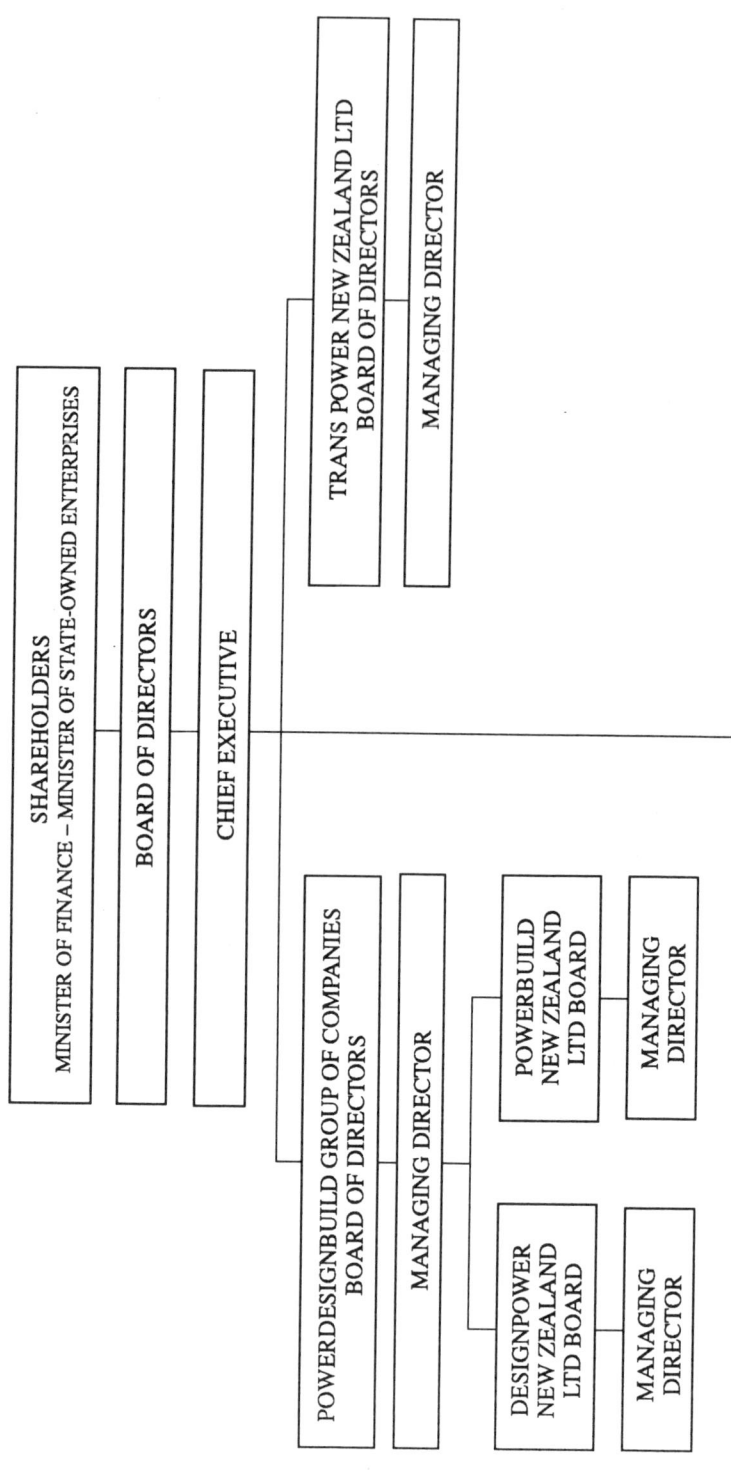

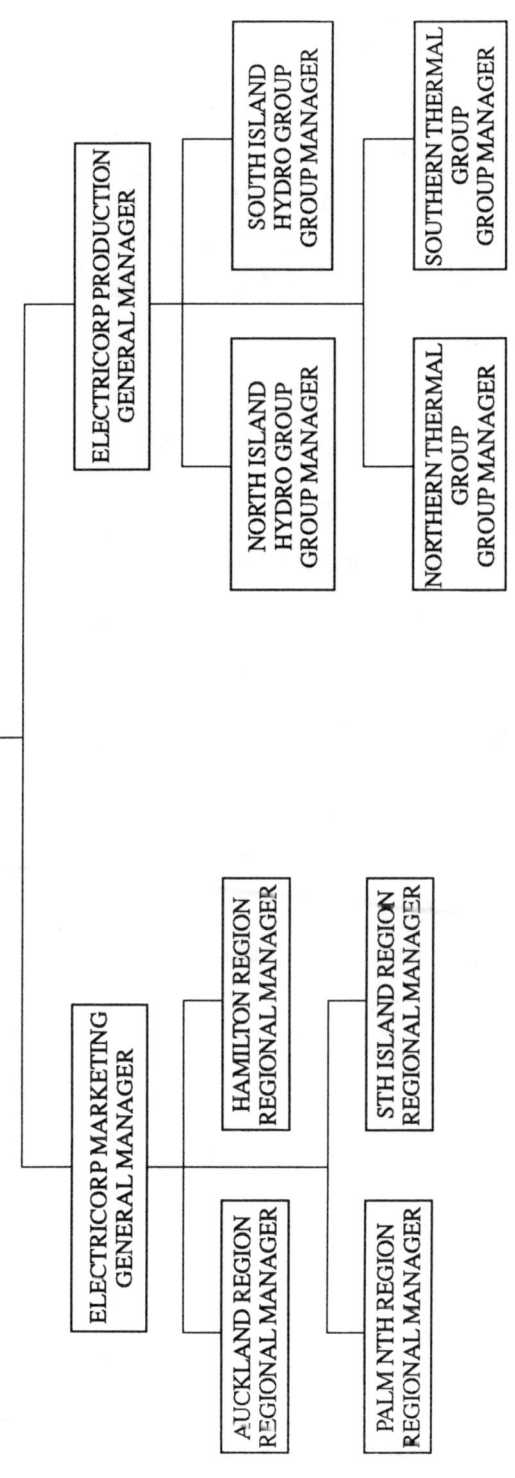

Appendix C

Financial Performance Data

Description of adjustments made to published accounts of NZED and ECNZ

(1) NZED accounts 1980–1987

These adjustments fall into three categories:

(1) Retail Distribution expenses which relate to SEPS were added back to profit.

(2) Extraordinary items relating to Marsden A (1981–1986) were eliminated by adding them back to profit.

(3) Prior Year items which had been included in the General Reserve Account were reclassified under Interest and Operating Expenses. These related to realignment of currencies and the writing off of abandoned projects and suspensory loans.

(2) ECNZ accounts 1988–1990

These adjustments fall into two categories:

(1) Interest relating to capital work in progress is capitalized in the ECNZ accounts but had previously been expensed in the NZED accounts. To obtain comparability, therefore, capitalized interest has been eliminated from the fixed assets of ECNZ and expensed.

(2) The increase in asset valuation when ECNZ was created has been eliminated by reducing the fixed assets and shareholders' funds balances. Details are given in Table 7.1, Panel F. The effect of this is to reduce depreciation expense, relative to that reported in ECNZ's accounts, for 1988–1990.

The rates of depreciation used by ECNZ differ from those used by NZED. All ECNZ's depreciation items have been restated using NZED's rates. The effect of this has also been to reduce depreciation expense, relative to that reported in ECNZ's accounts, for 1988–1990.

Details of the difference in depreciation methods are given in the table opposite.

Comparative Depreciation Methods: NZED with ECNZ

Asset Description	ECNZ	NZED
Geothermal Stations	4% SL	3⅓% SL*
Fuel Stations	4% SL	2½% SL*
Hydro Stations: Civil	1% SL	1% SL*
Electrical	4% SL	1% SL*
Transmission Lines	2% SL	1% SL*
Plant	10% SL	10% DV
Light Vehicles	20% SL	20% DV
Heavy Vehicles	10% SL	20% DV
Loose Tools	15% SL	20% DV
Machine Tools	8% SL	20% DV
Furniture	10% SL	25% DV
Office Machines	20% SL	25% DV
EDP Equipment	20% SL	25% DV

Key
SL: Straight Line
DV: Diminishing Value

* Plus 4% of the Provision for Depreciation Account balance at the end of the previous financial year.

Table 7.1 Financial data based on adjusted time series
Panel A: Profit and loss statements 1980–1990

	1980	1981	1982	1983	1984	1985	1986	1987	1988	1989	1990
Sales of Electricity	472,907	535,748	597,758	711,069	759,872	827,064	1,032,676	1,209,832	1,317,172	1,433,947	1,513,207
Operating Expenses											
Fuel	25,377	32,324	40,373	83,824	78,823	97,180	140,893	135,600	147,000	134,115	150,000
Other Generation (1)	38,125	41,728	54,907	62,926	74,749	83,924	132,544	139,445	185,065	379,420	345,930
	63,502	74,052	95,280	146,750	153,572	181,104	273,437	275,045	332,065	513,535	495,930
Transmission (1)	19,976	25,133	31,821	43,371	35,266	37,504	43,713	55,545	58,000		
Administration (1)	28,758	35,405	45,775	53,205	58,733	59,152	72,100	106,304	133,033		
Adjustments (2)			4,163	1,158						3,742	4,778
Expenses before Depn	112,236	134,590	177,039	244,484	247,571	277,760	389,250	436,894	523,098	517,277	500,708
OPERATING EARNINGS	360,671	401,158	420,719	466,585	512,301	549,304	643,426	772,938	794,074	916,670	1,012,499
Depreciation (3)	38,812	41,622	42,215	45,076	61,662	72,422	80,657	90,601	95,823	108,313	116,095
EARNINGS BEFORE INTEREST & TAXES	321,859	359,536	378,504	421,509	450,639	476,882	562,769	682,337	698,251	808,357	896,404
Interest (4)	198,646	201,316	217,466	236,331	231,830	270,690	334,410	327,207	574,615	414,528	391,108
PROFIT BEFORE TAX	123,213	158,220	161,038	185,178	218,809	206,192	228,359	355,130	123,636	393,829	505,296
Other Income	1,609	4,933	4,550	3,899	2,567	3,471	4,401	6,976	8,491	21,334	19,157
NET PROFIT BEFORE TAX	124,822	163,153	165,588	189,077	221,376	209,663	232,760	362,106	132,127	415,163	524,453

These figures are from the published accounts of ECNZ and NZED and include the adjustments outlined at the start of this appendix.

Notes
1 It was not possible to obtain a breakdown of operating expenses into Other Generation, Transmission, and Other Expenses for 1989 and 1990. Therefore, figures for Other Generation in 1989 and 1990 of 379,420 and 345,930 are total figures for all three categories and do not compare with the figures for 1980 to 1988.
2 These adjustments relate to prior year adjustments which were included in retained profits in the accounts of NZED.
3 Depreciation has been recalculated for the period 1988 to 1990 using the rates of NZED and excluding the revaluation in 1987.
4 Interest has been adjusted in 1988 to 1990 to include interest capitalized in the ECNZ accounts in order to obtain comparability with NZED.

Table 7.1 Panel B: Balance sheet 1980–1990

	1980	1981	1982	1983	1984	1985	1986	1987	1988	1989	1990
Fixed Assets	2,767,785	3,014,472	3,287,092	3,577,237	3,860,512	4,092,015	4,326,674	4,589,525	6,406,371	6,764,625	7,172,502
Less Revaluation (1)									(1,410,475)	(1,410,475)	(1,410,475)
Interest (1)									(99,843)	(194,520)	(272,928)
	2,767,785	3,014,472	3,287,092	3,577,237	3,860,512	4,092,015	4,326,674	4,589,525	4,896,053	5,159,630	5,489,099
Less Depreciation (2)	382,316	425,640	470,342	518,348	583,036	658,564	732,978	823,375	919,198	1,027,511	1,142,332
	2,385,469	2,588,832	2,816,750	3,058,889	3,277,476	3,433,451	3,593,696	3,766,150	3,976,855	4,132,119	4,346,767
Current Assets											
Stocks	68,538	71,319	81,803	92,938	136,183	156,673	162,604	180,073	167,042	141,572	145,915
Debtors/Prepaid	96,736	110,707	128,636	153,585	163,159	174,013	207,862	252,456	317,580	201,114	231,224
Bank	4,087	8,315	9,479	5,900	4,542	5,581	676	9,031		2,259	228
	169,361	190,341	219,918	252,423	303,884	336,267	371,142	441,560	484,622	344,945	377,367
Current Liabilities											
Creditors	22,313	20,124	24,088	40,428	24,207	30,820	43,680	85,473	165,276	217,362	297,044
Proposed Dividends								42,000	48,000	148,797	255,615
	22,313	20,124	24,088	40,428	24,207	30,820	43,680	127,473	213,276	366,159	552,659
Working Capital	147,048	170,217	195,830	211,995	279,677	305,447	327,462	314,087	271,346	(21,214)	(175,292)
Loans/coal contracts					5,227	20,706	41,967	83,682			
	2,532,517	2,759,049	3,012,580	3,270,884	3,562,380	3,759,604	3,963,125	4,163,919	4,248,201	4,110,905	4,171,475
Shareholders Funds (3)	268,661	426,794	587,176	770,483	985,755	1,188,752	1,428,265	1,596,569	1,035,359	1,043,027	1,136,085
Deferred Tax									54,918	142,286	210,458
Financing											
Crown Liability	2,083,019	2,150,718	2,259,066	2,353,420	2,464,706	2,452,719	2,457,343	2,487,239	2,811,000	2,765,512	500,000
Term Liabilities	180,836	181,537	166,337	146,981	111,923	128,136	106,308	80,113		160,080	2,031,791
Short Term Loans/Deposits	0	0	0	0	0	(10,000)	(28,788)	0	346,924		293,141
	2,263,855	2,332,255	2,425,403	2,500,401	2,576,629	2,570,855	2,534,863	2,567,352	3,157,924	2,925,592	2,824,932
	2,532,516	2,759,049	3,012,579	3,270,884	3,562,384	3,759,607	3,963,128	4,163,921	4,248,201	4,110,905	4,171,475

Notes

1 These adjustments were made to eliminate the revaluation and capitalized interest as outlined at the start of this appendix.

2 Accumulated depreciation for 1988 to 1990 has been adjusted by the balance brought forward from NZED.

3 The Revaluation of Fixed Assets and accumulated depreciation have been deducted from the share premium account for 1988 to 1990.

Table 7.1 Panel C: Common sized profit and loss statements 1980 – 1990

	1980	1981	1982	1983	1984	1985	1986	1987	1988	1989	1990
Sales of Electricity	100%	100%	100%	100%	100%	100%	100%	100%	100%	100%	100%
Operating Expenses											
Fuel	5%	6%	7%	12%	10%	12%	14%	11%	11%	9%	10%
Other Generation (1)	8%	8%	9%	9%	10%	10%	13%	12%	14%	26%	23%
	13%	14%	16%	21%	20%	22%	26%	23%	25%	36%	33%
Transmission (1)	4%	5%	5%	6%	5%	5%	4%	5%	4%	0%	0%
Other (1)	6%	7%	8%	7%	8%	7%	7%	9%	10%	0%	0%
Adjustments	0%	0%	1%	0%	0%	0%	0%	0%	0%	0%	0%
Expenses before Dep	24%	25%	30%	34%	33%	34%	38%	36%	40%	36%	33%
OPERATING EARNINGS	76%	75%	70%	66%	67%	66%	62%	64%	60%	64%	67%
Depreciation	8%	8%	7%	6%	8%	9%	8%	7%	7%	8%	8%
EARNINGS BEFORE INTEREST & TAXES	68%	67%	63%	59%	59%	58%	54%	56%	53%	56%	59%
Interest	42%	38%	36%	33%	31%	33%	32%	27%	44%	29%	26%
PROFIT BEFORE TAX	26%	30%	27%	26%	29%	25%	22%	29%	9%	27%	33%
Other Income	0%	1%	1%	1%	0%	0%	0%	1%	1%	1%	1%
NET PROFIT BEFORE TAX	26%	30%	28%	27%	29%	25%	23%	30%	10%	29%	35%

This table shows each item as a percentage of Sales.

Notes
1 The percentages for 1989 and 1990 do not compare to the percentages for 1980 to 1988 for the reasons outlined in Table 7.1 Panel A.

Table 7.1 Panel D: Ratio analysis 1980 – 1990

	1980	1981	1982	1983	1984	1985	1986	1987	1988	1989	1990
SALES	472,907	535,748	597,758	711,069	759,872	827,064	1,032,676	1,209,832	1,317,172	1,433,947	1,513,207
EBIT	321,859	359,536	378,504	421,509	450,639	476,882	562,769	682,337	698,251	808,357	896,404
NPBT	124,822	163,153	165,588	189,077	221,376	209,663	232,760	362,106	132,127	415,163	524,453
ASSETS	2,554,830	2,779,173	3,036,668	3,311,312	3,586,587	3,790,424	4,006,805	4,291,392	4,461,477	4,477,064	4,724,134
SHAREHOLDERS' FUNDS	268,661	426,794	587,176	770,483	985,755	1,188,752	1,428,265	1,596,569	1,035,359	1,043,027	1,136,085
NPBT/EBIT	39%	45%	44%	45%	49%	44%	41%	53%	19%	51%	59%
EBIT/SALES	68%	67%	63%	59%	59%	58%	54%	56%	53%	56%	59%
SALES/ASSETS	19%	19%	20%	21%	21%	22%	26%	28%	30%	32%	32%
ASSETS/SHF	951%	651%	517%	430%	364%	319%	281%	269%	431%	429%	416%
EBIT/ASSETS	13%	13%	12%	13%	13%	13%	14%	16%	16%	18%	19%
NPBT/SHF	46%	38%	28%	25%	22%	18%	16%	23%	13%	40%	46%

This table summarizes the information contained in Table 7.1 Panels A and B and includes the adjustments outlined at the start of this appendix.

Notes

	1980	1981	1982	1983	1984	1985	1986	1987	1988	1989	1990
Fixed Assets	2,385,469	2,588,832	2,816,750	3,058,889	3,277,476	3,433,451	3,593,696	3,766,150	3,976,855	4,132,119	4,346,767
Current Assets	169,361	190,341	219,918	252,423	303,884	336,267	371,142	441,560	484,622	344,945	377,367
Loans/Coal Contracts					5,227	20,706	41,967	83,682			
Assets	2,554,830	2,779,173	3,036,668	3,311,312	3,586,587	3,790,424	4,006,805	4,291,392	4,461,477	4,477,064	4,724,134

Table 7.1 Panel E: Operating ratios in cents per kWh 1980–1990

	1980	1981	1982	1983	1984	1985	1986	1987	1988	1989	1990
Sales Volume in GWh	19,040	19,833	20,365	20,651	23,214	23,923	24,241	25,187	25,772	26,436	27,374
Sales per kWh	2.48	2.70	2.94	3.44	3.27	3.46	4.26	4.80	5.11	5.42	5.53
Op Exps per kWh	0.59	0.68	0.87	1.18	1.07	1.16	1.61	1.73	2.03	1.96	1.83
Op Earnings per kWh	1.89	2.02	2.07	2.26	2.21	2.30	2.65	3.07	3.08	3.47	3.70
EBIT per kWh	1.69	1.81	1.86	2.04	1.94	1.99	2.32	2.71	2.71	3.06	3.27
NPBT per kWh	0.66	0.82	0.81	0.92	0.95	0.88	0.96	1.44	0.51	1.57	1.92

Operating ratios in $000s per employee 1980–1990

	1980	1981	1982	1983	1984	1985	1986	1987	1988	1989	1990
Number of Employees	5,416	5,598	5,705	5,760	5,858	5,895	6,076	5,999	4,403	4,100	3,913
Sales per employee	87.32	95.70	104.78	123.45	129.72	140.30	169.96	201.67	299.15	349.74	386.71
Op Exps per employee	20.72	24.04	31.03	42.45	42.26	47.12	64.06	72.83	118.80	126.17	127.96
Op Earnings by employee	66.59	71.66	73.75	81.00	87.45	93.18	105.90	128.84	180.35	223.58	258.75
EBIT per employee	59.43	64.23	66.35	73.18	76.93	80.90	92.62	113.74	158.59	197.16	229.08
NPBT per employee	23.05	29.14	29.03	32.83	37.79	35.57	38.31	60.36	30.01	101.26	134.03
kWh per employee	3.52	3.54	3.57	3.59	3.96	4.06	3.99	4.20	5.85	6.45	7.00

These ratios are calculated using the information contained in Table 7.1 Panels A and B, and include the adjustments outlined at the start of this appendix. Information on the number of employees and Sales Volume was obtained from ECNZ and the annual accounts.

Table 7.1 Panel F: Reconciliation of asset revaluation at 31 March 1987

	($000) 31 March 87	($000) 1 April 87
Fixed Assets at Cost	4,589,525	6,000,000
Depreciation	823,375	
	3,766,150	
Current Assets	441,560	300,000
	4,207,710	
Loans for Local Hydro Schemes	43,711	
Coal Contracts	39,971	
	4,291,392	6,300,000
Net Change	2,008,608	
Asset Revaluation	6,000,000	
Fixed Assets	3,766,150	
	2,233,850	
Comprising:		
Increase in Cost	1,410,475	
Reduction in Accounts Depn	823,375	
	2,233,850	
Increase in Fixed Assets	2,233,850	
Decrease in:		
Current Assets	(141,560)	
Loans	(43,711)	
Coal Contracts	(39,971)	
	$2,008,608	

Table 7.2 Time series to calculate return on Crown investment

	1980	1981	1982	1983	1984	1985	1986	1987	1988	1989	1990
SALES	472,907	535,748	597,758	711,069	759,872	827,064	1,032,676	1,209,832	1,317,172	1,433,947	1,513,207
EBIT	321,859	359,536	378,504	421,509	450,639	476,882	562,769	682,337	698,251	808,357	896,404
NPBT (*)	298,955	349,839	364,941	405,879	453,888	453,952	588,564	719,144	132,127	415,163	524,453
ASSETS	2,554,830	2,779,173	3,036,668	3,311,312	3,586,587	3,790,424	4,006,805	4,291,392	4,461,477	4,477,064	4,724,134
SHAREHOLDERS' FUNDS (*)	2,351,680	2,577,512	2,846,242	3,123,903	3,450,461	3,641,471	3,885,608	4,083,809	1,035,359	1,043,027	1,136,085
NPBT/EBIT	93%	97%	96%	96%	101%	95%	105%	105%	19%	51%	59%
EBIT/SALES	68%	67%	63%	59%	59%	58%	54%	56%	53%	56%	59%
SALES/ASSETS	19%	19%	20%	21%	21%	22%	26%	28%	30%	32%	32%
ASSETS/SHF(*)	109%	108%	107%	106%	104%	104%	103%	105%	431%	429%	416%
EBIT/ASSETS	13%	13%	12%	13%	13%	13%	14%	16%	16%	18%	19%
NPBT(*)/SHF(*)	13%	14%	13%	13%	13%	12%	15%	18%	13%	40%	46%

This table is similar to Table 7.1 Panel D except that interest on the Crown loan account has been added back to Net Profit Before Tax (NPBT) and the Crown loan account has been included in Shareholders' Funds for the period 1980 to 1987. (These items are marked with an asterisk.) This has been done to show the total return and investment by the Crown in NZED.

Notes

	1980	1981	1982	1983	1984	1985	1986	1987	1988	1989	1990
Fixed Assets	2,385,469	2,588,832	2,816,750	3,058,889	3,277,476	3,433,451	3,593,696	3,766,150	3,976,855	4,132,119	4,346,767
Current Assets	169,361	190,341	219,918	252,423	303,884	336,267	371,142	441,560	484,622	344,945	377,367
Loans/Coal Contracts					5,227	20,706	41,967	83,682			
Assets	2,554,830	2,779,173	3,036,668	3,311,312	3,586,587	3,790,424	4,006,805	4,291,392	4,461,477	4,477,064	4,724,134

Table 7.3 Time series restated in $March 1987 units of purchasing power
Panel A: Profit and loss statements 1980–1990, restated in $March 1987

	1980	1981	1982	1983	1984	1985	1986	1987	1988	1989	1990
Sales of Electricity	1,198,640	1,168,659	1,128,218	1,157,393	1,184,024	1,191,064	1,284,427	1,312,202	1,263,019	1,307,071	1,287,027
Operating Expenses											
Fuel	64,321	70,510	76,201	136,439	122,821	139,950	175,241	147,074	140,956	122,248	127,579
Other Generation (1)	96,632	91,024	103,632	102,423	116,473	120,860	164,856	151,244	177,456	324,673	277,254
Transmission (1)	160,953	161,534	179,833	238,362	239,294	260,810	340,097	298,318	318,413	446,921	404,833
Administration (1)	50,632	54,824	60,059	70,594	54,951	54,010	54,370	60,245	55,615	3,411	4,064
Adjustments (2)	58,444	60,867	70,349	66,027	78,019	73,803	74,680	98,467	103,458		
			7,857	1,885							
Expenses before Depn	270,029	277,225	318,098	377,368	372,264	388,623	469,147	457,030	477,486	450,332	408,897
OPERATING EARNINGS (3)	928,610	891,433	810,120	780,025	811,760	802,442	815,280	855,172	785,533	856,738	878,130
Depreciation	307,099	325,527	335,325	314,941	315,349	305,164	289,910	284,238	270,605	259,543	218,900
EARNINGS BEFORE INTEREST & TAXES	621,512	565,907	474,796	465,084	496,411	497,278	525,371	570,934	514,929	597,195	659,230
Interest (4)	503,492	439,142	410,449	384,671	361,235	389,824	415,934	354,894	550,991	377,850	332,649
PROFIT BEFORE TAX	118,020	126,764	64,347	80,412	135,176	107,454	109,436	216,040	(36,062)	219,344	326,581
Other Income	4,078	10,761	8,588	6,346	4,000	4,999	5,474	7,566	8,142	19,446	16,294
NET PROFIT BEFORE TAX	122,098	137,525	72,935	85,758	139,176	112,453	114,910	223,606	(27,920)	238,790	342,875

This table shows the figures in Table 7.1 Panel A restated in $March 1987 purchasing power using the Consumer Price Index. March 1987 was chosen as it was at this date that NZED became ECNZ.

Notes

1 It was not possible to obtain a breakdown of operating expenses into Other Generation, Transmission and Other Expenses for 1989 and 1990. Therefore, figures for Other Generation in 1989 and 1990 of 324,673 and 277,254 are total figures for all three categories and do not compare with the figures for 1980 to 1988.

2 These adjustments relate to prior year adjustments which were included in retained profits in the accounts of NZED.

3 Depreciation has been recalculated for the period 1988 to 1990 using the rates of NZED and excluding the revaluation in 1987.

4 Interest has been adjusted in 1988 to 1990 to include interest capitalized in the ECNZ accounts in order to obtain comparability with NZED.

Table 7.3 Panel B: Common sized profit and loss statements 1980 – 1990, restated in $March 1987

	1980	1981	1982	1983	1984	1985	1986	1987	1988	1989	1990
Sales of Electricity	100%	100%	100%	100%	100%	100%	100%	100%	100%	100%	100%
Operating Expenses											
Fuel	5%	6%	7%	12%	10%	12%	14%	11%	11%	9%	10%
Other Generation	8%	8%	9%	9%	10%	10%	13%	12%	14%	25%	22%
	13%	14%	16%	21%	20%	22%	26%	23%	25%	34%	31%
Transmission	4%	5%	5%	6%	5%	5%	4%	5%	4%	0%	0%
Other	5%	5%	6%	6%	7%	6%	6%	8%	8%	0%	0%
Adjs	0%	0%	1%	0%	0%	0%	0%	0%	0%	0%	0%
Expenses before Depn	23%	24%	28%	33%	31%	33%	37%	35%	38%	34%	32%
OPERATING EARNINGS	77%	76%	72%	67%	69%	67%	63%	65%	62%	66%	68%
Depreciation	26%	28%	30%	27%	27%	26%	23%	22%	21%	20%	17%
EARNINGS BEFORE INTEREST & TAXES	52%	48%	42%	40%	42%	42%	41%	44%	41%	46%	51%
Interest	42%	38%	36%	33%	31%	33%	32%	27%	44%	29%	26%
PROFIT BEFORE TAX	10%	11%	6%	7%	11%	9%	9%	16%	-3%	17%	25%
Other Income	0%	1%	1%	1%	0%	0%	0%	1%	1%	1%	1%
NET PROFIT BEFORE TAX	10%	12%	6%	7%	12%	9%	9%	17%	-2%	18%	27%

This table shows each item as a percentage of Sales.

Notes
1 The percentages for 1989 and 1990 do not compare to the percentages for 1980 to 1988 for the reasons outlined in Table 7.3 Panel A.

Table 7.3 Panel C: Operating ratios in cents per kWh 1980 – 1990, restated in $March 1987

	1980	1981	1982	1983	1984	1985	1986	1987	1988	1989	1990
Sales Volume in GWh	19,040	19,833	20,365	20,651	23,214	23,923	24,241	25,187	25,772	26,436	27,374
Sales per kWh	6.30	5.89	5.54	5.50	5.10	4.98	5.30	5.21	4.90	4.94	4.70
Op Exps per kWh	1.42	1.40	1.56	1.83	1.60	1.62	1.94	1.81	1.85	1.70	1.49
Op Earnings per kWh	4.88	4.49	3.98	3.78	3.50	3.35	3.36	3.40	3.05	3.24	3.21
EBIT per kWh	3.26	2.85	2.33	2.25	2.14	2.08	2.17	2.27	2.00	2.26	2.41
NPBT per kWh	0.64	0.69	0.36	0.42	0.60	0.47	0.47	0.89	-0.11	0.90	1.25

Operating ratios in $000s per employee 1980 – 1990, restated in $March 1987

	1980	1981	1982	1983	1984	1985	1986	1987	1988	1989	1990
Number of Employees	5,416	5,598	5,705	5,760	5,858	5,895	6,076	5,999	4,403	4,100	3,913
Sales per employee	221.31	208.76	197.76	200.94	202.12	202.05	211.39	218.74	286.85	318.80	328.91
Op Exps per employee	49.52	49.52	55.76	65.52	63.55	65.92	77.21	76.18	108.45	109.84	104.50
Op Earnings by employee	171.46	159.24	142.00	135.42	138.57	136.12	134.18	142.55	178.41	208.96	224.41
EBIT per employee	114.75	101.09	83.22	80.74	84.74	84.36	86.47	95.17	116.95	145.66	168.47
NPBT per employee	22.54	24.57	12.78	15.06	23.76	19.08	18.91	37.27	-6.34	58.24	87.62
kWh per employee	3.52	3.54	3.57	3.59	3.96	4.06	3.99	4.20	5.85	6.45	7.00

These ratios are calculated using the information contained in Table 7.3 Panel A and include the adjustments outlined at the start of this appendix. Information on the number of employees and Sales Volume was obtained from ECNZ and the annual accounts.

Table 7.4 ECNZ data 1988 – 1990

Panel A: Summary financial statement information — ECNZ Annual Reports 1988 – 1990

	1988	1989	1990
Income	1,325,663	1,455,281	1,532,364
Expenses,excluding finance costs	654,757	639,619	702,727
Profit before finance and taxation	670,906	815,662	829,637
Net finance costs (1) (See opposite page)	474,772	323,261	312,700
Profit before taxation	196,134	492,401	516,937
Taxation	54,918	139,305	177,780
Profit after taxation	141,216	353,096	339,157
Extraordinary loss	0	21,393	0
Profit less taxation and extraord. loss	141,216	331,703	339,157
Preference dividend	48,000	48,000	48,000
Profit available to ordinary shareholder	93,216	283,703	291,157
Profit (excl. extraord. item) to ord. s/h	93,216	305,096	291,157
Current Assets	571,704	804,000	387,205
Fixed Assets	6,274,712	6,507,214	6,714,346
Total Assets	6,846,416	7,311,214	7,101,551
Current Liabilities	1,458,282	1,985,294	1,355,638
Term Liabilities	2,000,000	1,765,512	2,031,791
Deferred Taxation	54,918	142,286	210,458
Total Liabilities	3,513,200	3,893,092	3,597,887
Ordinary Shareholders Funds	2,533,216	2,618,122	2,703,664
Preference Shareholders Funds	800,000	800,000	800,000
Shareholders Funds	3,333,216	3,418,122	3,503,664
Liabilities and Shareholders Funds	6,846,416	7,311,214	7,101,551

Table 7.4 Panel B: Summary financial statement ratios — ECNZ Annual Reports 1988–1990

	1988	1989	1990
RETURN ON ASSETS, EBIT/ASSETS (1)	9.80%	11.16%	11.68%
RETURN ON SHAREHOLDERS' FUNDS,			
PRE TAX (1)	5.88%	14.41%	14.75%
RETURN ON SHAREHOLDERS' FUNDS,			
AFTER TAX (2)	4.24%	10.33%	9.68%
RETURN ON ORDINARY			
SHAREHOLDERS' FUNDS (3)	3.68%	11.65%	10.77%
RETURN ON NET FUNDS, EBIT/NF (3)(4)	12.45%	15.31%	14.44%

Notes
1 Measurements used for NZED and ECNZ comparisons.
2 Measurements used for comparisons with other corporations.
3 Contracting measures from the Statement of Corporate Intent.
4 Net Funds (NF) is measured as Total Assets less Current Liabilities.

Notes to Panel A
1 Net Finance Costs (See Panel A)

Loan Interest　Crown	601,000	372,437	205,376
Other	4,867	135,026	325,816
Gross Finance Costs	605,867	507,463	531,192
Less Interest Capitalized	99,843	94,677	78,408
Less Investment Income	506,024	412,786	452,784
Interest on Government Stock	0	11,331	13,308
Interest on Other Investments	31,252	78,194	126,776
Net Finance Costs	474,772	323,261	312,700

Figure 7.1   Ratio of net profit before tax to earnings before interest and taxes

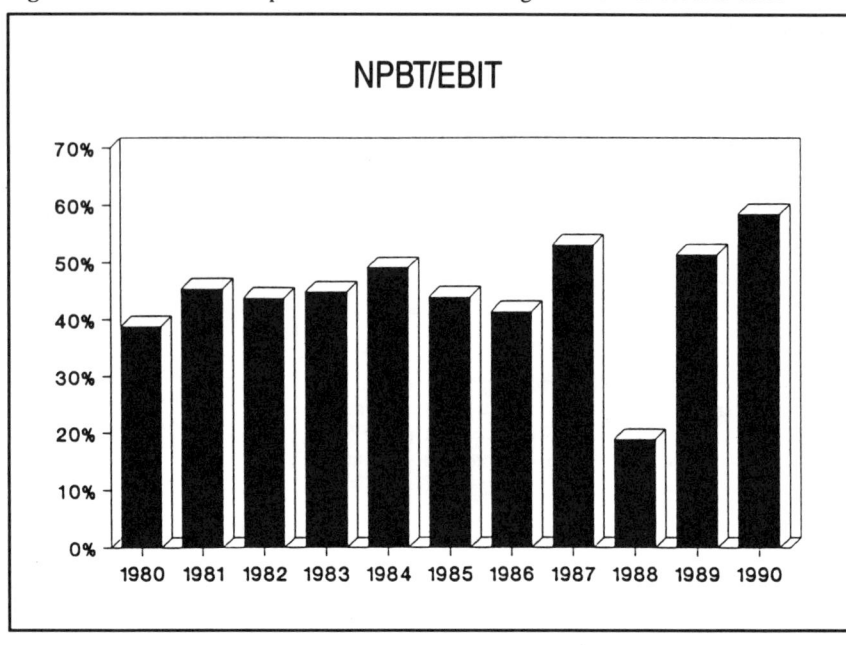

Figure 7.2   Ratio of earnings before interest and taxes to sales

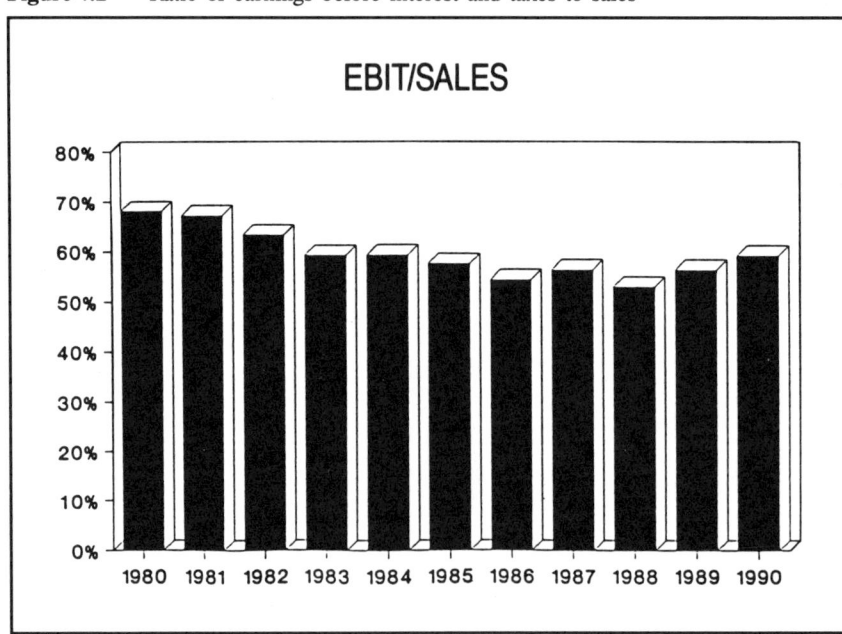

Figure 7.3 Ratio of sales to assets

Figure 7.4 Ratio of earnings before interest and taxes to assets

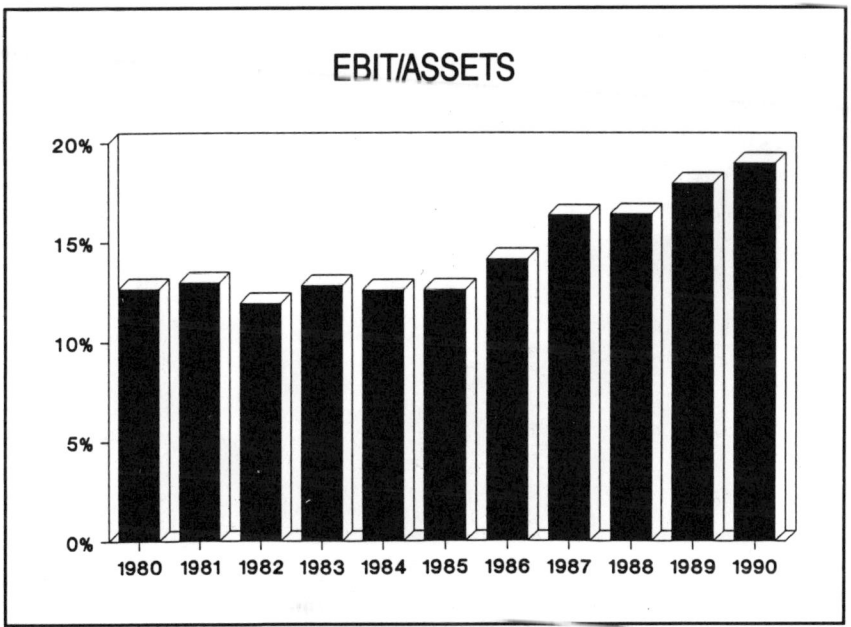

Figure 7.5 Ratio of assets to shareholders' funds

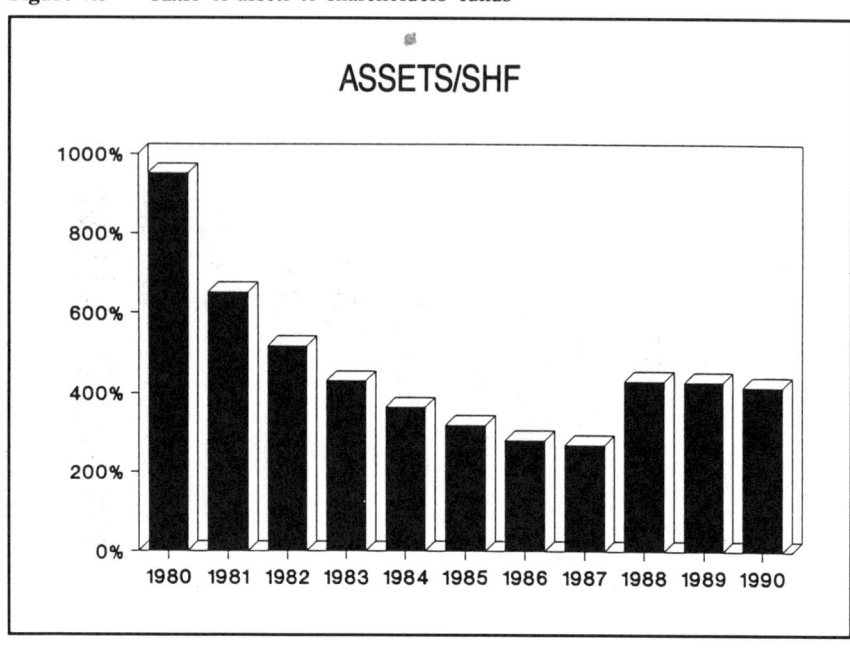

Figure 7.6 Ratio of net profit before tax to shareholders' funds

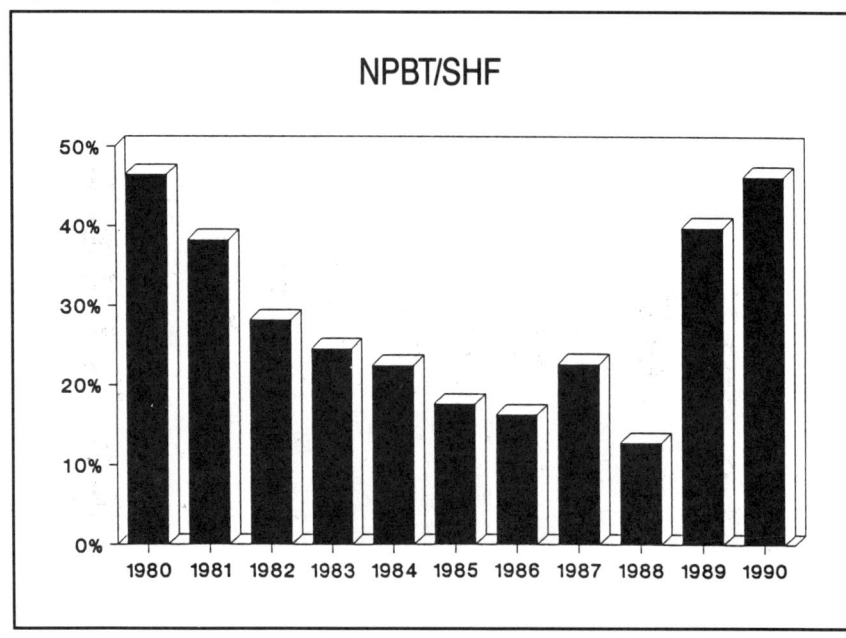

Figure 7.7   Ratio of net profit before tax to Crown investment

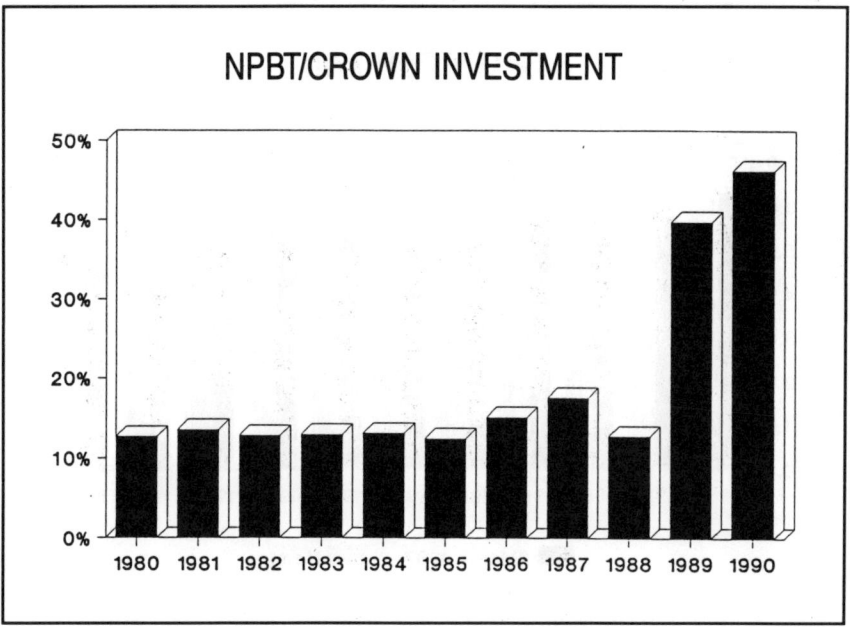

Figure 7.8

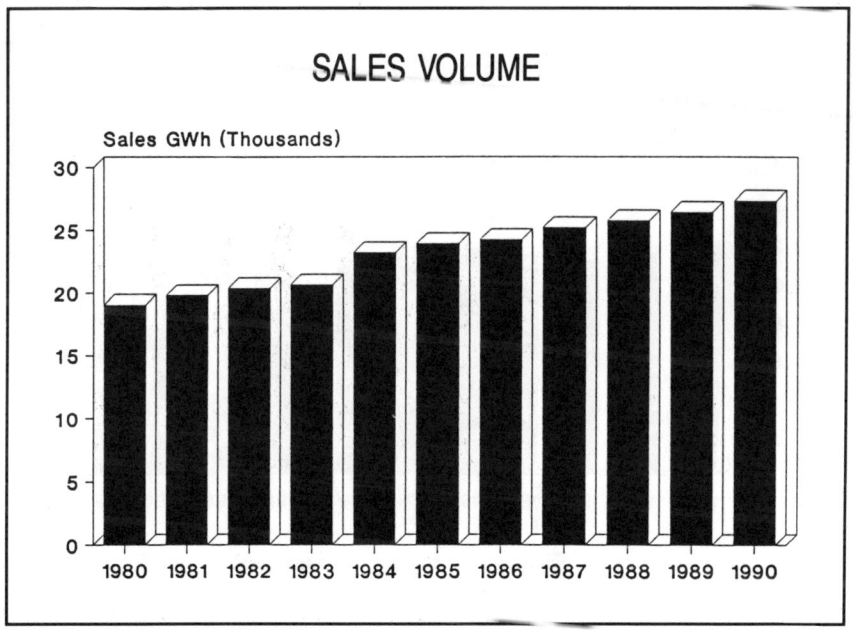

Figure 7.9

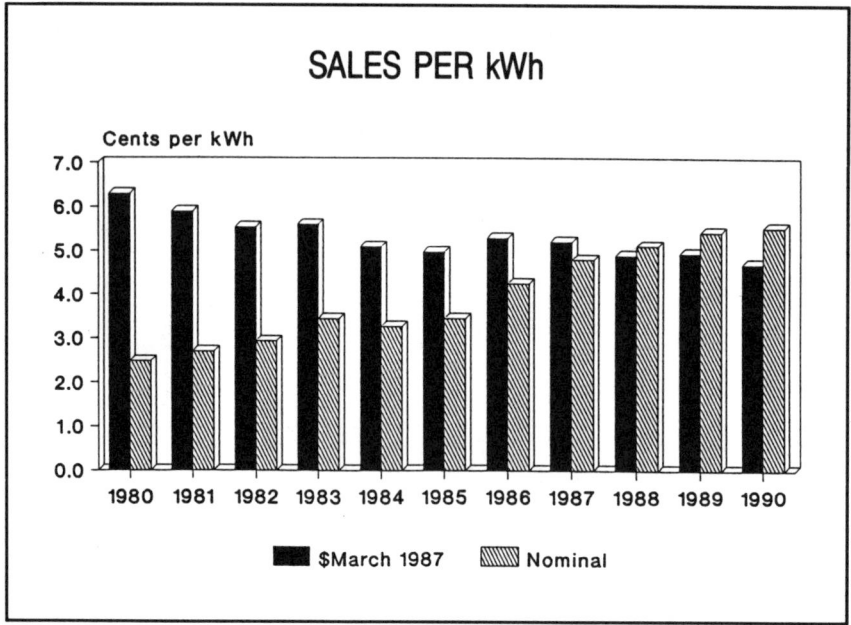

Figure 7.10

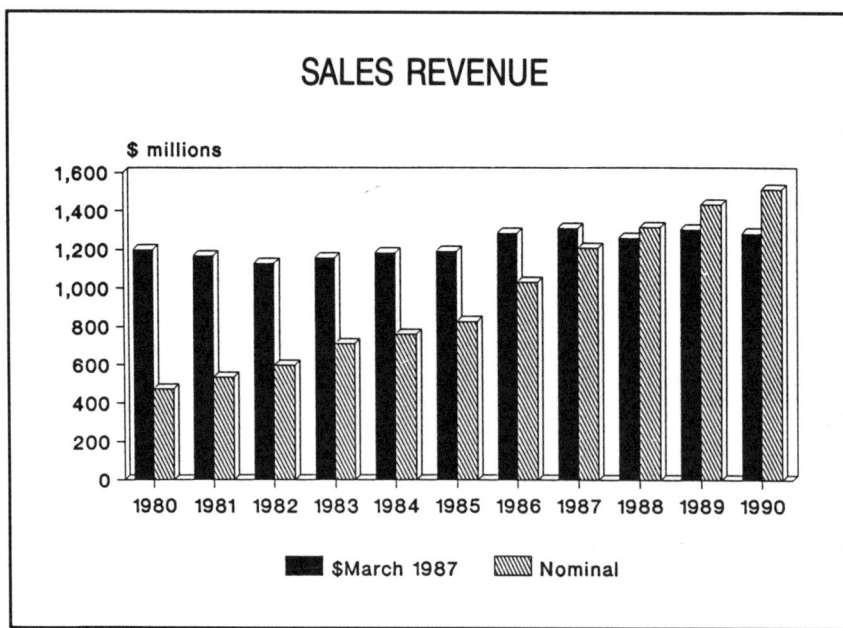

Figure 7.11

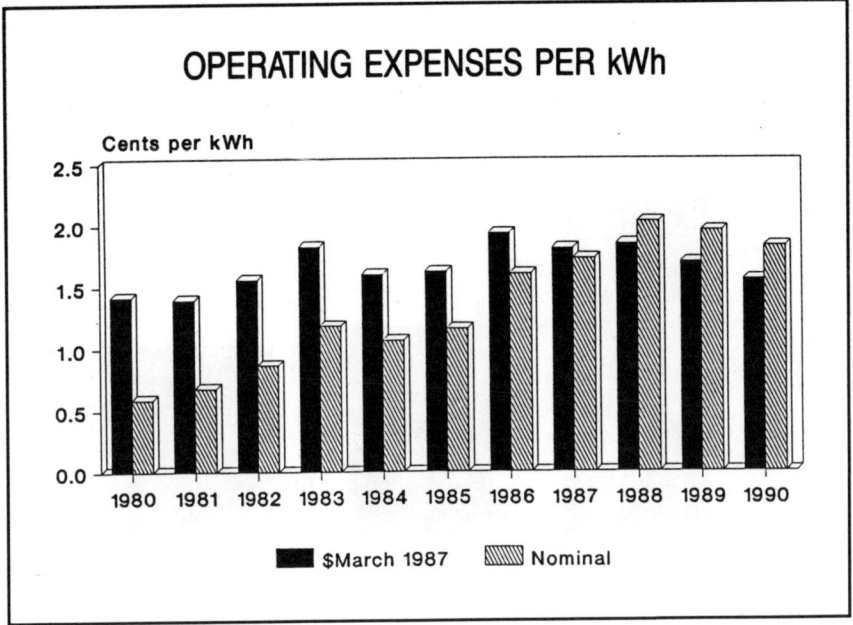

Figure 7.12

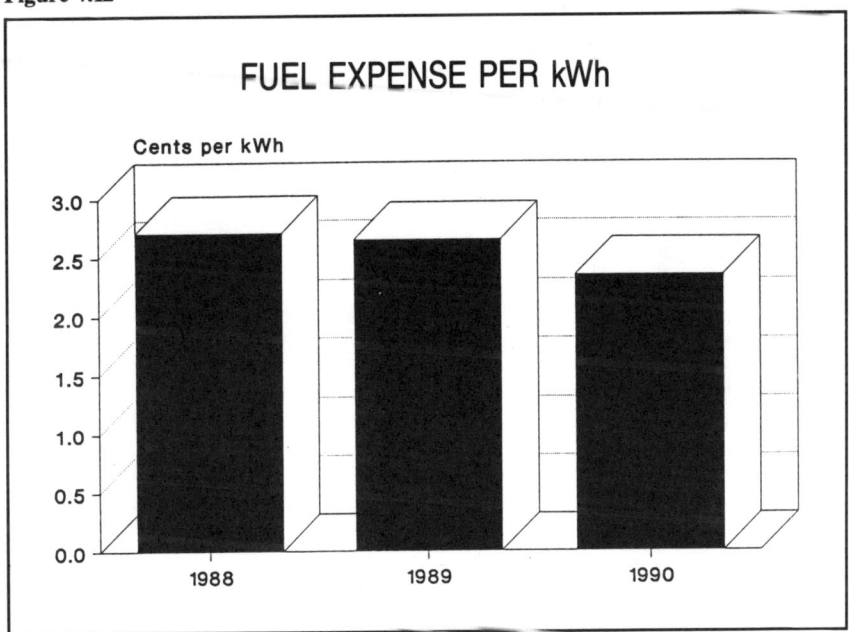

Figure 7.13

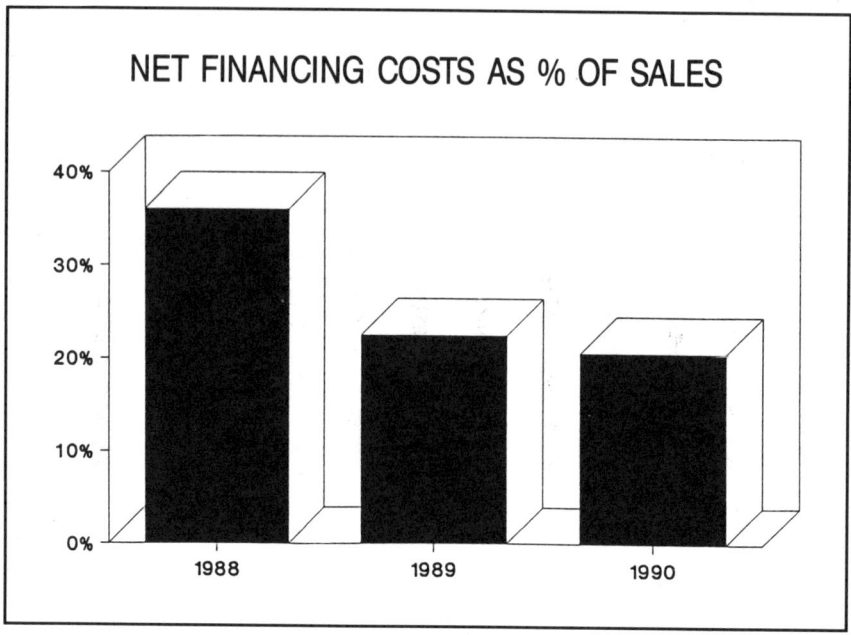

Figure 7.14

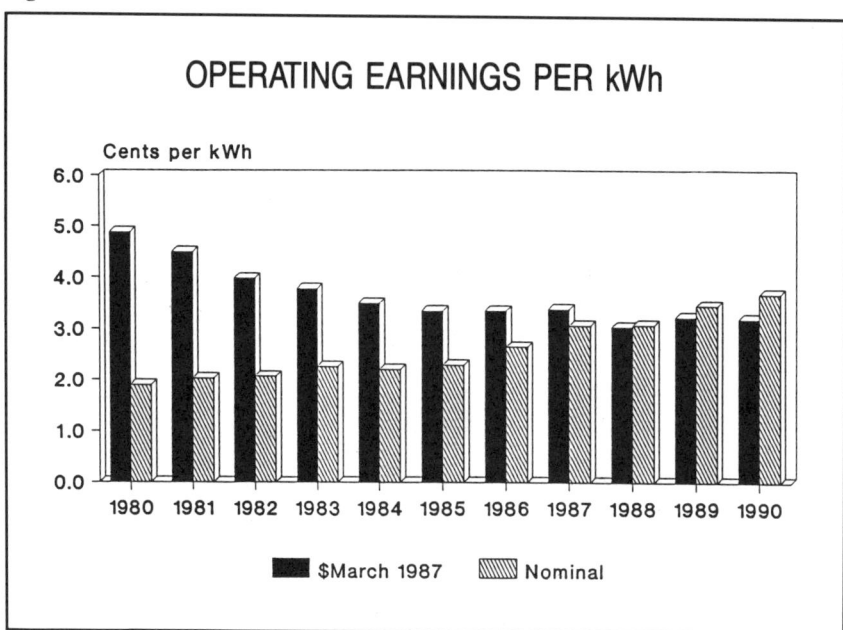

Figure 7.15   Earnings before interest and taxes per kWh

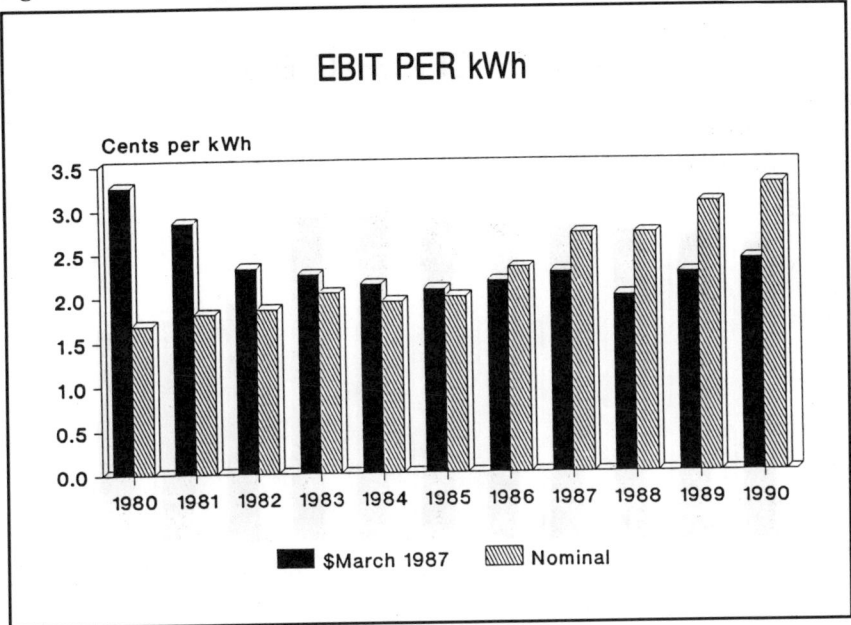

Figure 7.16

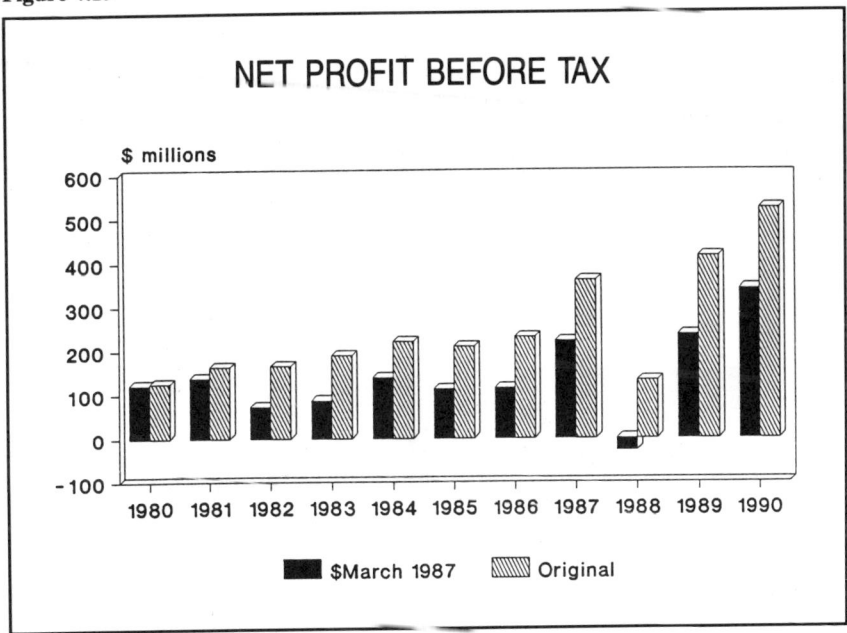

Figure 7.17

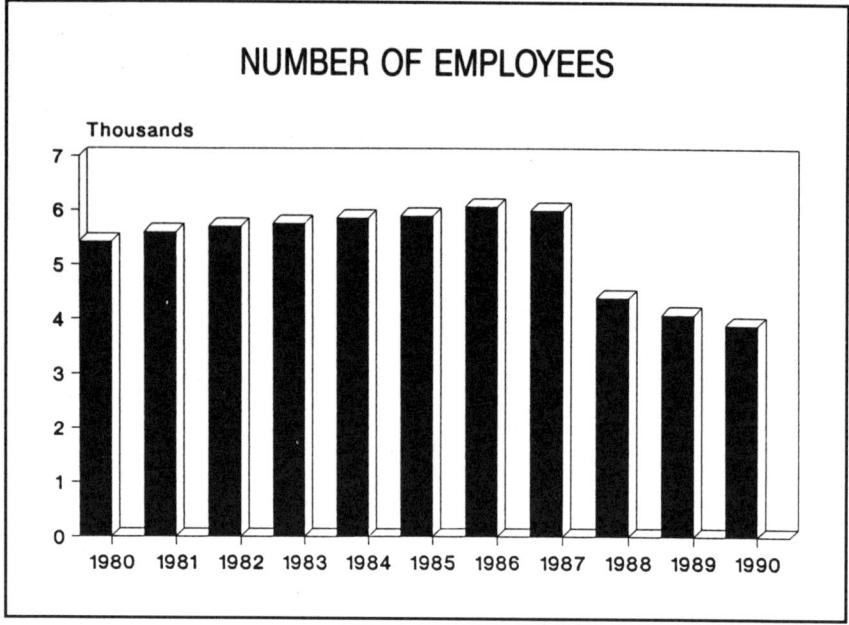

Figure 7.18

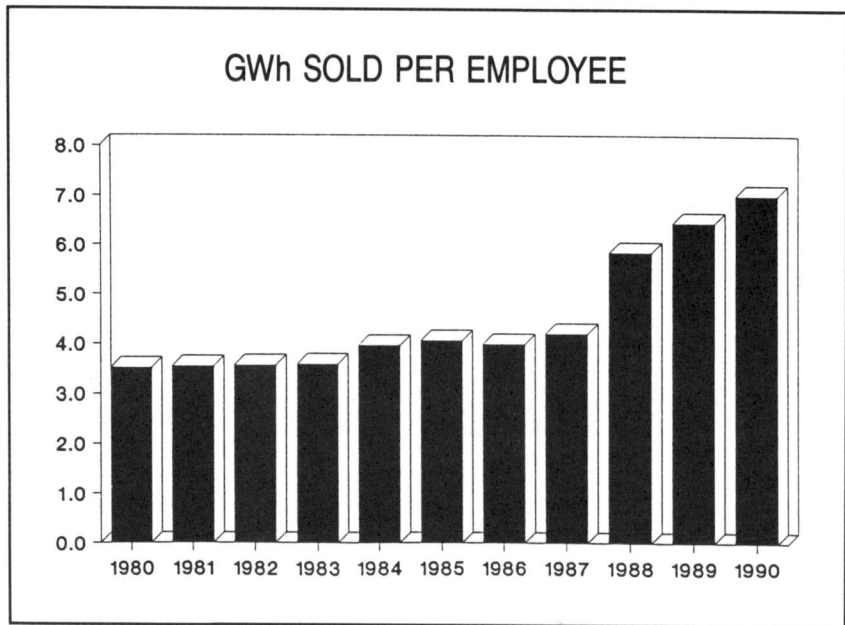

Figure 7.19   Sales and operating expenses per employee

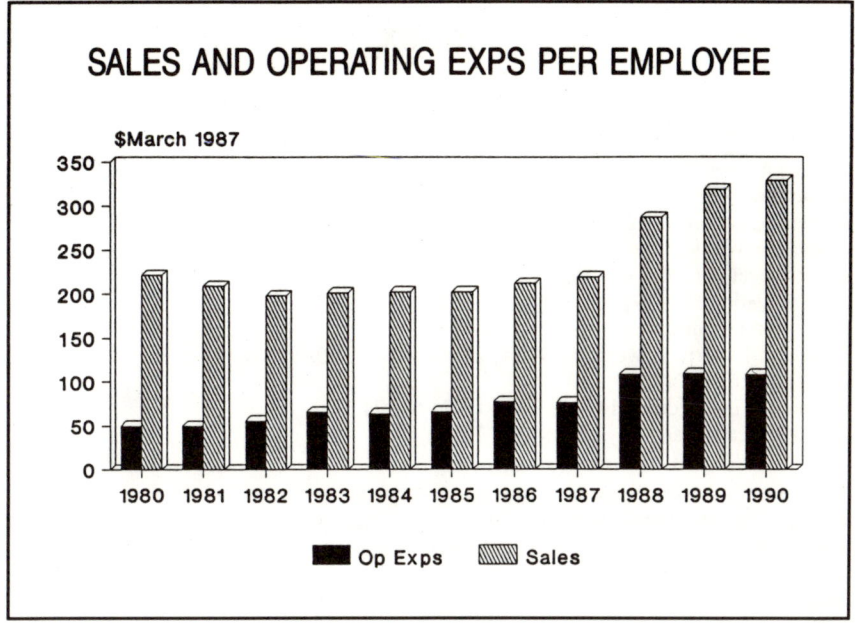

Figure 7.20   Operating earnings and earnings before interest and taxes per employee

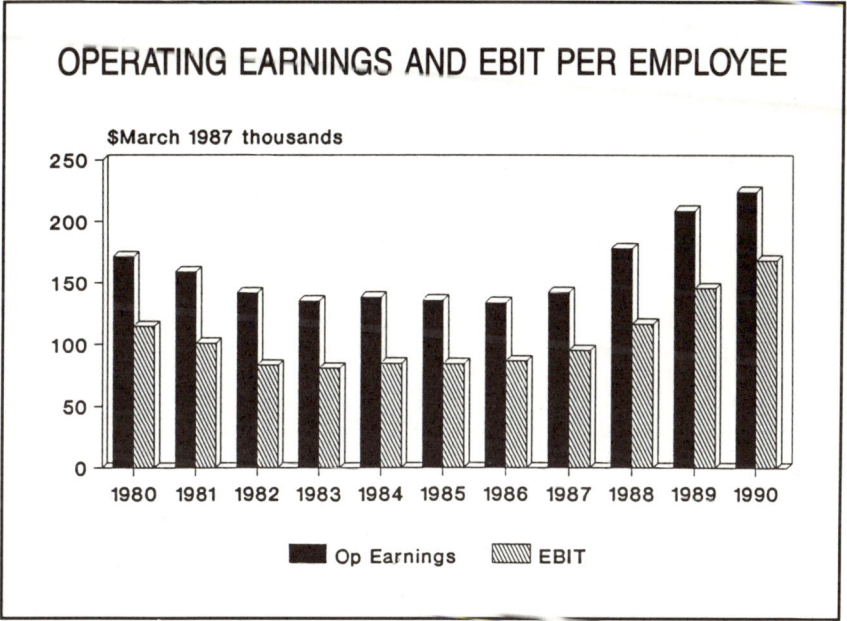

Index